Discovering and Restoring Antique Furniture

Discovering and Restoring Antique Furniture

A practical illustrated guide for the buyer and restorer of period antique furniture

Michael Bennett

CASSELL

This edition 1995 by
Cassell
Wellington House
125 Strand
London, WC2R OBB

Reprinted 1996, 1997

Distributed in the United States by
Sterling Publishing Co., Inc.
387 Park Avenue South
New York
NY 10016-8810

British Library Cataloguing in Publication Data
Bennett, Michael
Discovering and restoring antique furniture.
1. Antique furniture, Restoration – Amateur manuals
I. Title
749'.1'0288

ISBN 0-304-34740-x

Printed and bound in Portugal by Tilgráfica, S.A.

Preface
Acknowledgements

BUYING ANTIQUE FURNITURE

CHAPTER 1
Sources of antique furniture 1

CHAPTER 2
Are you getting value for money? 1
Provenance 1
Style and rarity 1
Condition 1

CHAPTER 3
Is it really antique? 2
Woodworking methods 2
Nails and screws 2
New and reused wood 3
Veneers 3
Brass handles 3
Locks 3
Anatomy of a fake 3

Contents

RESTORATION OF CABINETWORK

IAPTER 4
e bases of cabinetwork 42
ie tools 42
ie wood 50
ie glue 53

IAPTER 5
ructural repairs 56
ose and broken joints 56
lits and warps 67
rawer stops, runners and rails 68
et of case furniture 70

IAPTER 6
pairs to surfaces and ecorative features 74
iips, blisters and dents 74
ouldings and beads 79
ecorative inlay and veneers 81

RESTORATION OF FINISHES

CHAPTER 7
Reviving a tired finish 90
Washing 90
Revivers and cleaners 90
Wax polish 91

CHAPTER 8
Preparation for finishing with shellac 93
Raising the grain 93
Preparation of a sound existing finish 93
Stripping 94
Bleaching 99
Stopping and grain filling 101

CHAPTER 9
Rebuilding a finish 104
Shellac polishing 104
Burnished beeswax 109

CHAPTER 10
Matching colour and surface features 111
Colouring 111
Pigmenting 115
Staining 118

THE FINISHING TOUCHES

CHAPTER 11
Metal fittings 126
Handles and escutcheons 126
Hinges 130
Castors 131
Locks and keys 131

CHAPTER 12
Leather and baize liners 137

CHAPTER 13
Glazing 140

CHAPTER 14
Woodworm treatment 142

APPENDICES
Checklist of machinery, tools and equipment 144
Checklist of miscellaneous materials and equipment 146
Woods used for the construction and decoration of English furniture 147
Checklist for a basic stock of woods 149
Checklist for stock of finishing materials 150
Suppliers of materials and services 152
Summary of recipes 153

Recommended Reading 154

Index 155

Preface

Only a few years ago you could set out with a couple of pounds in your pocket to buy a piece of furniture to fill that odd corner and, as like as not, return with an antique. You probably were not aware that it was an antique, as you would be today, thanks to Arthur Negus, the 'Antiques Roadshow' and innumerable auctioneers' valuation days, but were just pleased to find a nice piece of second-hand furniture which suited your home. Nowadays, when you set out to buy antique furniture, bear in mind that you are well and truly outnumbered by rogues and the ill-informed, and you *might* just survive unscathed. In the world of antiques, *caveat emptor* applies more than ever before.

Before going any further, let's define the word 'antique'. *The British Antique Dealers' Association* defines antique furniture as that made before 1830, after which increased mechanization introduced more and more mass-produced furniture. *Antiques fairs organisers* make much of limiting their exhibitors' stock to specified datelines, that for furniture often being 1850, which lets in the lighter designs of the early Victorian period. *The '100-years old' rule – ie* any object over a century old – is becoming generally accepted as a guide to antiquity. It does, however, allow an awful lot of junk to be described as antique, stuff which will never measure up to the modern interpretation of the word:

> **Antique**. A decorative object, piece of furniture, or other work of art created in an earlier period, that is valued for its beauty, workmanship and age.
>
> (*Collins Concise English Dictionary*, 1982)

This must surely be the essence of all definitions of fine furniture. Commit it to memory and every time you reach for your cheque book recite those words: 'beauty, workmanship and age'.

You don't have to be a master cabinet-maker to do your own restoration; the most accomplished restorer is the one who Nature has endowed with a problem-solving turn of mind, deft hands and an unerring eye for line and colour. However, the acquisition of the skills necessary to practise the restorer's art may come easier to those with woodworking experience, and this book assumes that you have not only some basic woodworking knowledge but also the basic tools and materials, and reasonable workshop facilities – not much restoration can be successfully accomplished on the kitchen table!

The professional restorer will, in the course of a year, deal with many hundreds of different problems, although their solutions may involve variations of only a couple of dozen well-tried techniques. It is this collection of basic techniques, together with their applications to common problems, which have been brought together in this book. In what combination you will be confronted with them is impossible to forecast; in what order you will actually have to tackle them is a matter for your judgement.

Some of the methods described in these pages might reasonably be considered as faking, so perhaps some justification is required for publishing them:

1. The ethics of restoration in general will continue to be debated long after this book has turned to dust. The arguments are outlined in Chapter 2, but one of those points is worth emphasizing: a piece of furniture which is marred by unrepaired damage or by a repair which is itself an eyesore is as much devalued as a fine painting which is damaged and begrimed.
2. The attainment of the results possible by using the described techniques will probably take much longer than the converter or copyist is prepared, or can afford, to spend.
3. If you know how this sort of work is done you will be better able to spot it when you are examining furniture.

How far *you* go in making your repairs disappear is a matter for your conscience.

MICHAEL BENNETT

Acknowledgements

My first thanks are to Keith Connah for his dedicated work in photographing, processing and printing nearly all the material for the illustrations in this book (he is not responsible for the few somewhat hazy 'work in progress' shots, for which I apologize to the reader!).

My thanks also to the management and staff of the following firms and organizations who assisted in my research into patents and manufacturing methods of locks, wood screws and nails: European Industrial Services Ltd (Guest, Keen and Nettlefolds' Fasteners Division after being bought by its management); the Liverpool Central Library's Science and Technology Reference Department; the City of Birmingham Science Museum; the Willenhall Lock Museum, the Chartered Institute of Patent Agents; Patents Research and Documentation (Mr R. I. Rosenfelder).

I am also grateful to Unwin Hyman Ltd for permission to quote from *Antique or Fake?* by Charles Hayward and to Air Improvement Centre Ltd for permission to reproduce the diagram on page 68.

Finally, apologies to my wife and children for my long periods of isolation behind mounds of paper and photographs. 'Quoth the Raven . . . .' (Edgar Allan Poe, *The Raven*, 1845)

Buying Antique Furniture

Now that the word 'antique' is synonymous with 'valuable' and the demand for a dwindling supply ensures that prices move inexorably upwards, the buyer of antique furniture is in danger of being landed with pieces which don't, and perhaps never will, represent value for money. It is regrettable that a large proportion of furniture on the antiques market today is either spurious or in poor condition, sometimes both: so it is to the buyer of antique furniture that the first chapters of this book are addressed. Whether buying a piece in pristine condition or 'in the rough' to restore yourself, you may be glad of a few pointers to guide you through the somewhat murky marketplace. And for those who already own antique furniture, they may help to resolve that vexed question: 'Is it genuine?'

CHAPTER 1

Sources of antique furniture

Principal sources of antique furniture will usually be the **auction room**, **antique shop** or **antiques fair**. The occasional piece might come to light at a collectors' fair, car boot sale or through your local paper, but to make a habit of searching these seldom repays the effort.

The large, international **auction houses** which offer the world million-pound treasures will probably not be frequented by you on your furniture-hunting expeditions, but it'll certainly be worth attending one of their sales if only to see just how much loose cash there is about. Their provincial auctions may be less daunting but you will still need a well-filled pocket, for there will be few items of furniture which are knocked down for less than three figures, and four-figure prices are common.

Most towns have their own auction rooms, holding sales of 'antiques and household effects' on a regular basis. Many of them have felt the effect of the competition from London-based auctioneers, whose advertising budgets and valuation days continue to attract those who find Rembrandts in their lofts. Your local auction is well worth attending, though, for many decent pieces are still sold through them.

The price you pay for a piece of furniture at auction depends on several factors in addition to those which are the main determinants of value, as discussed in Chapter 2. More often than not, the price realized will also depend on how many people are interested in the lot which you have got your eye on (and if trade bidders are present, whether they will let it go to you, for one or two of them have been known to push the bidding way past expected prices in order to keep a private buyer out). The number of competing bidders can in turn depend on such simple things as the weather (how many are keen enough to turn out on a cold, wet day), on how well laid out the lots are (your prize piece may be hidden amongst others in a 'junk lot') and on how well publicized the auction is by advertisements and catalogues. Not least, the price will depend on the expertise of the auctioneer, the best of whom can get the bidding going with a momentum which exposes the 'just-one-more-bid' syndrome in the most hardened auction-goer. And when you have beaten off the opposition and the lot is yours there is still likely to be a commission (the buyer's premium) to pay the auctioneer, with Value Added Tax on the commission. Carriage or storage charges may also be levied if you cannot remove your purchase at the end of the sale.

You will doubtless ensure that you get a receipt for your purchase. Unfortunately, however, you will be unable to use this document as anything other than a simple receipt for the money paid for that lot. No matter what information finds its way from the sale catalogue (if, indeed, there is a catalogue – at the smaller sales you might only be going on the auctioneer's announcement as the lot is put up) onto your receipt, it does nothing to validate the auctioneer's description of the goods. Have a look at the fine print in the 'Conditions of Sale' which may be printed in the catalogue or displayed in the room. You will usually find a clause to the effect that goods are sold with 'all errors of description' and, furthermore, that the auctioneer is acting as agent for the seller and neither one of them is responsible for the authenticity of the items sold. In other words, the auctioneer's expert is offering an opinion only, or even using the vendor's words to describe the goods. So if you end up with a well-worn Victorian reproduction instead of the Queen Anne period piece described in the catalogue, you will usually have no redress, legal or otherwise, unless you can prove that the piece is a deliberate fake. The 'errors of description' can sometimes work in your favour: that set of chairs catalogued as 'George III-style, *c*1880' *could* turn out to be George III, *c*1780. If no-one else notices the error, it's your lucky day!

Bear in mind that the auctioneer's job is to sell things in the condition in which they are presented to him. Most items of furniture put into auction are going to require some attention. Such problems as damaged veneers and mouldings or missing handles are hardly noticed and certainly don't rate a mention in the catalogue, so when you do see the words 'in need of restoration', or are told that goods are sold 'as found', you may be sure that the piece is in pretty poor condition. All said and done, patience will always be rewarded with a bargain in the auction room, but it is important to take advantage of viewing days to make as thorough an inspection as possible of your intended purchase.

Antique dealers range from the specialist, who may even concentrate on one period of furniture, through the general dealer who always has a few nice pieces in stock, to the bric-a-brac dealer who *might* sell you the table on which he displays the tea-sets. Not everyone will have the first category of dealer within reasonable travelling distance, but there will be a few of the second category and maybe several of the third. Your chances of finding a nice piece at bargain price at the junk shop end of the market are fairly remote these days – many such dealers have consulted the latest price guide and stuck on the highest price they think they can get away with, regardless of quality or condition.

The price you will pay to a reputable dealer may be little more than you would pay for a similar item in the saleroom, for as auction prices continue to rise not all dealers adjust their prices to follow the trend. Nor will you always pay the highest price to the specialist dealer, whose particular knowledge will not only ensure that what you buy is good of its kind but also that it represents value for money. The general dealer may also be knowledgeable about more than one of the categories of his stock, but he cannot be expected to know all about everything. His price will, therefore, tend to be influenced by what he has had to pay: if he bought well, his price will tend to be low; if he paid too much, his price may be such that he will have to wait until inflation catches up before he can sell. Unlike auctioneers, many dealers, particularly the specialists, ensure that their wares are in good condition before they sell them, which is obviously not an advantage if you are hoping to buy cheaply and do your own restoration.

The antiques trade has its share of rogues (well, perhaps one or two more than average), so it is most important to get to know your dealer. He will doubtless recognise your gambit but will usually not object, as he in turn wants to get to know his potential customer. Your first approach will tell you a great deal. Are you welcomed and asked if there is anything in particular you are looking for? If your answer is no, but you would like to look around, are you left to browse in peace or do you feel eyes following you round the shop? Does a question get a ready and friendly answer or a supercilious response ('This is my stock, take it or leave it.')? If a question cannot readily be answered, does the dealer go to a well-filled shelf of reference books and look up the answer with you or does he try to waffle his way round it?

Find the dealer with whom you can establish a friendly relationship where trust is mutual and you can reasonably expect to get value for money. Even so, when the deal is done, do get a receipt. The issuing of a receipt will be automatic with most antique dealers but in the excitement of the moment it might be forgotten. Even in the most honest and straightforward transactions, things can and do go wrong and you will then welcome the protection afforded by the Trades Description Act, from which antique dealers may *not* exclude themselves. To benefit from this protection you must have a receipt which adequately describes and dates the piece, details which the reputable dealer will have on his price tag and transcribe onto the receipt. The content of the ideal receipt is described on p. 14.

Some antique dealers are members of the British Antique Dealers' Association (BADA), others are members of the London and Provincial Antique Dealers' Association (LAPADA), both of which have their own codes of business practice. The theory is that you will be better off dealing with a member of one of the professional associations, but this overlooks the fact that there are many dealers in a smaller way of business who do not qualify for membership, or have no wish to be members, who are no less reputable.

That modern phenomenon, the **antiques fair**, does seem to be a good place to buy antique furniture: dozens of dealers all under one roof, competing to sell you a greater variety of wares than you could find in any one town. Many of these dealers specialize in selling at fairs and have no shops to look after, leaving them free between events to scour the land in search of fresh stock. All the exhibitors strive to make their stands as attractive as possible and restorers are kept busy making sure that every piece is in first class condition for the fair. Every dealer knows that before he can display his goods to the public they will be examined by a committee of experts – the vetting committee – which will reject any item which is not within the fair's dateline and, now that the '100-years old' rule is becoming widely accepted, that they will also be vetted for quality. Or so goes the theory.

One problem at many fairs is that the vetting committee may largely consist of dealers who are themselves exhibiting. All are perfectly honest, to be sure, but can they be *entirely* unbiased? Even if they are unbiased they will simply not have time to examine every piece thoroughly, and some subjective decisions are bound to be taken. The vetting scheme is probably, therefore, best regarded as a deterrent which will make the dealer more careful about his exhibits, but if *he* is not aware that some of his things are suspect (only the cynical would suggest that he might try to slip them through knowingly), there's a good chance that they will end up on sale as bona fide antiques. You, the buyer, now have to determine if the piece is as described on the price tag. Whereas you would have a reasonable opportunity to examine it thoroughly in an antique shop, it is difficult to do so at a fair, for there may be the distraction of many people about the stands and the furniture will be under a battery of spotlights. Even the most insensitive will hesitate to give pieces more than a perfunctory check, relying instead on an assessment of style and observation of basic and accessible constructional features – and on the dealer's label. Antiques fairs are certainly not places for the novice buyer of furniture. They are wonderful places to look and learn – but cheque books should be left at home.

CHAPTER 2

Are you getting value for money?

What makes one piece of antique furniture valuable and another almost worthless? The true value depends on several factors. Is it known when and by whom the piece was made, and where it has been since? Is the piece in keeping with recognized stylistic features? Is it a fairly common design, or unique? Is its construction compatible with that of pieces with which it is supposed to be contemporary, or is it altered or 'made up'? Is it functional and are its decorative features intact? Are colour and patina fine and mellow or can you not even see the wood? Has some botcher made a nonsense of the repairs? (*Botcher* not to be confused with *bodger*. The chair bodgers who worked with the simplest of tools in the beech woods of the Chiltern Hills until comparatively recent times are survived by furniture of a standard of craftsmanship which the botcher could never emulate.)

Your search for many of the pointers you need to check in order to establish antiquity will be bound to catch someone's eye – you can't crawl about underneath things, pull out drawers and turn chairs over without drawing attention to yourself. Whilst this sort of inspection is accepted as normal in most auction rooms on viewing days, some antique dealers might not be so amenable. So when you visit an antique shop, do ask permission if you want to do more than look at a piece *in situ*; it will seldom be denied, but if it is you will have reasonable grounds for suspecting that the purchase might be unwise anyway. Some investigation will only be possible once you have got your purchase home. The removal of screws, dismantling of locks and other such checks involving the use of tools (which are the subjects of later chapters), obviously cannot be expected to be acceptable either in the auction room or the antique shop, let alone at the antiques fair.

Provenance

Confirmation of the origin of a piece of antique furniture in the form of the cabinet-maker's bill is seldom found, except for items in the collections of stately homes or museums. The best confirmation of origin which is likely to be discovered in most pieces appearing on the open market will be a maker's label, stamp or signature. Stamps and labels are most often located in accessible places such as the top of a drawer front or cupboard door, on the swing legs of card and tea tables, and inside or beneath the seat rail of a chair. Signatures and other handwritten gems are usually in less obvious places such as back boards, backs or bottoms of drawers and the undersides of table tops.

1. A substantial trade label. This boldly engraved brass plate in the rail of a patent-action dining table proclaims the high quality of the products of Mr Titter's workshops (see also Fig. 96, p. 65).

Usually there is nothing in or on a piece of furniture to indicate its origin, and you have to rely on the information given on your receipt. Apart from this, it is not reasonable to expect much by way of written evidence of origin for a piece of furniture which is likely to have changed hands several times

2. An unusual means of establishing provenance. The back rail of a chair bears the stamped abbreviation for House of Peers (top), a leg another stamp indicating the period of William IV (bottom). Research confirmed the provenance and established that this is one of the few pieces of furniture to have survived the 1834 fire at the Palace of Westminster.

without any accompanying documents. Hence the importance of the receipt; if the history of the piece is nonexistent, you will be doing your bit for posterity by getting some details on paper. The minimum information on the receipt should be:

The accepted name for the type of furniture
Maker's name, if known
The woods used in its construction and decoration
The salient features
An approximate date
The price paid

An 'approximate' date is often all that can be recorded because the dating of a piece of furniture with absolute precision can be difficult, even for the most expert. Provincial furniture has often followed the styles set by the London designs and continued in production for many years, even decades, so a specific date is most unusual. '*Circa* 1755' is to be expected for a piece which has obviously been made by highly-skilled craftsmen to a design in Chippendale's *The Gentleman and Cabinet-Maker's Director* (originally published in 1754). For a piece of the same design which is likely to have been made later by provincial ('country') craftsmen then 'third quarter of the eighteenth century' is more than adequate. 'Early eighteenth century' and 'late eighteenth century' will also be seen, as will the name of the appropriate monarch, with or without an approximate date, eg, 'George III, *c*1780' or 'George III', all of which are reasonably acceptable. Just 'Georgian', which is often seen, is *not* good enough, for the description covers a period of more than a hundred years. And do look out for that word 'style', which indicates a later imitation. Millions of pounds must have changed hands for pseudo-antiques with 'Chippendale-style' writ large on their labels.

Style and rarity

Is that really a piece of period antique furniture you're looking at or is it a later imitation which the maker has not got quite right? Is the style typical of the period and fairly common or is it a rarity? To be completely sure of the answers to these questions, you must have a comprehensive knowledge of furniture styles and methods of construction down the ages. This will require considerable reading, since the subject fills hundreds of volumes, and the beginner could be put off for life. But, fortunately, the weightiness of the reading does not necessarily increase in proportion to the scholarliness of the works available. (See **Recommended Reading**, p. 154)

When you have done the required stint of reading, furniture will need to be seen and, wherever possible, handled, to get a true feeling of what is 'right'. Visits to museums and collections are essential, preferably in the company of someone who can point out the features which are the keys to identification.

The learning process is endless; there will always be something new to fascinate, particularly when you come across the handiwork of the late nineteenth- and early twentieth-century copyists. Amongst several who have owned up is Charles Hayward who, in his book *Antique or Fake?*, writes: 'My thoughts go back to my apprenticeship days before the First World War, when a great deal of hand work was still being done . . . . We were an antique shop; that is we made reproductions and fakes, repaired old pieces, and did something quite remarkable in the way of conversions

. . . and it is an interesting thought that some of them may be the treasured possession of folk happy in the thought that they possess authentic work of the golden age of cabinet-making.' Just about perfect in every detail of style, construction and decoration, such pieces have had many decades to mellow to a fine colour and patina, and even now many hundreds of them are lurking around to beguile the unwary. Whilst much of the botcher's work is incompetent and will soon be revealed to the trained eye, you will have to look deeper than the pointers which books on style and construction teach you, if you are to discover the work of those crafty copyists, or that of today's fakers who have, in many cases, so skilfully taken up their trade.

Special attention should be paid to small pieces of furniture, particularly those which are also decorative, as such items have gone up in price spectacularly, to the level where the faker now finds it very profitable to 'improve' and convert large pieces and make things up from old wood – and he can afford to spend longer on making his work look convincing. Be wary of chests of drawers and kneehole desks which are less than three feet wide, lowboys, canterburys, pembroke tables, sewing tables, tea and card tables, sets of shelves, corner cupboards, stools and rare styles of chairs.

Condition

The features described in the rest of this chapter are usually easily observed but frequently overlooked by the buyer in his enthusiasm to acquire the piece of furniture, or dismissed by the seller as having no bearing on value. Antique furniture is subjected to more abuses than perhaps any other category of antiques. Anything functional is bound to get knocked about a bit, but much furniture is never cleaned or polished; loose and broken joints are botched rather than go to the expense of having a restorer do a proper repair; the piece is exposed to the over-dry atmosphere caused by heating systems and is stressed beyond any limits envisaged by its maker. Then, perhaps out of fashion as well as half-wrecked, it is relegated to the garden shed or garage, there to languish for a decade until someone spots it and thinks it will make a few pounds. Small wonder that so much antique furniture coming onto the market is in terrible condition.

If both seller and buyer are aware of the cost of good-quality restoration work, there is a lot to be said for buying things 'in the rough' (before the botcher gets his hands on them), at a price which reflects the forthcoming outlay on restoration. Too often, though, problems are overlooked, making estimates for restoration costs pathetically low. The buyer ends up paying over the odds for the piece and then faces a stiff bill for the work needed to put it in decent condition. Specific points to look out for in order to establish the condition of a piece are:

Firmness of construction

Any piece of furniture is likely to work loose at the joints, even the sturdiest case furniture. Anything with drawers should have these removed before testing the structure – if it sways about without them you will have a rebuilding job on your hands. Glazed doors can be a problem, too, for often it is only the glass and putty which are keeping glazing bars and frame together. Pay particular attention to pieces with mortice and tenon construction, especially that most abused of all furniture, the poor old chair, for what appear to be just loose joints could be broken, requiring not a simple

3. A sign of hidden problems. That small patch indicated by the arrow is stopping which has been used to fill the hole made by sinking the head of a nail beneath the surface. When this is disguised with a tinted finish it becomes extremely difficult to spot. Such a 'repair' to a loose joint is not only totally ineffective but leads to much unnecessary work for the restorer.

gluing operation but a large-scale, costly reconstruction. You can't afford to be shy – give each piece a good going-over, joint by joint and then, if there is no movement detected, make a visual inspection in the area of every joint. You are looking for tell-tale patches, usually circular but maybe quite small, which could mean that filler or plugs of wood have been put in to cover screws, nails or dowels used to 'strengthen' loose joints, indicating major problems to be tackled when the inevitable happens and the piece falls apart (Figs. 3 and 4).

Colour and patina

Colour and patina are most important features. They are, after all, fundamental to that first impression of the otherwise fine piece of furniture in which you are about to invest.

As a general rule, the darker woods such as walnut, mahogany (except some West Indian mahoganies) and rosewood fade when exposed to light, whilst the pale woods darken. Most take on a mellow golden-brown colour, which is enhanced by their own particular characteristics of grain and figure markings. This natural process affects the wood to the most minute depth below the surface and it can easily be destroyed by over-enthusiastic cleaning or careless restoration work. Nothing looks so stark as a piece of period furniture which has been stripped, sanded down to raw wood and refinished to a high gloss with a tinted varnish. You may as well have a modern reproduction, and not only from the aesthetic point of view, for the value of such a piece is drastically reduced. The rectification of such appalling treatment *is* possible with many hours of patient work, employing the techniques described in following chapters, but you'd need to be virtually given the thing to make the exercise worthwhile.

When discussing patina we venture into one of the grey areas of the antiques world. The dictionary defines patina as 'the sheen on the surface of wood, produced by long handling'. It is the word 'sheen' which is important. This view seems to have been lost somewhere along the way, judging by the number of dirt-encrusted items which are offered for sale described as 'nicely patinated'. Could it be that those who urge us to look on a thick layer of accumulated muck as patina, and therefore a desirable feature which is proof of antiquity, are so unknowledgeable that they must rely on supposedly centuries-old filth as authentication? If so, they overlook two points: firstly, their precious accumulations can build up rapidly in the less than fastidious household, as evidenced by the number of smoke- and grease-blackened pieces of Victorian and Edwardian furniture to be found; secondly, such 'patina' *can* be faked.

So, when considering colour and patina, be wary of pieces on which the condition of the wood is obscured by dirt and oxidized finishes, for whilst the processes required to clean, revive and polish are reasonably simple (and described in Chapter 7) you can't be sure what lies beneath until you've got them home. Firmly reject pieces which are as sharp and clean as reproductions and go for the ones which have a warm, mellow glow to the wood, unless you are able to negotiate a handsome reduction in price to compensate for the cost and time required for restoration.

Missing parts

Excessive loss of veneer (which can point to structural damage as well) and missing pieces of moulding, beading and inlay do mar the appearance of a piece of furniture and can cost a lot to have put right by the professional

4. An example of botched workmanship. Judging by the variety of glues, screws, dowels and brackets, there have been many attempts made to secure the leg of this chair. The costly repair which is now necessary would have been avoided if the job had been done properly the first time.

5. A pleasure to behold. The fine, natural colour and patina of this late eighteenth-century chest of drawers greatly add to its value. (By courtesy of Jon David Fine Furniture Ltd)

restorer. To do this sort of cosmetic work properly often takes more time in the matching of woods than it does to cut the pieces and glue them in, for bunging in pieces of any old roughly-matched wood that comes to hand results in repairs which look worse than the original damage. So if your stock of timber is not varied enough to cope with the repairs required, think twice before buying such a piece.

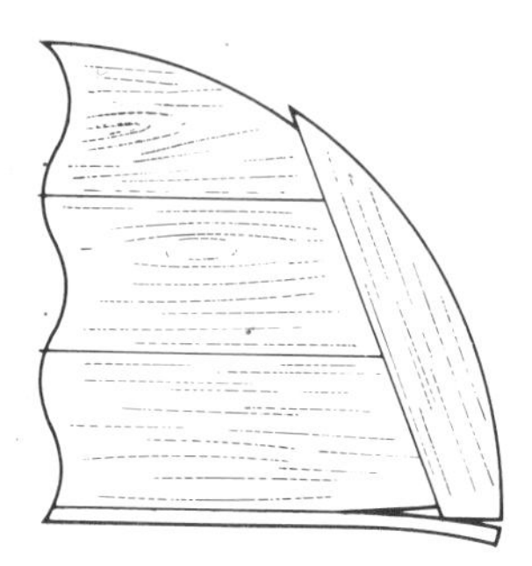

6. The effects of shrinkage.
a. Typical construction of a card-table top. Shrinkage of the boards between the clamping strips can result in damaged crossbanding and stringing, protruding clamping strips and torn veneer.

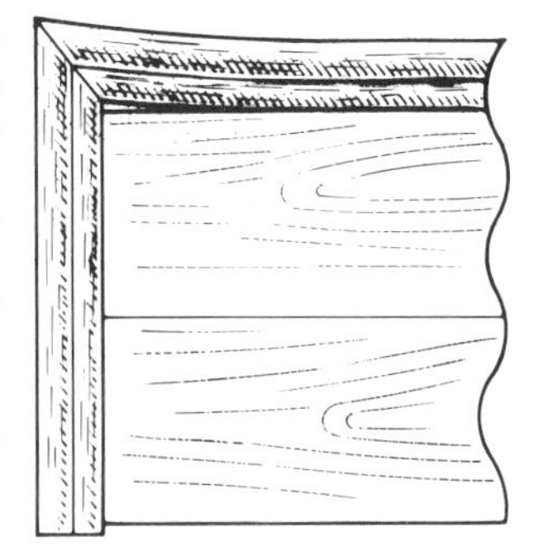

b. Construction of the top of a piece of case furniture, which will have veneer overlapping the applied mouldings. Shrinkage across the grain of the ground wood can force the front moulding forward, splitting the veneer, and distort the veneer where it has remained attached to the side moulding.

7. A major restoration job. The damage to this card table illustrates one of the problems associated with the construction in Fig. 6*a*. The end clamping strips have obviously been unable to restrain the shrinkage of the ground wood, particularly on the lower leaf.

8. This photograph of an edge of the top of an architect's table clearly illustrates the effect on veneer of the shrinkage of ground wood.

Splits and warps

Many veneered surfaces, such as the folding tops of tea and card tables, have a ground which is made of boards held with clamping strips, as in Fig. 6, the intention being to avoid distortion of the top by shrinkage and warpage. In some cases this has obviously not been successful, when the ends of the clamping strips protrude at front and back and the veneer over the joins between clamping strips and board ends is distorted and split, the veneer on the clamping strips having stayed put while that on the boards dragged past it.

The same problem can occur with the tops of tables, chests of drawers and other case furniture, where the veneer of the top overlaps mouldings which have been applied to the edges of the ground wood. Splits in the veneer occur where the ends of the front moulding are forced away from the ground and the same zigzag splits show along the join of ground to end moulding. Such excessive movement of ground wood can play havoc with marquetry and inlay, and metal inlay in particular; it can also cause the separation of the gesso beneath gilding and the cracking and loss of material from painted and lacquered surfaces.

All the above damage caused by wood movement can be prohibitively expensive to put right so it is wise to check with a restorer if there is any evidence of such problems. Almost the same can be said for panels and table tops which are warped. Since they are impossible to rectify without great expense, unless the piece is otherwise in nice condition and you are sure that you can live with the warp, don't buy it. Causes of these problems are discussed in Chapter 5.

9*a*. From a distance a piece of furniture which has the multitude of dents, scratches and small repairs shown in the illustrations on the left might give the appearance of well-patinated age. But take a look at the enlarged picture of a section of a drawer front (right) the marks on which are enough, by themselves, to raise questions about the antiquity of the piece.

To the trained eye, this sort of fakery will be obvious. However, the chest of drawers which bore these marks was auctioned recently as an eighteenth-century piece.

9*b*. How many times has this one small area of drawer front been struck with the same object, from the same angle, with about the same amount of force? One small area with a few similarly uniform marks might be regarded as reasonable, being the consequence of the activity of a child wielding a toy, but when a piece of furniture bears such gatherings of marks all over, and has a label describing it as a period antique, it should be regarded with the utmost suspicion.

Wear and tear

Every piece of furniture in daily use is going to get a bit worn, dented and scratched, even in the most careful household. A couple of hundred years of this and the result will be a myriad minute (and some not so minute) marks and stains, corners and rails rubbed and all, to be hoped, beautifully polished. The copying of this effect is probably the most uneconomical proposition for the restorer, but it has to be done to some extent if repairs are to match their surroundings (see Chapter 10). Most fakers haven't the patience to do a proper job of 'distressing', and their attempts at it usually stand out horribly (Fig. 9) and are nearly always impossible to rectify without going back to bare wood, with all the costly work that is then entailed in recreating the colour and patina. Look out for such botched work and use it to negotiate a reduction in price if you otherwise like the piece.

Wear and tear of fabrics is another matter. Leaving the last remaining shreds of an original, rare cloth on the seat of a museum piece is one thing, but for day-to-day use it would be neither pleasing nor practical. Reupholstery using traditional methods and materials is desirable for chairs which are still expected to fulfil their function. No foam rubber or stapled-on material should be accepted unless, of course, the price you are paying for chairs in this condition is low enough to allow you to get the work done again properly.

Think twice before accepting the often-made suggestion to reline a table or desk which has leather in poor condition. There are two good reasons to hesitate: firstly, the quality of leather tooling offered by many suppliers of liners is not what is used to be, and nothing looks worse than a pristine

10. The leather liner on a writing slope. The embossing shows the highly skilled workmanship of nineteenth-century craftsmen. Much of the work done today is of very poor quality but a few exponents of the art remain.

11. One of the better examples of the leather embosser's workmanship which is available nowadays.

leather with shallow, inaccurate embossing and patchy gilt-effect (gold leaf is seldom used these days); and, secondly, even crumbling leather may perhaps be restored. Reviving and relining are discussed in Chapter 12.

Glass is another material which is almost certain to suffer sometime or other. Replacement of the old, rippled glass of an antique cabinet should be avoided for just a small crack in a pane, as it will be difficult to get real old glass to do the job. Reglazing is described in Chapter 13.

Woodworm

There is no reason to dismiss a piece of furniture just because of a few old woodworm holes. However, signs of extensive activity beneath the surface might not be apparent from the dozen or so flight holes on the outer, polished surface, so look on the corresponding inside surface to see what has been going on there. Try poking a sharp needle into the worm-damaged wood (no-one can object, surely what's one more hole?) and if it goes in with little effort there's a good chance that structural failure is imminent.

Flight holes in decorative surfaces do look bad but they can be effectively disguised. Those hidden away round the back are often welcomed as proof of great age, but beware, for not only could the infestation have been comparatively recent but they may have been faked, as described in 'Anatomy of a fake', p. 36. In the early stages of infestation, real flight holes will usually be found in the vicinity of a joint or other dusty crack in which the beetle laid its eggs. Left untreated, future generations of larvae will travel further and the flight holes will spread, but the majority will still usually be found in the area of the original attack (Fig. 12). The faker is not likely to take the time to place his 'worm holes' in the natural pattern of the beetles, nor to drill them so carefully as to leave sharp, clean holes. He is more likely to take a few stabs at the wood with a bodkin, making holes with rounded edges which are passable to the naked eye but are particularly distinctive when viewed through a magnifying glass.

Look out, too, for exposed woodworm galleries in the surface of the wood (Figs. 13 and 14). Woodworm larvae *never* work along an exposed surface (although galleries may be found where two pieces of wood have remained pressed together for a long time), so these winding trenches are evidence that the original surface has been planed off. Any such indications that the wood has been reworked should make you very suspicious.

Let us dispel the notion that woodworm holes are not to be found in mahogany, oak or other hard woods. The larvae love the sweet sapwood which is frequently found in oak furniture, and where hardwood veneers are applied to pine, birch, beech and other such tasty structural timbers, any woodworm pupating beneath will have only one way out when they eventually become beetles – straight through the veneer, tough as it is (Fig. 15). Treatment for woodworm is described in Chapter 14.

Previous restoration

Perhaps, before you even start your own investigation into the piece of furniture in the antique shop, you should look the dealer straight in the eye and ask: 'Has this piece had any work done to it before?' When he has got to know you he'll be waiting for the question and have his story ready, otherwise his reaction may vary from a bit of spluttering while he adjusts to this straightforward approach, to a haughty: 'We don't approve of restoration!', implying that all the stock around you is in untouched, original condition. It is a rare dealer who will volunteer information about restoration work

a

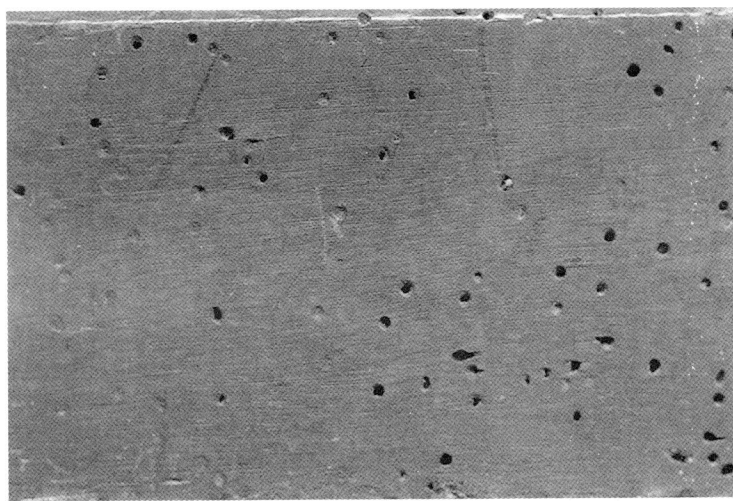

b

12. The effects of woodworm in a beech chair. The few dozen flight holes visible on the outside and inside (*a* and *b*) of a seat rail give little indication of the larvae's voracious activity beneath the surface (*c*).

c

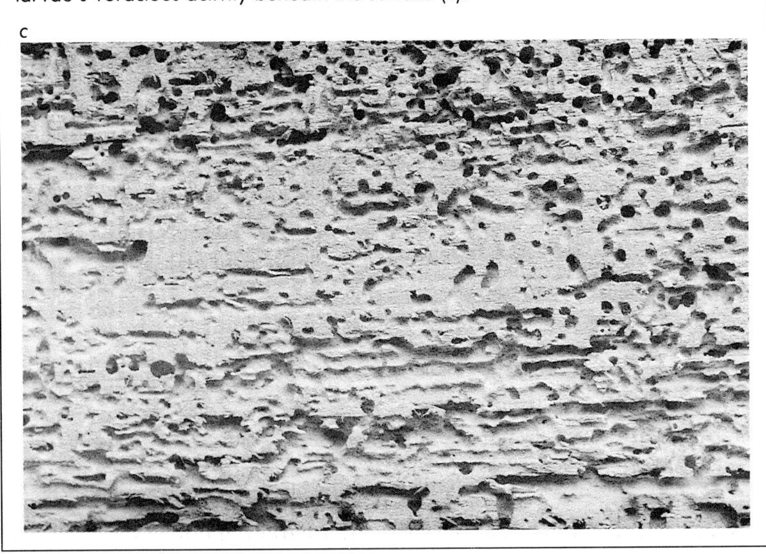

13. Exposed woodworm galleries. The side of a walnut-veneered clock case has suffered from the heavy use of abrasives, revealed not only by galleries which are now on the surface but by the extensive scoring of the wood.

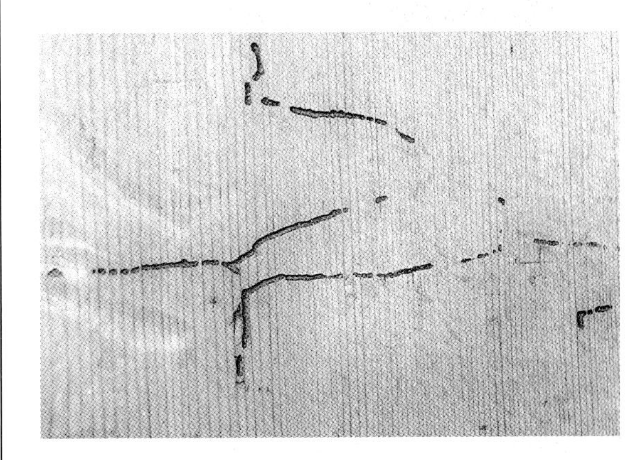

14. Evidence of reworked wood. The inside of the case door of the clock illustrated in Fig. 13 leads to the suspicion that the veneers have been relaid on a new ground.

15. Flight holes in mahogany veneer. The mature beetles have no other way out if they have pupated near the wrong surface.

which he knows has been done. In fact there is no good reason for such reticence, for first-class, sympathetic restoration is unlikely to affect the value of a piece significantly. The pundits may argue this point, but anyone who regularly attends auctions of antique furniture will have noted the trend in prices which supports this view. It is when botched workmanship and deliberate fakery are discovered that prices are reduced and 'restoration' becomes a dirty word. The botcher will not be concerned with the accuracy of his work, nor will he bother to match the colour or even, sometimes, the sort of wood he uses. You will not need much experience to spot this sort of job, or the drips of coloured wax and stained varnish which have found their way into out of sight places, or the dust which proves to be glued in place – all the botcher's trademarks.

Almost as alarming is the attitude, albeit well meant, of that school of conservation which insists that repair work, if it is to be allowed at all, must be entirely visible in order to protect the integrity of the piece. The principle behind this argument is entirely laudable, for if a repair is invisible some scallywag might pass the thing off as being in original condition. Also, they say, natural wear and tear should not be reversed and only that work may be done which ensures no further deterioration. Unfortunately, the results of this policy can be extremely unattractive, as evidenced by some of the nation's treasures on public display in major collections. On your visits to these collections, look out for decorative panels with gaps and splits filled with pink joiner's stopping or white glue, for superb chairs with worm-damaged legs built up with car body filler, for gaps in fretted brass inlay filled with yellow wax and for crude and ill-matched patches in veneered surfaces. The proponents of such 'conservation' overlook the point that a piece of furniture may reasonably be regarded as having artistic merit as well as function (remember those words in the definition of 'antique': *beauty*, workmanship and age'?). There is no more reason why the artistry of the cabinet-maker should be allowed to stay in a state of neglect than that of the painter of a masterpiece in oils. The ideal repair, whether functional or cosmetic, should be unobtrusive – visible on close inspection, by all means, but not eye-catching.

CHAPTER 3

Is it really antique?

Most books dealing with the styles of antique furniture also discuss the constructional features of the various periods. These features are usually the most obvious ones, which are linked to the designs of the periods, but there are others that, requiring rather more investigation, will be perhaps more useful in confirming the true age of a piece of furniture. The copyist or faker may be well aware of these features but, suspecting that many dealers and their customers are not, will not waste his time and effort in attending to them.

Woodworking methods

Marks left by tools of the timberyard and the cabinet-maker's workshop tell us much about the age and quality of a piece of furniture. It will be unusual to find signs of primary timber conversion, in which the log is reduced to manageable boards, on high-quality work of the city cabinet-maker, but they are not uncommon on provincial furniture. The methods used in the timberyards of England were for centuries less mechanized than those on the Continent, where water- and wind-powered saw mills were operating on a substantial scale in the fifteenth century, using reciprocating-action frame saws. The marks of the early mechanized frame saw (Fig. 16) are fairly regular, coarse cuts, usually at right angles to the direction of the grain (Fig. 17). In England, most primary conversion was still being done by hand during the nineteenth century and, in fact, the pit saw (Fig. 21) persisted in some small yards well into this century. Hand-sawn timber is easily identified by its irregular, often overlapping, cuts which are usually at an angle to the direction of the grain (Fig. 18). Less often found, but most welcome, is the sight of riven oak (split along the medullary rays to form the most stable 'cut' for panelling) or a surface with adze or plane marks (Figs. 19 and 20), for whilst the faker might have been lucky enough to come across sufficient wood so worked, he certainly would not go to the trouble of working it himself.

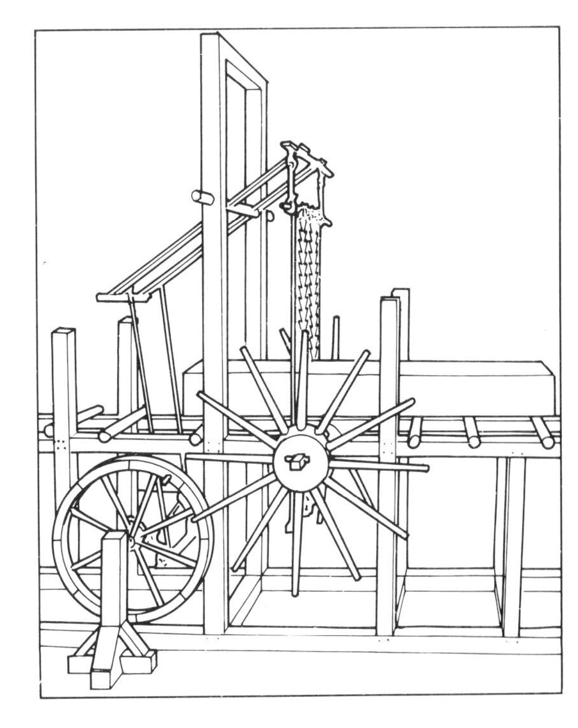

16. A reciprocating-action frame saw. This 15th-century example of a mechanized saw was probably driven by wind- or water-power, operating a belt to the large wheel (bottom left).

During the late eighteenth century, the invention of the circular saw and the steam engine inevitably led to a change in approach to woodworking, but it was not until the second quarter of the nineteenth century that the quality of steel and the manufacturing methods for blades improved to the point where the circular saw could be reliably employed in the manufacture of furniture. Even then, this machine would only have been used in large, wealthy centres of employment, the country craftsman still relying on manual methods. The invention of the bandsaw did not come until the early nineteenth century and it was not until the middle of the century that a reliable working machine was available. Again, this was due to the poor quality of steel from which blades could be made, and also to the fact that a

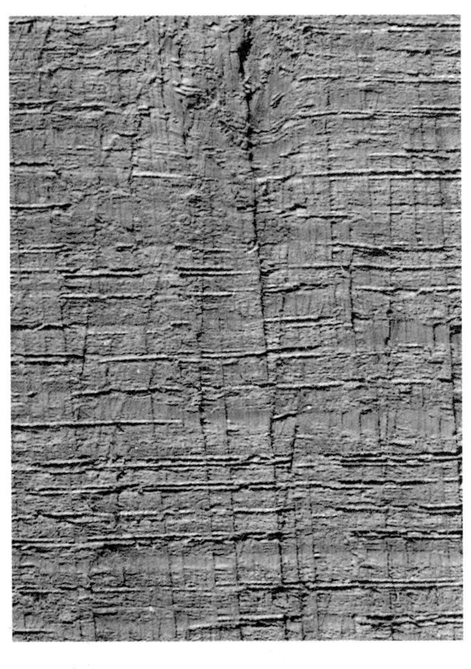

17. The signs of a frame saw (left). The marks on boards cut by a frame saw are more evenly spaced than those made by a handsaw, are more or less parallel to each other and at right angles to the general direction of the grain.

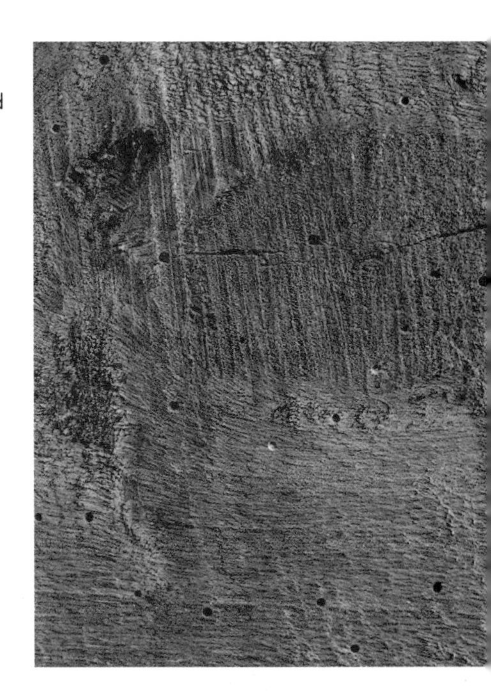

18. Handsawn timber (right). The unmistakable marks of a handsaw on the back board of an eighteenth-century dresser base.

19. Riven oak used for the bottom boards of a drawer.

20. Evidence of handwork. The top of a clock hood shows the signs of individual workmanship.

21. A pit saw in operation. How many years did the poor pitman have to work down there before he could aspire to be top sawyer?

satisfactory means of joining and repairing the blades had not been developed. With the improvement in the quality of steel and of brazing techniques, by the third quarter of the nineteenth century, the bandsaw was in use for cabinetwork, but it was not until the end of the century that it was accepted in general use for mill work.

By comparison to the marks of the early frame saw or the handsaw, the marks of modern machine saws are very regular. Most distinctive is the pattern made by the circular saw (Fig. 22), while that of the bandsaw cannot be confused with the marks of a handsaw. Large bandsaws for converting timber into boards will show coarse marks (Fig. 23); the cabinet-maker's bandsaw will show finer but equally uniform marks (Fig. 24). In either case, any fault in the blade will show up at regular intervals. The mill blade here shows a series of major faults while the cabinet shop blade, although much truer and better set, still reveals a pattern which distinguishes it from other types of saw.

Evidence of woodworking machinery having been used in the manufacture of furniture will usually only be found in out of the way places where the maker either thinks you won't look or just has not been careful enough – most copyists, however, did take care to remove all machine marks with the hand plane. Remove the drawers of case furniture and look closely round the back, sides and underneath of each, and while they are out check inside the carcase – sides, top, back boards, dust boards and drawer runners. Look inside and beneath seat rails of chairs, beneath stretchers and table rails, and at any surface which is not seen in day-to-day use. All are possible places in which to find the odd square inch of wood which the plane has missed, revealing the tell-tale marks of woodworking machinery. Of course, that one drawer back or chair rail with marks of machining could be a perfectly legitimate repair, but if this is the case it will usually be easily identified as such, for while the repairer would use a similar piece of wood if he had it, he wouldn't attempt to disguise his work on hidden, unpolished surfaces. So, if the machined area is on a piece of wood which matches all similar parts around it for type, grain and figure, colour, wear and grime, then it is likely to be original work and, therefore, the piece of furniture could not have been made much before the middle of the nineteenth century.

Look out, too, for the smooth, evenly-spaced ripples left by a planing machine on the surface of boards (Fig. 25) and similar marks of a spindle moulder in the grooves and hollows of mouldings where the sandpaper cannot easily reach, both evidence of modern (and hasty) production.

Nails and screws

Nails and screws which are used to secure joints, panels and fittings are often most revealing about the antiquity (or lack of it) of a piece of furniture. Under the general heading of nails may be included the pegs (treenails) which were commonly used to secure joints until the second quarter of the eighteenth century and for several decades after that in country-made furniture. Such pegs are never perfectly round, uniform lengths, as might be cut from a length of dowel, but were split, roughly rounded and tapered. When mortice and tenon joints were cut, holes for the pegs were drilled slightly closer to the shoulders of the tenons than those across the mortices (Fig. 26), so that when the piece was assembled (no glue was used) the pegs drew the tenons right home, ensuring rigid joints. Over the centuries, shrinkage has usually caused these joints to loosen, sometimes enough to allow a peg to be withdrawn for inspection, revealing its typical form with

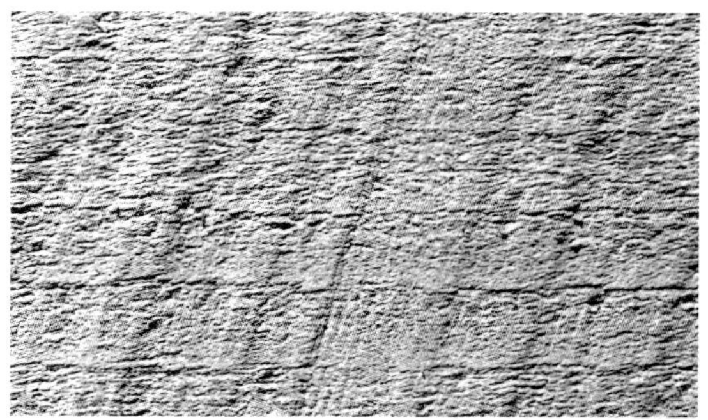

22. The distinctive concentric arcs cut by a circular saw are the signs of mass production, indicating that the work was most likely to have been done in Victorian times, or later.

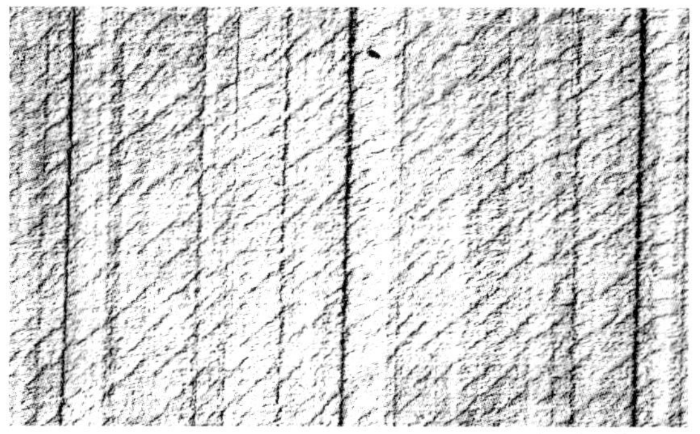

23. Marks of the sawmill bandsaw. Note the absolutely parallel cut and the repeated sequence of marks made by faults in the blade.

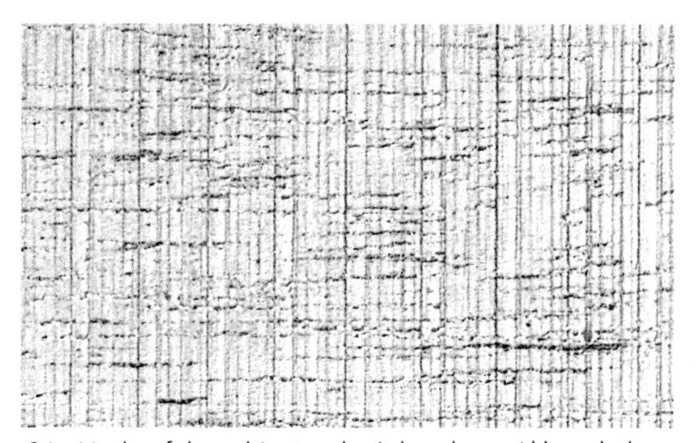

24. Marks of the cabinet-maker's bandsaw. Although the finer blade of this saw has been well set it still shows the sequence of faults which distinguishes its cutting pattern from those of handsaw and frame saw.

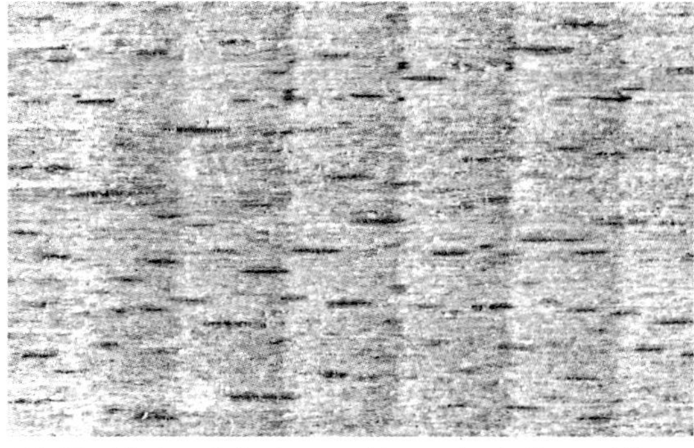

25. The blades of planing machine and spindle moulding machine can leave unique marks if the wood is fed through them incorrectly. Look out for regular, smooth ripples such as these made by a planing machine on beech.

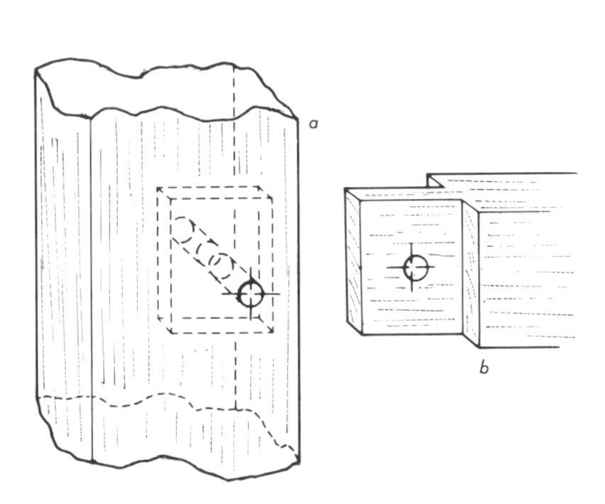

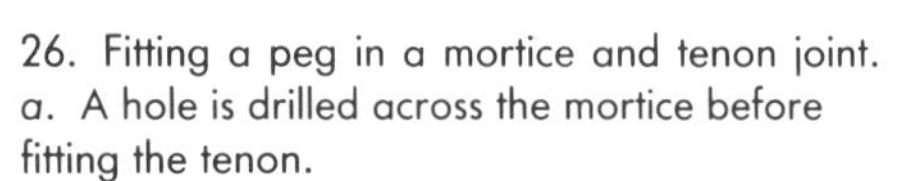

26. Fitting a peg in a mortice and tenon joint.
a. A hole is drilled across the mortice before fitting the tenon.
b. The tenon is inserted into the mortice and the centre of the predrilled hole is marked. The hole in the tenon is then drilled a fraction of an inch closer to the shoulder, ensuring that the joint will be tight when the peg is driven through.

27. A peg (or treenail). This peg has been removed from a joint in a panel frame. The typical kink is formed where the peg went through the offset hole in the tenon.

28. The point of a peg. Nearly an inch of the peg is showing on the inside of one of the joints in an elm chair; the other has been broken off.

the kink where it went through the tenon (Fig. 27). Outward evidence of shrinkage of a rail or leg into which the mortice is cut will be the slight protrusion of the head of the peg above the surrounding surface, which is sometimes better revealed to the fingertip than the eye. This protrusion is even detectable on walnut-veneered chairs of the late seventeenth and early eighteenth centuries, showing as a slight bump in the veneer covering the peg, and is a valuable pointer to the authenticity of such pieces (see 'Anatomy of a fake', p. 36). Also, the peg would usually be taken right through the joint, with its point either trimmed off or perhaps left with as much as an inch showing on the inside of the framework (Fig. 28), but the absence of this last feature should not be taken as conclusive evidence of fakery unless associated with other evidence, such as an obvious lack of shrinkage.

Screws and iron nails will only reveal all their characteristics, and so give an idea of their age, when taken out, and therefore preliminary examination will have to be confined to their heads. The faker knows this and concentrates on those features which show on the surface, making a detailed examination of samples essential for complete peace of mind. Obviously, the removal of screws and nails must be left until you get your purchase home, as it is a time-consuming operation which has to be done carefully to avoid damage (and the wrath of the antique dealer). Screws which resist initial attempts with the screwdriver (you *must* use one which fits the slot of the screw perfectly, or the edges of the slot may be torn, making it even more difficult to remove, and make sure that the slot is cleared of dust and rust) should be treated as follows. First, try turning the screw a fraction clockwise, as if to tighten it, then, if that doesn't free it, hold the blade of the screwdriver in the screw slot and tap the end of the handle smartly with a mallet (if the piece of furniture is up to such treatment). If the screw will still not budge then heat will have to be applied. This may be accomplished safely by applying the hot tip of an electric soldering iron to the screw head and leaving it there for a few minutes. When the screw has cooled, the grip of the rust deposit will almost certainly have been broken, enabling the screw to turn freely. Nails, of course, present a different problem – only when the point of a nail is exposed will it be possible to drive it back out. This is, in fact, more common than one might imagine; the nails holding backs of furniture and drawer bottoms in place usually have to go through a board into a fairly thin edge and at least one will have missed somewhere. With a little persuasion (the soldering iron on the nail head will loosen it if it is rusted in), it can be removed for detailed examination.

Again, the search is for signs of handwork or evidence of the simple mechanical devices of the late eighteenth and early nineteenth centuries. In view of the continuing production of hand-forged pins and nails of all descriptions well past any of the antique datelines mentioned earlier, the identification of such nails removed from furniture cannot really be taken as positive evidence. However, it will be of more than passing interest if all the samples taken from that eighteenth-century piece (which has no other nail holes to indicate repair work) prove to be stamped out. So it is worth comparing examples of both hand-forged and stamped nails (Figs. 30 and 32), and keep your eye open for that faker's favourite, the five-clout nail, so called because its head was formed by five well-aimed clouts of hammer on molten metal (Fig. 31). It's popular because it is so easy to fake by adapting the head of a modern tack, which then, short as it is, can be used to secure the thickest board by the simple expedient of concealing a long panel pin beneath the

29. Hand-forged nails or machine-made? The inaccurate fastening of this drawer bottom makes it easier to establish the method of manufacture of the nails and so estimate the date of construction of the piece of furniture.

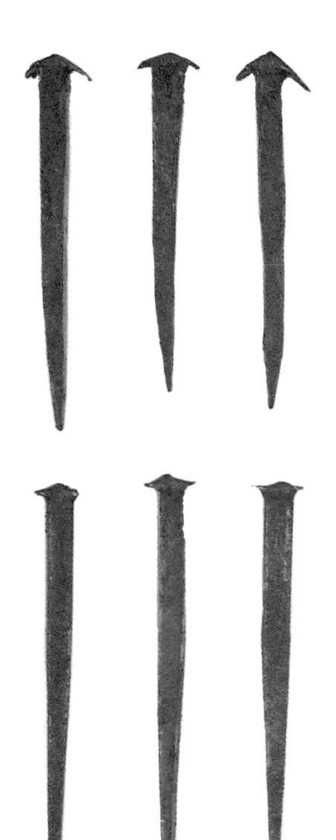

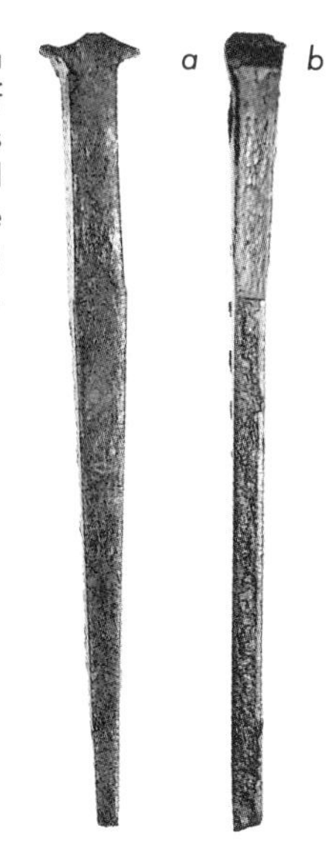

30. Close-up photographs of a cut clasp nail. The narrow faces of the nail show that the metal was sheared (*a*), whilst the broad faces are slightly convex on one side and concave on the other (*b*) due to the force of the press.

32. Samples of clasp nails from two periods. The top row shows the variation in size and shape which is typical of hand-forged nails, whilst the regular size and form of those on the bottom row indicates that they have been stamped from sheet metal and their heads formed by machine.

31. The head of a 'five-clout' nail, showing the five facets from which it gets its name.

33. A group of fake 'five-clout' nails. These have been made from ordinary upholstery tacks. Once they have been rusted, they will be almost indistinguishable from the real thing.

Development of the English wood screw

Wood screws are much more revealing than nails and, whilst they cannot be used for precise dating, some significant inventions transformed their features in a relatively short period of history. The shape and accuracy of manufacture are the clues to dating wood screws, which thus fall roughly into these categories:

34. **Pre-1760** (but continuing as a cottage industry until about 1800). The screw blank was hand-forged, probably by the nail-maker, with varying degrees of taper. The slot was cut with a saw and the thread filed to a point by hand. Needless to say, such screws were not turned out in large quantities, so although their use in furniture making is recorded from about 1700, it was not until some mechanical methods were introduced that they became a common feature for securing metal fittings and fixing table (and other) tops.

35. ***c*1760–1820**. The screw blank is still hand-forged, and there is sometimes a slight taper to the core but not the thread. Thread and slot are cut with the aid of simple mechanical devices, usually with no great accuracy. Close inspection will reveal the marks of the cutters used to clean up the bevel of the screw head, the marks left by the dies used to hold the blank, and varying degrees of precision in thread cutting (*a*). The file marks on the head, and the off-centre slot (*b*), often lead such screws to be described, from this one view alone, as handmade.

36. ***c*1820–50**. The screw blank is now often formed from drawn wire or rod, the signs of which are evident on the shank. Threads are usually more accurately cut and head trimming cleaner but there is still little or no taper and no point.

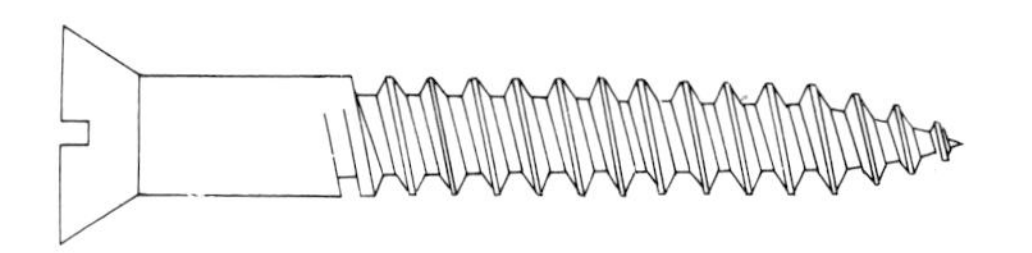

37. A drawing based on that accompanying the British patent of Thomas J. Sloan of New York, taken out by patent agent William Edward Newton (number 11,791) in 1847.

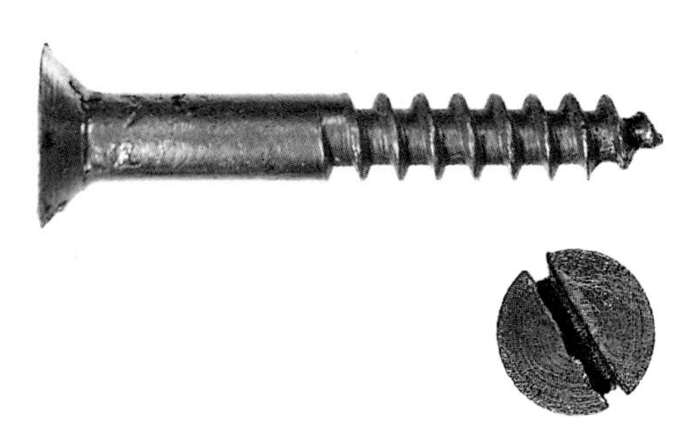

38. ***c*1850**. A wood screw of basically the same design as specified in Sloan's patent. Note the lack of taper from thread into the shank (*a*) which was a point of weakness when driving the screw in. The head of the screw (*b*) by now shows the pattern of lathe marks familiar on today's product.

39. ***c*1860**. By now the thread core is tapered into the shank. The wood screw as we know it today has arrived.

spread-out tack head (Fig. 33). Nor should you be convinced by every rusty nail surrounded by blackened wood; these features *can* be faked and should only be considered as positive evidence if everything else looks right.

Contrary to an opinion often expressed, those antique wood screws with irregular threads and sheared tips were *not* handmade. The first wood screws used in the construction of English furniture, in the first half of the eighteenth century, were virtually handmade – a piece of roughly-forged iron was held in the end of a treadle-operated spindle and all parts of a screw formed with hand-held files. And the result was a pointed screw.

Figure 34 shows a screw produced from a hand-forged blank, probably about 1780 (as in most English trades, old methods die hard). Flat and bevel of the head, the shank and the thread, are all filed. Note the slight taper to the thread and the tapered core, both features inventors of mechanized methods of wood screw production were to fail to achieve for the best part of a hundred years. The slot in the head is handsawn and shows the lack of precision common to this type of screw and many generations of machine-made screws which were to follow it.

The first, and only eighteenth-century, British patent for devices intended specifically for the manufacture of wood screws was granted in 1760; the next was taken out in 1817. In the intervening years, the product changed little and is the screw commonly called 'handmade'. Still using the hand-forged blank, the screw-maker filed the head and shank, but a system of cutters, wheels or dies cut the thread with a greater or lesser degree of accuracy (Fig. 35).

It was in about 1820 that drawn iron wire began to replace hand-forged blanks or rod as the basic material for the production of wood screws, and evidence of the drawing process is often to be seen on the shank of screws made after this time. However, the means of manufacture still restricted the screw's shape to a bolt-like appearance (Fig. 36).

The search for improvements continued without success until 1847, when the latest in an increasingly efficient series of machines constructed in the decade managed to produce pointed screws in commercial quantities. The pointed screw itself was the subject of an American invention (Fig. 37), the manufacturing rights for which were purchased by John Sutton Nettlefold, who started production of the 'new' screw in 1854. Its type is illustrated in Fig. 38. There was, however, still a design problem – the lack of taper in the area where thread meets shank created a weakness.

A patent of 1858 put an end to this problem and the wood screw was once more the tapered and pointed article that it had been a hundred years earlier (Fig. 39).

40. Six screws used to secure a hinge. No two are exactly the same size but all bear identical lathe and tool marks, establishing them as being early machine-made screws. The faker might be able to make the heads of modern screws look like those of this set but imitation of the shanks and threads would be difficult, if not impossible.

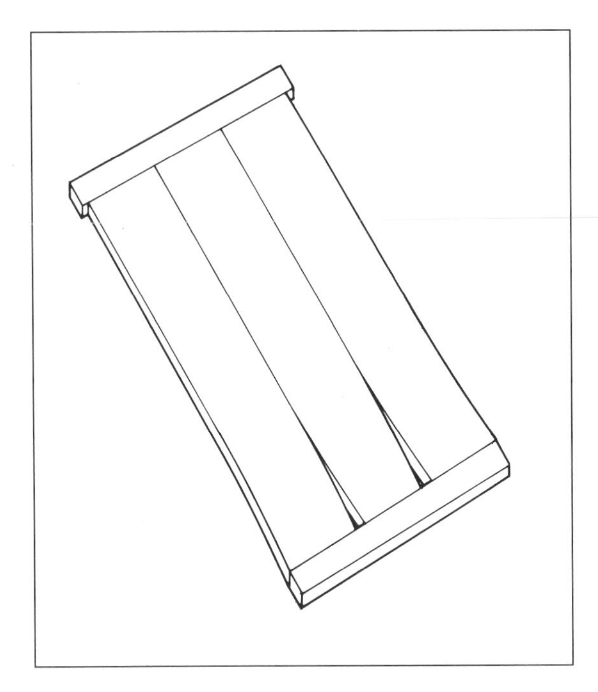

41. The effects of shrinkage on a clamped-board table top. Since shrinkage along the grain is a fraction of that across it, the clamping strips may now protrude beyond the edges of the top if the boards have been free to move. Where boards have been held more firmly, gaps are likely to appear between them, as at the bottom of the diagram.

New and reused wood

The odd piece of freshly-cut wood found in a piece of furniture – a new drawer runner, for example – is one thing: lots of fresh wood, sharp edges and shavings is another. The one is evidence of a legitimate repair, the other that extensive repairs or alterations have been done. Use your nose as well. The smell of freshly-cut wood doesn't last long, so if you can smell wood and/or the solvents used in stains and varnishes instead of that musty, dusty aroma of age, and can see recently-sawn edges, start asking questions.

Another sign of new wood or the reuse of old, well-seasoned wood is the lack of evidence of shrinkage (see the comments about pegged joints in the previous section). A circular table top made years ago will not now be circular: check the diameter along the grain and across it and if they are the same there's something wrong, for the measurement across the grain should be $\frac{1}{8}$th of an inch or more shorter, per foot of the diameter, than along it. Table tops and doors made of a number of boards with their ends held by clamping strips may show the effects of shrinkage in two ways (or a combination of both): the boards may shrink uniformly and stay together, leaving the ends of the clamping strips protruding, or the ends of the boards may be held more or less firmly, shrinkage showing across the centre with separation of the boards somewhere along the joins, often at the ends (Fig. 41).

The amount of shrinkage which occurs does depend on the moisture content of the wood when the piece of furniture was made and on how quickly it dried out. Furniture made of unseasoned wood is likely to show considerable shrinkage and, depending on how the timber was cut from the log, some distortion, but radial cuts of well-seasoned timber will produce furniture which is subject to minimal movement (see Chapter 5).

Veneers

One thing the faker seldom copies is the thickness of the eighteenth-century veneers, probably only because he can no longer get supplies of thick enough veneer and hasn't got the solid wood, or the energy, to handsaw the stuff. The earliest veneer was more of a facing of wood than the thin ($\frac{1}{32}$") sheet which is standard today. It is not uncommon to find an early veneer of $\frac{1}{8}$" or more, or rather average $\frac{1}{8}$" in thickness, for it seems that it would often be glued on straight from the saw, with scant regard for irregularities in it or the ground wood to which it was applied, and then sanded flat. The result can be a veneer which varies in thickness from $\frac{1}{16}$" to $\frac{3}{16}$".

42. Eighteenth-century mahogany veneer. This composite picture of the edge of a panel shows the extreme variations in thickness of veneer.

There will nearly always be an exposed edge of a veneered top, drawer front or panel which you can inspect. The thicker veneers just mentioned will indicate eighteenth-century workmanship, but in the later years of that century more accurate methods of cutting veneer were developed, permitting a thinner veneer of uniform thickness. Veneer of at least $\frac{1}{16}$" thick will be found on furniture made up to the second quarter of the nineteenth century, after which thinner cuts became common, some of them paper-thin. So if you see what purports to be an early Georgian chest of drawers with veneer so thin that glue has seeped through the pores of the wood, leave it alone.

Check also for variations in the thickness of veneer from panel to panel in the same piece of furniture and to see if even veneered panels are combined with solid wood panels. Fakers who make up 'antiques' from pieces of old furniture often assume that the customer's interest is limited to the exterior appearance of their wares and trust to a coat or two of stain on the edges and insides of panels to disguise their tricks.

Brass handles

This, of all the pointers, is probably the least positive, but it must be included in order to correct some misunderstandings about the ease with which the authenticity of brass handles may be established. Dealers and auctioneers make much of being able to describe a piece of furniture as 'having original handles', which helps them obtain a good price. One suspects that most of them give the handle plate a cursory look ('in period, nice and thin, edges bevelled and well worn with polishing'), peer inside to establish that there are no other holes to indicate changes of handles and that the post threads and nuts are of brass and not obviously modern steel, then pronounce the handles original.

In fact, very few pieces have survived with their original sets of handles intact. Handles and posts of heavily-laden drawers break and if matching replacements cannot be obtained a complete new set is fitted; or fashions change and another style of handle is used to bring the piece up to date. So long as the present handles are of the correct period design and construction, and fit in the original holes, you will probably not be able to tell if they are old or new without more extensive examination at home (see Chapter 11). There are some fine copies of cast handles about nowadays which are correct in virtually every detail, made of brass which even metallurgical laboratory tests might not distinguish from old metal. Don't be persuaded that it is simple to identify old brass by its colour. It is true that brass used for casting did have a higher copper content than nowadays, about 75% copper to 25% zinc against about 60/40 today, but this is a difference which the average eye might have difficulty in detecting if well-polished samples were held side by side, let alone when comparing brasswork in varying stages of tarnish. In any event, it is only in recent times (in antique terms) that the proportion of copper in brass was reduced, so those handles could have been cast in the 1920s and now be so well buffed and naturally patinated that no one can tell them from antique. Don't be swayed, either, by the colour and patination of tarnished brass, for these effects can be produced on brass of any composition (see p. 129). The one detail which might identify a modern casting may be revealed if you can remove a handle post and examine its thread through your magnifying glass. You may find that it has been cast (or stamped) into the metal instead of cut (Figs. 43 and 44).

43. An old brass handle post. This bears the marks one would expect to find on a late eighteenth- or early nineteenth-century lathe-made screw.

44. A twentieth-century handle post. Although outwardly almost identical to its predecessor, this post is given away by the fine seam which is just visible one-third the way in from the left of the thread.

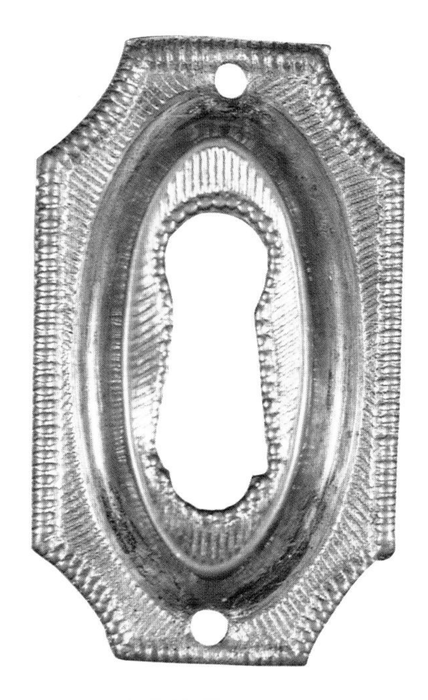

45. An early pressed brass escutcheon plate. Compare the detail on this with that of the modern one of the same design.

46. A modern pressed brass escutcheon plate. Even from a distance the lack of sharpness of detail will be apparent.

In the case of pressed handle plates and escutcheons, which came into vogue in the late eighteenth century, the difference between antique and modern is easily detected, particularly with the aid of the magnifying glass. The crispness of details of early examples is completely absent in their twentieth-century successors (Figs. 45 and 46).

But does the date of a handle matter? If the handles fit and are correct for the period and the piece of furniture is established as period by all your other investigations, then it does seem unreasonable to reject it because of a suspicion that the handles might be later replacements. Your suspicions and the reasons for them, however, should be pointed out to the person claiming 'original handles'. Replacing handles is discussed in Chapter 11.

Locks

A fitting which *can* tell you something about the age of a piece of furniture is its lock. The pointers here are primarily concerned with the external appearance of a lock, it being unreasonable to expect to be able to remove it and inspect its innards while negotiating a purchase. The comments and photographs relating to mechanisms and internal features will assist you in your fireside investigation later and will hopefully confirm your original opinion.

Eighteenth-century English furniture locks made up to about 1780 usually have a thin-gauge steel case with a chamfer around the edge of the back, particularly on small locks. The bolt is also of steel and often not exactly rectangular in section but the case opening will fit it perfectly nonetheless (Fig. 47a). Sometimes the lock will be secured by four screws and the case will be drilled with four countersunk holes for the purpose. Others have two countersunk holes for screws at the top and two small holes at the bottom for nails (they were perhaps made this way to save on cost, as screws were expensive items before the introduction of machinery for their manufacture). When the lock is removed (note methods of removing rusted-in nails and screws on page 26), its front cover plate (the cap) may be lifted from its retaining lugs by sliding a stout knife blade beneath it, to reveal the characteristic forged steel bolt with integral spring. Many of these back-spring locks are fitted with wards to provide a measure of security; these are the thin, curved lengths of metal fitted to the inside of the case and cap, centred on the pin, making a barrier which must be matched by slotted wards in the key bit before the key will move the bolt (Fig. 47b).

Brass-cased locks came into production in the late eighteenth century, some still with steel back-spring bolts and wards but, with fierce competition to produce the ultimate in secure locks, the mechanisms became more complex. First came variations on the common tumbler lock. The arrangement of wards surrounding the pin of such a brass-cased lock is usually clearly visible on the outside of the case (Fig. 48). A distinctive feature of many tumbler locks is the accurately made steel bolt which shows one or two parts through the case of a small lock used for a drawer or small door (Fig. 49*a*), or three or four parts on a lock for a large door or bureau fall. When this type of lock is removed, a cap will be found which is similar to that on a steel-cased type, but it will usually be secured by two small steel bolts in addition to the lugs. Removal of the cap will reveal the tumbler with a spring bearing on its pivot end, a lug on the tumbler locating in notches in the edge of the bolt (Fig. 49*b*) or, sometimes, in a form of gating in the bolt (Fig. 50). Some later versions of the tumbler lock have contoured wards of brass (Fig. 51) which cannot be detected from the outside. The cap of this type of tumbler lock will most often be of cast brass, secured by two or three small bolts.

The lever lock came into production in the second quarter of the nineteenth century. The first ones were brass cased with a steel bolt of large section and often the words SECURE and/or LEVER are stamped on the bolt face of the case (Fig. 52). PATENT is found on all sorts of locks which were not, in fact, blessed with the Royal Letters Patent. Removed from the piece of furniture, the cast brass cap is seen, secured by two or three steel bolts and with a hole cut in it in front of the levers. Early lever locks are distinguishable by the comb of springs bearing against the fulcrum ends of the levers (Fig. 53). In those made after about 1870 each lever is fitted with its own spring and most have bolts of brass (Fig. 54), completing the transition to the lever lock which is still made today.

Both back-spring and common tumbler locks continued in production right through the Victorian period and it is sometimes not possible to detect these later ones by means of an external examination. Inspection with a magnifying glass may reveal that the case has been stamped out of sheet metal but confirmation of a later date of manufacture will be in the discovery of roughly cast or stamped components (Figs. 55 & 56).

While you have the lock out, check to see if there are screw holes in the wood other than those which align with those on the lock. If there are, then the lock has been changed, and identifying and dating it will be interesting but not evidence; if there are no other screw holes there is a reasonable chance that the lock is original and can confirm that you have a period piece of antique furniture.

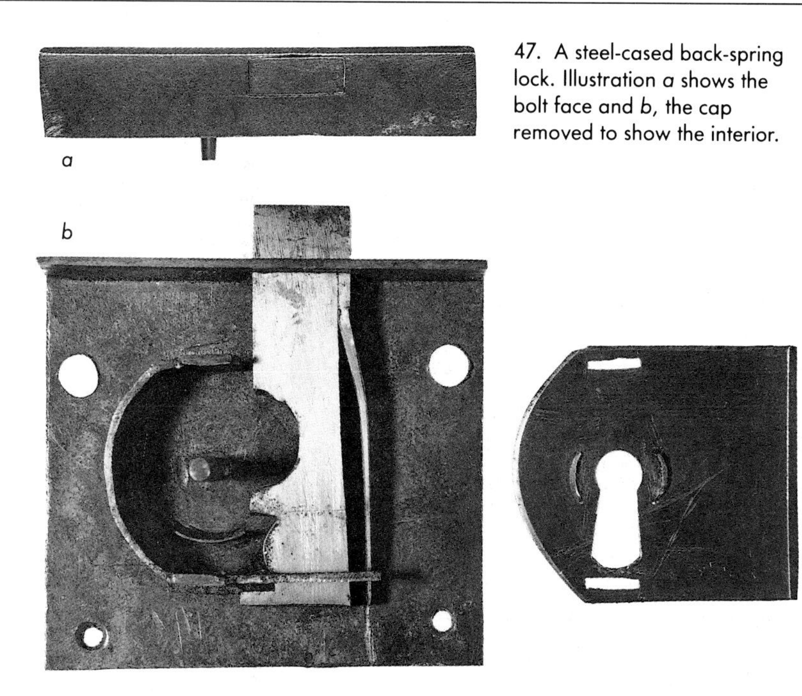

47. A steel-cased back-spring lock. Illustration *a* shows the bolt face and *b*, the cap removed to show the interior.

A key will only fit right down the pin if the ward on the case fits a matching slot (also called a ward) in the front of the bit of the key, and will only turn if the wards on the cap are matched by the back of the bit. The bolt is thrown by pressure of the key bit on the semicircular section (the talon) of the bolt, which raises it against the resistance of the integral spring, clearing the first notch in the tail of the bolt and relocating the second notch onto the rim. This lock is secured by screws in the top pair of holes in the case and by nails in the bottom holes.

48. The pattern of steel parts showing through this brass case tells us that it is a warded tumbler lock (see Fig. 49)

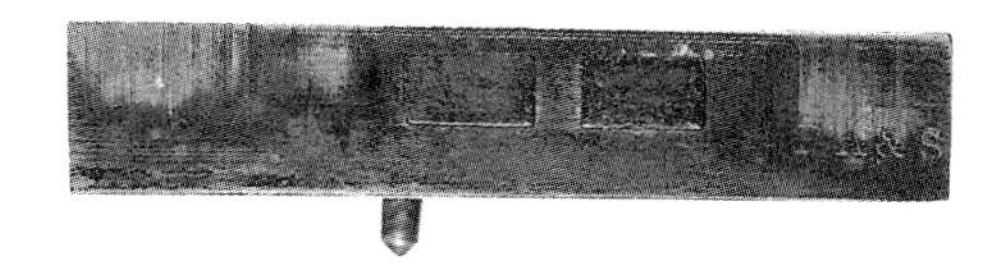

49. A tumbler lock. Illustration *a* shows the bolt face of a typical drawer lock with tumbler mechanism and *b* shows the interior. Note the spring bearing on the pivot-end of the (brass) tumbler, where less wear will occur because movement is least. Not only will the wards on the case and cap have to be matched by the key but the tumbler must be lifted far enough to disengage the lug beneath the tumbler from notches in the edge of tbe bolt, the first of which is visible with the bolt in the thrown position (as shown here).

50. A Barron's patent type (invented by Robert Barron in 1778). The system of gates cut into the bolt would later be adapted to operate in the tumbler, creating what is now known as the lever lock. There are comparatively few of this type of lock to be found in furniture.

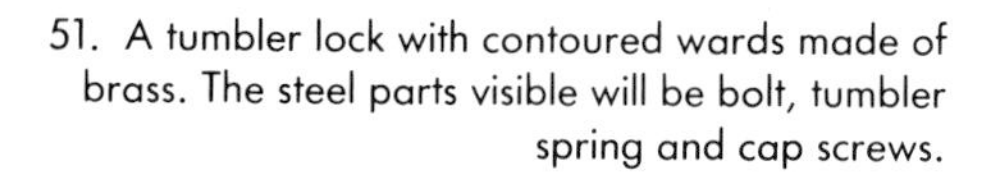

51. A tumbler lock with contoured wards made of brass. The steel parts visible will be bolt, tumbler spring and cap screws.

52. Although brass-cased with a steel bolt, this might not be a tumbler lock. The more stamped lettering on the bolt face, the later it is likely to be and this one is, in fact, a lever lock.

53. A Victorian Chubb patent lever box lock. Illustration *a* shows the bolt face with several informative stamps, including a serial number which puts the approximate year (part of the number is obliterated) of manufacture at 1864. Illustration *b* shows the interior with the notches in the lever gating and the spring-loaded lug which comprise the 'detector' mechanism. If an attempt is made to pick the lock or even open it with a key which does not operate each of the seven levers absolutely precisely, the mechanism will jam, only to be freed with the correct key. Illustration *c* shows one piece of steel forms the comb of springs which bears against the levers – an extraordinary example of nineteenth-century craftsmanship.

54. A standard Victorian lever lock. Each lever has its own spring bent round the fulcrum end. Only when the key bit has lifted all the levers to the precise height will the lug on the bolt be allowed to pass through the gating to unlock the mechanism.

55. A Victorian steel back-spring lock. A first glance at this lock while it is still fitted in a drawer will probably persuade the eye that it is of eighteenth-century origin. Once it has been removed, the shaped keyhole tells of a later date of manufacture and this is confirmed when the cap is removed to reveal the cast bolt with its separate spring.

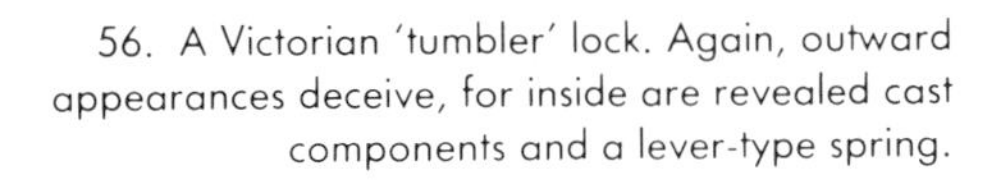

56. A Victorian 'tumbler' lock. Again, outward appearances deceive, for inside are revealed cast components and a lever-type spring.

Anatomy of a fake

57. This pair of chairs was taken to the restorer's workshops only for a check over and a coat of wax polish.

Once in a while you may come across something which accumulates so many black marks that you wonder how it could have slipped onto the market unnoticed, as have so many nineteenth- and early twentieth-century copies. Such signs of recent deliberate faking are evident on two walnut chairs which came into circulation purporting to be from the early eighteenth century (Fig. 57). Apart from any question of correctness of style, the first thing which catches the eye is the wear on the arched cross-stretcher. Close inspection, with the aid of a profile copier (Fig. 58), shows that the front hollow of the moulding had never been cut right along: just a couple of inches are cut at each end. If the man had completed the moulding and *then* rounded it off it would be less obvious, but even then the wear would not have been reasonable, as it would be impossible to rest the feet on the rail without performing the most uncomfortable contortions.

Inspection of the cross-stretcher at close quarters focuses attention on another alarming feature. Under a magnifying glass, it is clear that all those scratches are on top of the 'wear' and beneath a thick layer of varnish, which is not thinner in the area where the heaviest wear is supposed to have been. There are no fresh marks or partly-rubbed old marks to testify to ongoing wear and tear, and an examination of all other varnished surfaces shows the same. Without a laboratory test it is not possible to establish the type of varnish used and therefore its likely age, but it is evident that two tinted finishes were used: a pale ochre for tops of rails, sides and front and a dark one for the back. Not a trace of wax polish is to be found but under magnification every varnished surface shows signs of abrasion, probably the result of being dulled down with fine steel wool – so much for the patina resulting from centuries of hand polishing! To further undermine the case for 'antique colour and patina', the finish has been rubbed so thin in places that pale, raw wood shows through, confirming that the colour is in the finish.

Turning a chair over reveals more. That 'patination' which looks so like crackled, old varnish (compare Figs. 59 and 60) is rather a skilfully-applied hard wax, as samples proved: the stuff crumbled off instead of reducing to a resinous powder, and it melted when warmed, giving off the distinctive aroma of carnauba wax. It would have been more convincing, visually, if there had been some signs of wear and tear instead of a completely unbroken crust – a couple of hundred years

58. Checking the profile of the cross-stretcher reveals the extent of the false wear.

59. Beneath the stretchers is the 'crackled varnish' which turned out to be hard wax.

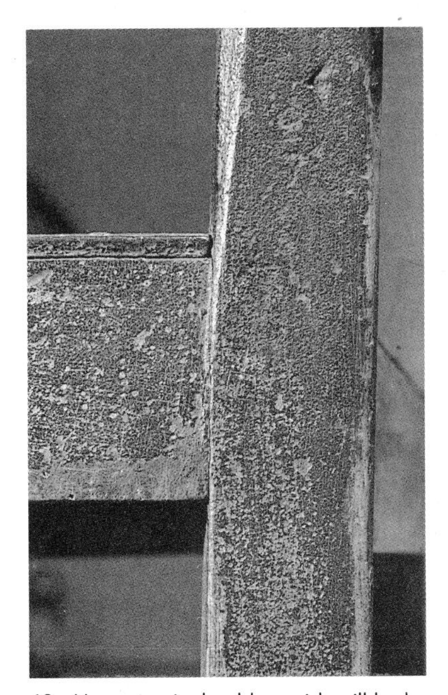

60. How genuinely old varnish will look after scores of years of wear and tear.

61. To the casual observer these two different brackets might indicate separate and ancient repairs.

of housework and handling would surely have left their marks.

The odd brackets at the back joints (Fig. 61) start off another train of checks. They may be there to persuade us that repairs have been carried out at various times in the past, but the brackets perform no useful function. Remove them and the chairs are absolutely rigid, with no hint of the movement which is to be expected in chairs of this construction (pegged mortice and tenon) and supposed age. These chairs have been glued together, which no restorer with a grain of sense would do.

There is also a question about the pegs through the joints. Under *Nails and screws*, two pointers were mentioned: shrinkage would leave the head of each peg just proud of the surface of the leg, detectable as a small bump in the veneer; and the point of the peg would usually be visible on the inside of the leg. Neither is the case on these chairs (Figs. 62 and 63).

As the eye passes over the veneer of the front of the legs looking for signs of pegs and then checks inside for the pegs showing there, something else jangles a nerve. There are worm holes on the outside of the legs but none inside. A search for the other worm-damaged areas reveals a series of holes in the splat shoes – an almost identical pattern of holes on top, front and back of both

62. A 'centuries-old' chair with no small bump to indicate the position of the head of a joint peg?

63. No pegs showing on the inside of the top of a leg. And that rail, despite showing the marks of a handsaw, looks very clean and sharp.

64. 'Wear and tear' and 'worm holes' on the splat shoes of one chair...

chairs' shoes and veneered back rails (Figs. 64 and 67). A further coincidence is the large chip of veneer out of both rails in almost the same position on each and with identical wear to the edges of the gaps. Such coincidences must be worthy of a closer look and, once again, the magnifying glass reveals all: the holes and chipped veneer are not filled with the accumulated grime of centuries but with the same black wax as has been used to 'patinate' beneath the frame and stretchers. Could those worm holes be fakes?

There is nothing for it but to remove a piece of veneer and see if there is any worm-damage behind it. An area of veneer at the top of a front leg, which has a couple of holes in it, will probably be doubly interesting, for this is where the peg

65. A piece of veneer removed from the top of one of the legs. The 'worm holes' on the outside are obviously made with a bodkin.

66. The top of the leg, with matching traces of the bodkin marks and all the evidence of modern manufacture.

67. . . . and remarkably similar 'evidence of age' on the other.

should be. When a small piece of veneer is removed and the glue washed off it is clear that a bodkin made the holes; the impression is on both veneer and the top of the leg. The peg is no more a roughly-rounded treenail than the bodkin marks are worm holes and, as if further proof of jiggery-pokery were necessary, that extra large 'worm hole' contains a modern panel pin (Figs. 65 and 66). Without removing the veneer from the other legs it is not possible to prove that the other joints have suffered similar treatment, but a metal detector does indicate a small metal object in the appropriate position on each.

The chairs are clearly fakes.

Restoration of Cabinetwork

Eighty per cent of the time which the professional restorer spends in the cabinet shop is taken up with the rectification of a handful of fairly standard problems. Most of the remainder of the time is occupied by rooting about for just the right piece of wood for the job and getting tools and equipment ready to do the work. This second part of the book, therefore, is about life in the cabinet shop.

CHAPTER 4
The bases of cabinetwork

68. A metal detector finds a concealed nail. This inexpensive gadget is an essential part of the restorer's tool kit.

69. A boxed set of oilstones and slipstones.

The tools

Your tool kit may not be extensive at the moment but this doesn't matter, although of course it may limit the scope of the work you can undertake; just so long as when you add to your collection you get the best you can find. You do not have to buy the hand-crafted products of the specialist tool-makers, or the top of the range of the well-known names, to get the best. There are lots of old tools about which, in spite of considerable use, have survived because of their high quality, and many of these may be obtained for relatively modest sums. Unfortunately, the days are gone when your local auction room regularly had boxes full of all sorts of old tools; now you will have to visit second-hand tool shops and antique dealers who specialize in tools to find a good selection. If you come across tools in a shop which stocks general antiques you must know exactly what you are looking at and also keep an eye on the prices, for these are often fixed at the highest guide book prices without regard to condition. A visit to a specialist's shop will be a worthwhile experience, if only to look and wonder, but you're bound to be tempted. Try to resist the fancy things (Fig. 71) on the first visit though, for whilst an ebony and brass mortice gauge looks splendid on your tool rack, it doesn't really perform much better than its beech cousin. Your first thoughts should be for those tools which do most of the hard work of restoration: the edge tools. Old wood is tough and requires fine steel to cope with it, and it does seem that an old chisel made from hand-forged steel holds its edge better than its plastic-handled descendant. Just try a couple of each sort in your work for a while and see which your hand reaches for most often.

Ancient or modern, your edge tools must be kept sharp. The sharper they are the cleaner they cut and the safer they are to work with; blunt tools not only give a less than perfect cut but they need more force to use, inevitably leading to injury to you and further damage to the piece of furniture you are restoring. Major damage to edges, as when you find a hidden nail the hard way, will need the attention of a whetstone, an expensive piece of equipment which may be justified in the professional's workshop but seldom otherwise, for the local sharpening services will surely oblige for a small sum. This sort of problem can usually be averted by the use of a small metal detector (Fig. 68) to check over old wood and any previous repairs to the piece you are working on.

For most grinding and honing a set of good-quality oilstones and slipstones will be all that you require. These should be boxed up together, for convenience and to keep them clean (Fig. 69). Separate stones for grinding (coarse) and honing (medium and fine) are ideal, but the double-sided combination stones will serve the purpose. These may be lubricated with thin mineral oil or a 50/50 mixture of household lubricating oil and paraffin. A honing guide is not recommended (but if you are accustomed to using one, so be it): apart from the time taken fiddling about setting the thing, the method of its use can result in wear being concentrated on one area of the oilstone, leading to chisels and plane blades with cutting edges out of square. There is a method of sharpening which is much kinder to the oilstones and ensures that you will achieve keen, square edges for longer before you have to trim the stones.

Traditionally, edge tools have been given two bevels, first the ground bevel and then the honed bevel, of about 25° and 30° respectively. Because of their size, this practice is the only reasonable one for most plane blades, as described below, but a true, sharp edge is easier to create and maintain on a chisel blade if it is ground and honed to one bevel only. The angle chosen depends on the quality of the steel from which the blade is forged, on how well the blade is tempered and also on what sort of work you will be doing with it. The finest steel, when well tempered, will hold a cutting edge if ground and honed to 25° and so be best for paring and other such fine work, whilst that which blunts quicker (perhaps it needs retempering, see p. 45) will need to be ground and honed to 30° and kept for rougher work. If you elect to adopt the single bevel for your chisels, start by getting them all ground to the selected angles. If you are unsure about the quality of the metal or its state of temper, make the firmer chisels 30° at first and bevel-edged 25°, then adjust them as working with them indicates.

To regrind a chisel which has suffered minor damage, you will probably get by with the coarse oilstone. Don't over-oil the stone: a few drops, spread evenly over the whole surface of the stone, will last a while. Rest the bevel of the chisel on the stone and check that it is sitting flat by rocking the blade back and forth very slightly – as it comes off the back edge of the bevel onto the flat a fine line of oil will appear at the cutting edge. When you are sure that the bevel is flat on the stone, start to move it in figures of eight. Cover the whole surface of the stone and maintain steady pressure to ensure that all the bevel stays in contact (Fig. 70*a*). Go on with the figures of eight until you can feel a burr forming on the back of the cutting edge. If the oil gets too thick with particles of metal, wipe it off and put on some more. When a decent burr is formed, turn the chisel over, place the blade absolutely flat on the far end of the stone and draw it towards you with one firm stroke to turn the burr back to the bevel side (Fig. 70*c*). As you do this you must prevent the blade lifting onto the cutting edge by even the smallest amount, or further deburring strokes will not be entirely effective, and that sharp edge will be impossible to achieve. It may be, if the damage was slight, that it will have all been removed by this operation. If not, go on with figures of eight, follow by the single deburring stroke, until it is.

The production of a fine cutting edge comes next, and this procedure is also used for its maintenance – whenever an edge needs reviving in the middle of a job. As your collection of tools enlarges it will not be necessary to abandon work to sharpen a blade as soon as it loses its cutting edge. A regular session of resharpening, when every edge tool is checked over and brought back to standard, will obviously save time.

If you have had to regrind the bevel you will be likely to have to go through the figure of eight routine on the medium stone before you can start the honing operation proper. Then, still on the medium stone, rest the bevel on the surface and make sure it is flat, as before, but this time move the blade in a series of small circles (Fig. 70*b*). Start with five or six circles, then turn the blade over and give one firm deburring stroke, as before (Fig. 70*c*). Turn the blade back over and do the circles – one less this time –

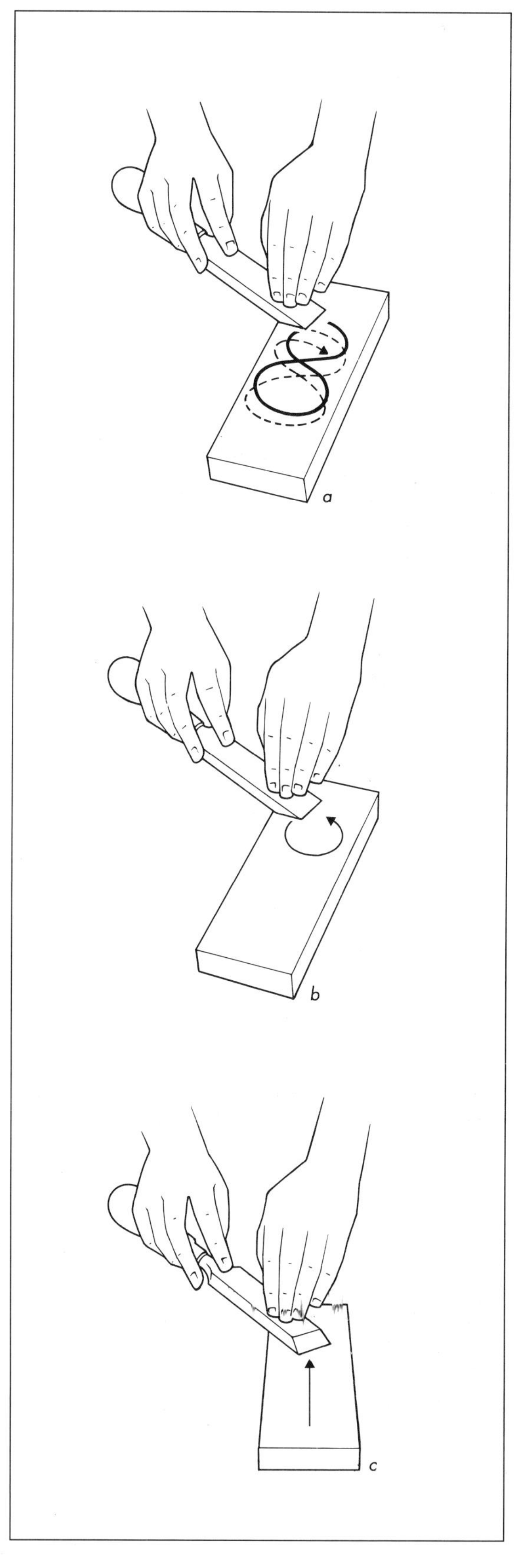

70. Honing a chisel.

followed by a deburring stroke. And so on, with reducing numbers of circles on the bevel, followed by one flat stroke on the back, until you finish with one circle and a last deburring stroke. The chisel will now be sharp enough for most work but if you need an extra-sharp edge then repeat the circles routine on the fine oilstone. Give the chisel a wipe with a meths-dampened rag and it is ready to be put to work again.

The sharpening of plane irons is achieved by the same series of steps, except that, having found the position of the ground bevel, the back of the blade is raised so that only the tip is resting on the oilstone, at an angle of 30°. (If you find this honing angle difficult to judge at first, try holding a 150° template on the stone in front of the iron to start you off.) An exception to this is the low-profile end grain plane, the iron of which is treated as a chisel and given one bevel of 25°.

Whether a gouge is to be given a single bevel or two – and if only one, the angle of that bevel – depends again on the quality of the steel, its use, and its size. Small, good-quality gouges for fine work can take one shallow bevel, large ones for rough work need a less acute bevel, or perhaps the two. The outer face of a gouge, whether bevelled (firmer gouge) or flat (scribing gouge), is treated on the oilstone by rubbing along the length of the stone while imparting a twisting movement to the blade to ensure that the whole of the cutting edge gets attention. This is easy enough with a scribing gouge, which is held flat, but is much more difficult with a firmer gouge, as the correct angle has to be maintained at the same time as the twisting motion. Perhaps even trickier is the treatment of the inner face. A slipstone of the appropriate arc must be given a steady side-to-side movement while maintaining the correct angle.

71. Collector's items as well as practical tools, made from brass and ebony.

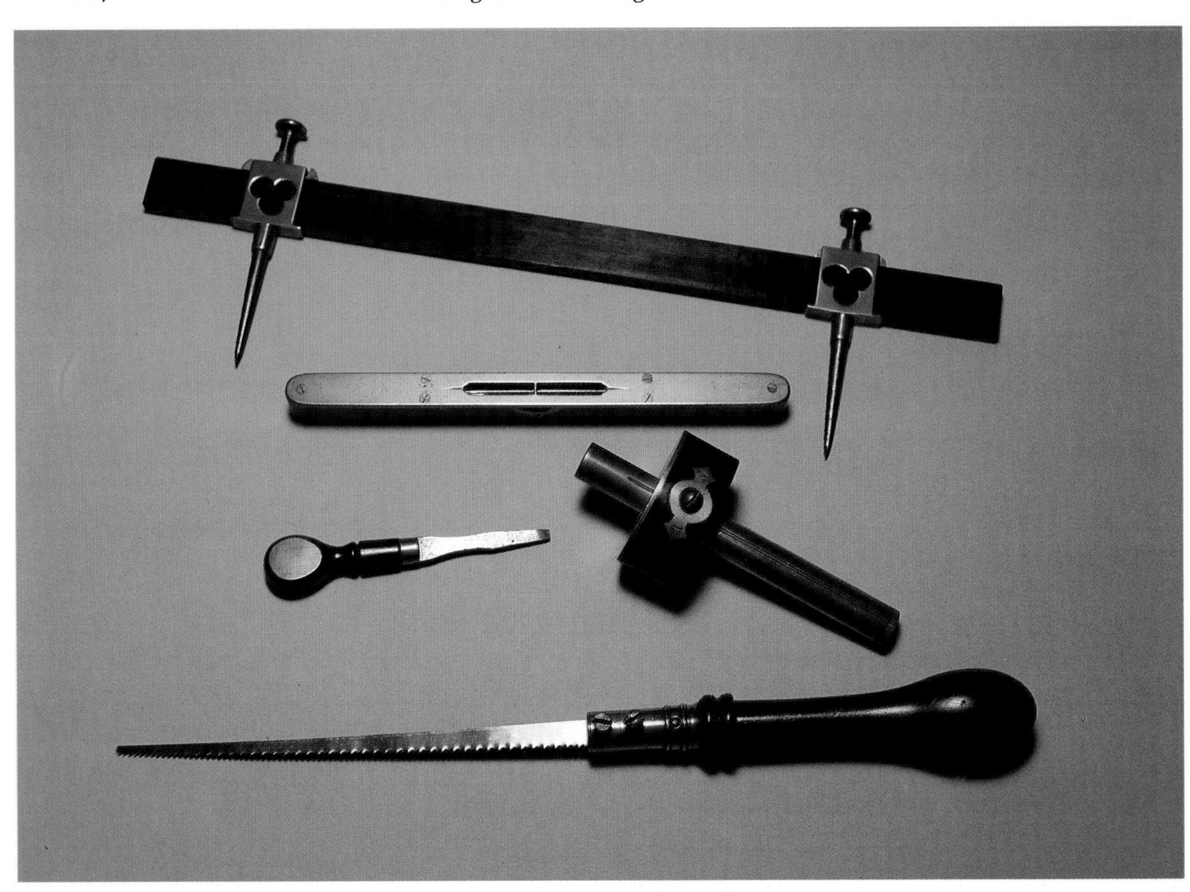

Eventually your oilstones will wear, even with the most careful use, sufficiently to upset the squared cutting edges of chisels and plane blades, and will need to be ground flat again. The way to do this is simple, if monotonous. Soak the offending stone in paraffin to remove the oil which has impregnated the surface. Set a slab of old marble or thick plate glass (make sure that *this* is flat) on your bench, sprinkle on a little 100-grit carborundum powder, add enough water to make a thin paste and you're all set. Grind the oilstone on the paste, using the whole area of the slab, and turn the oilstone round from time to time, adding more carborundum and water if you feel there isn't enough abrasion going on. Perseverance is required for this job, for it can take quite a while for the oilstone to get back to a proper state. When you are satisfied that you once more have a flat stone, rinse it and put it aside until it is completely dry.

There will come a time when you have reground a chisel to the point where its cutting edge is no longer at an ideal state of temper, being so soft that constant honing is required to maintain a usable condition. You may decide to leave retempering to the local blacksmith, but if you decide to have a go yourself, here is the method. To start with, you will need a gas blow-torch capable of producing a flame of variable heat. Then, as a first step, remove the handle from the chisel (this is not practicable with the plastic-handled variety). Holding the tang with pliers, heat the blade up in a good strong flame until it is cherry red (judge this away from bright light or you won't see the colour properly), paying particular attention to the cutting end, then quench it immediately in a bucket of cold water. It is important that this quenching operation is done precisely, with the blade plunged straight down into the water, cutting edge first, then immediately swirled about for several seconds. Remove the blade from the water and dry it, then polish its back (cutting-edge face) with emery cloth.

Now comes the really critical part of the operation. With a much reduced flame, heat the centre of the polished section of the blade until you can see the metal start to change colour. The first colour to appear will be a pale straw, darkening gradually to brown, then through shades of purple to bright blue. These colours will travel along the blade in succession, the speed depending on the amount of heat you are applying. You don't want the colours changing rapidly because the blade has to be quenched when the optimum colour is achieved at the tip, so keep the flame away from the blade once the colours have started to move and touch it back on again if they slow down too much. When the straw colour reaches the tip, stand by. The colour to quench at will come just before the brown – a reddish-brown (Fig. 72). If you quench before this, the tip will be a bit too hard for woodworking and will tend to break, particularly if an acute bevel is put on it. Quenching at purple to blue will leave the tip too soft for it to maintain a sharp edge for long. Polish the blade, put back the handle and it will be ready to receive the finest edge you can put on it.

72. Tempering colours demonstrated on a piece of scraper steel.

Tools to buy

Chisels and gouges: $\frac{1}{16}$″ (you will probably have to make something as small as this yourself), $\frac{1}{8}$″, $\frac{1}{4}$″, $\frac{3}{8}$″, $\frac{1}{2}$″, $\frac{3}{4}$″ and 1″ in firmer chisels and $\frac{1}{4}$″, $\frac{3}{8}$″, $\frac{1}{2}$″, $\frac{3}{4}$″ and 1″ in bevel-edged chisels, firmer gouges and scribing gouges. The requirements of the carver and the turner are not within the scope of this book for, although such work is often part of the restoration process, these subjects are already exhaustively covered by many specialist publications.

Planes: Jack, smoothing, jointer, a couple of block planes, including one with a low-angle iron, a small bullnose plane and an adjustable rebate plane, all metal. That should do for the basics, until you come to moulding planes, which you could spend a lifetime collecting and seldom find two the same. Attention should therefore be focused on matched pairs of rounds and hollows (the question as to which is the round plane – that which *is* round or that which *forms* the round – continues to be argued), a good range of which, together with the adjustable rebate plane, will manage just about every straight moulding you will need to copy. Curved and fine mouldings and beads can be produced with a scratch stock, which you can make yourself, as described on p. 48 (and see Chapter 6).

Saws: 18–24″ panel saw with 8–12 teeth per inch (tpi), 24–30″ rip saw with 4–6 tpi, 12″ heavy back saw (tenon) with 14 tpi, 6″ light back saw (gents) with 24–32 tpi, plus hacksaw, coping saw and piercing saw. Blades for the latter come in a number of sizes, the most useful to the restorer being those in the range 6 (33 tpi) down to 2/0 (58 tpi), which will manage most marquetry, boulle and fine metalwork (see Chapters 6 and 11, respectively). And if you don't have a bandsaw you will need a bowsaw.

Screwdrivers: Whilst you may manage very well with a limited range of some sorts of tools, you won't get by with just a couple of screwdrivers (or turnscrews, to the purist). Ideally, the screwdriver blade will fit the slot of the screw exactly, but since the slots of antique screws are extremely variable, you would need several dozen to guarantee a good fit every time. And then there's the question of the length of the screwdriver's blade. Generally, the larger the screw the longer the blade you will need in order to apply the required torque, especially when withdrawing well-rusted screws (see p. 26). However, the space in which to operate is often limited in restoration work and a shorter blade then has to be used; hence the number of screwdrivers you will eventually acquire. In the meantime, you will probably manage with ten or so.

WIDTH OF TIP	THICKNESS OF TIP	LENGTH OF BLADE
$\frac{1}{8}$″	$\frac{1}{64}$″ & $\frac{1}{32}$″	4–6″
$\frac{1}{4}$″	$\frac{1}{64}$″ & $\frac{1}{32}$″	4–6″
$\frac{3}{8}$″	$\frac{1}{32}$″ & $\frac{3}{64}$″	6–8″
$\frac{1}{2}$″	$\frac{1}{32}$″ & $\frac{3}{64}$″	8–10″
$\frac{5}{8}$″	$\frac{3}{64}$″ & $\frac{1}{16}$″	10″

Measuring and marking: 12″ and 6″ stainless rules. 8–10 foot tape measure. Steel straight edge, as long as you can afford. Mortice gauge and cutting gauge. Try square with 6″ arm. Sliding (adjustable) bevel. Steel compasses and calipers. Marking knife.

Drills: Ratchet brace with Jennings pattern bits sized $\frac{1}{4}$″, $\frac{5}{16}$″, $\frac{3}{8}$″, $\frac{1}{2}$″, $\frac{5}{8}$″, $\frac{3}{4}$″, $\frac{7}{8}$″ and 1″. Hand drill (enclosed). Electric drill, two-speed, preferably with variable speed controlled by trigger pressure – and the larger the chuck capacity the better. Set of high-speed steel bits, $\frac{1}{16}$″ to $\frac{1}{2}$″ in $\frac{1}{16}$″ steps, plus a countersink bit and plug cutters sized $\frac{5}{16}$″, $\frac{3}{8}$″, and $\frac{1}{2}$″. Archimedean drill and bits. Bradawl.

Hammers and mallets: Warrington pattern hammers, 10–12 oz. and 4 oz. (pin hammer). Wooden mallet (preferably with cylindrical head about 2$\frac{1}{2}$″ diameter by 5″ long). Hard-rubber or leather mallet.

Grippers: Pliers and pincers, large and small of each. Snipe-nosed pliers. Adjustable spanner. Tweezers.

Punches: $\frac{1}{16}''$ and $\frac{1}{8}''$ nail punches. Centre punch.

Spokeshave: Adjustable steel spokeshave, flat sole, with 2″ cutter (sharpened to one 30° bevel).

Cramps (or clamps): 3 sash cramps, 3–5 feet long (T-bar are best). At least 2 G-cramps of each size 3″, 4″, 6″ and 8″. 2 pairs cam (Klemmsia) cramps, 2 ft and 3 ft. Webbing cramp. Anything else you care to add to this list, from antique handscrews to some of the latest patent devices, will increase the scope and volume of work you can undertake yourself.

Knives: Swann-Morton no. 3 handle with 10A (straight-edged) and 15 (fine, curved edge) disposable blades. A couple of old, flexible steel table knives (pallet knives may be finer but are expensive and don't stand up so well to the rigours of restoration work).

Files: Assorted half-round, round, flat and rat-tail, and a file card to keep them clean.

Abrasives: Three sorts of paper and two of steel wool are the most you should need:

Garnet paper in 150 grit (4/0) and 320 grit (9/0); A OP (A weight, open coat)
Silicon carbide paper in 320 grit (9/0); A OP
Steel wool in 2/0 and 4/0 grades

Garnet paper is more expensive than glass paper but it lasts longer and does not clog easily. The silicon carbide paper is the only abrasive paper which should be used in finishing. Whichever paper you are using, do not use a sheet whole, nor pieces torn off at random. Divide each sheet into thirds across its width, draw the back surface of each strip across the edge of your workbench to take the stiffness out, then fold it into a three-thickness pad (Fig. 73). Check the quality of steel wool before you buy it, for manufacturers' gradings vary widely. Some brands have oil in them and sometimes strands of coarse stuff, and are clearly not intended for use in wood finishing.

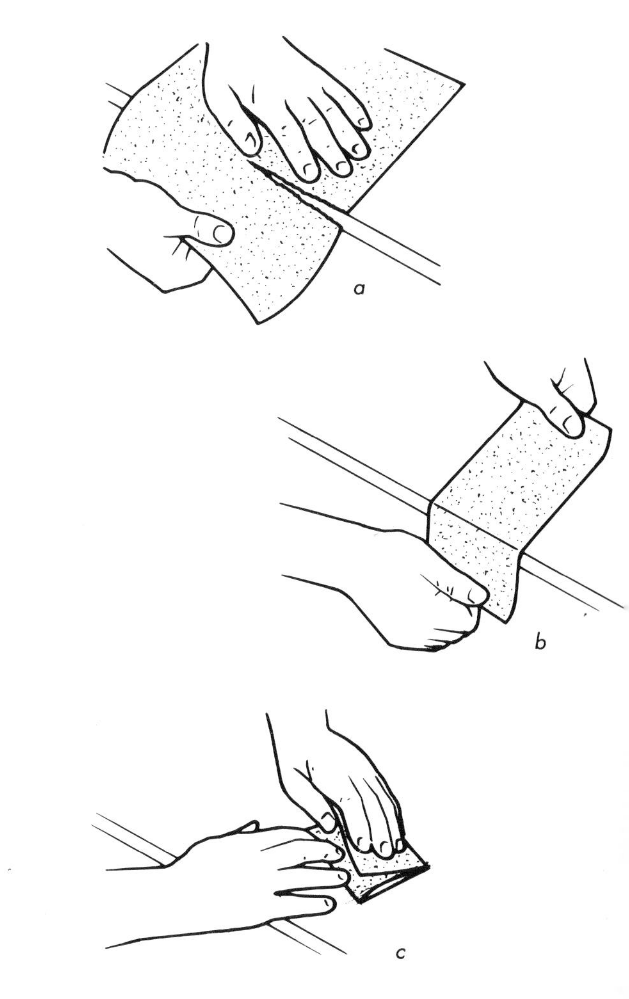

73. Preparing abrasive paper for use.
a. Tear off one-third of a sheet.
b. Rub the paper side over the edge of the workbench a couple of times.
c. Fold twice to make a handy pad.

Heating: Low-wattage electric soldering iron with $\frac{1}{8}''$ bit secured by a screw (and with a current regulator plug for certain jobs). Assorted flat irons. Electric hotplate. Heat gun (DIY paint stripper)

Workbench and vices: The bench does not have to be large so long as it is stable and able to support a good-sized vice – a quick-release vice is best and, ideally, an end vice and dogs. For metalwork, a 3″ engineer's vice mounted on a block of wood, which can be secured in the bench vice for use. A work trestle of 3–4 ft square by 12–15″ high is extremely useful – you will almost certainly do more work at the trestle than at the bench.

Power tools: Although the repairs described in following chapters may all be undertaken with hand tools, you will doubtless wish to take advantage of some of the wide range of power tools available today. The most versatile power tool for restoration work is the bandsaw.

Miscellaneous tools and equipment: Gluepot (see p. 53). Fire extinguisher: inert gas (halon) type. 6× magnifying glass. Heavy linen apron. Hypodermic syringe and as large gauge needles as you can get. Veneer hammer (or you can make one). Profile copier. Dust mask.

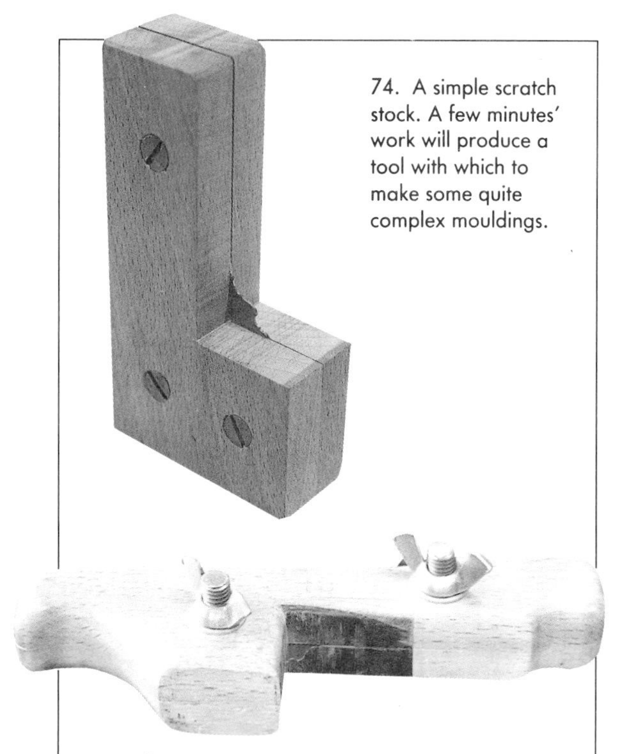
74. A simple scratch stock. A few minutes' work will produce a tool with which to make some quite complex mouldings.

75. A handled scratch stock. This version is better for heavier work or prolonged use and the wing nuts allow the quick fitting and adjustment of blades. The lignum vitae infill on the one illustrated was fitted when the sole had worn too far to permit accurate work.

76. Two forms of hardwood scraper which are useful in waxing and stopping operations.

77. A soldering iron bit adapted for softening old glazing putty.

Tools to make for yourself

Bench hook, mitre box and shooting board were perhaps the first things your woodwork teacher had you make. Here are some more:

Scratch stock: For making small mouldings and, in the absence of moulding planes, some quite large and complex designs can be produced with it. A simple scratch stock consists of two pieces of wood with a right-angle to form a fence, held together with three screws, as illustrated in Fig. 74. This is perfectly satisfactory for small work but for heavier or prolonged use the design with handles (Fig. 75) is preferable. Using wing nuts instead of the screws makes for rapid adjustment and replacement of blades. The cutting of blades to fit the scratch stock, and the method of its use, are described on p. 79.

Wax scrapers: Simple but essential tools made from scraps of hardwood, as illustrated in Fig. 76. The edge is not sharp but squared off to give two scraping edges – these will soon get rounded in use but they are easily restored by a couple of strokes on fine abrasive paper. Note the rounded corners, which prevent damage to the wood being treated.

Marquetry sawing table: The size of the table is determined by the size of work which your piercing saw can accommodate. The one illustrated in Fig. 82 is 9″ in diameter, to be used with a saw of 5″ capacity, and may be secured in the bench vice or bolted to the bench front at a comfortable working height.

Unless metalwork is one of your skills, you will be best advised to farm the following two tools out for manufacture – particularly the first, which does require precision engineering.

Holzer drill: A trepanning tool designed specifically for the task of removing embedded, broken and corroded screws and nails. The one for which measurements are given in Fig. 79 is the $\frac{1}{2}$″ version to cope with screw shanks up to about 14 gauge with $1\frac{1}{2}$″ embedded in the wood – a $\frac{3}{8}$″ version is useful for panel pins. Both versions are shown in Fig. 80 and their method of use is described on p. 57. The advantages of this design are, firstly, the centring guide ensures direct entry into the wood, with no skating about to damage surrounding surfaces; secondly, the hole which it cuts is clean and perfectly circular, which is seldom achieved when drilling objects out with twist drills; thirdly, it does its job very quickly – rusty metal can be removed and replaced with a precisely-fitting plug of wood in a few seconds. The simple design of this tool ensures that little maintenance is required. A small slipstone will usually be all that is necessary to keep the teeth in perfect trim. The inside of the cutter will benefit from an occasional gentle reaming to clear accumulated dust, followed by a light application of powdered graphite.

Putty softener: A bit for the electric soldering iron which is adapted for the purpose of softening old glazing putty quickly and safely. Consisting of a piece of copper bar with a soldering iron bit brazed into it (Fig. 77), this simple tool will greatly ease the task of removing putty which has hardened to the consistency of sun-baked clay, as described in Chapter 13.

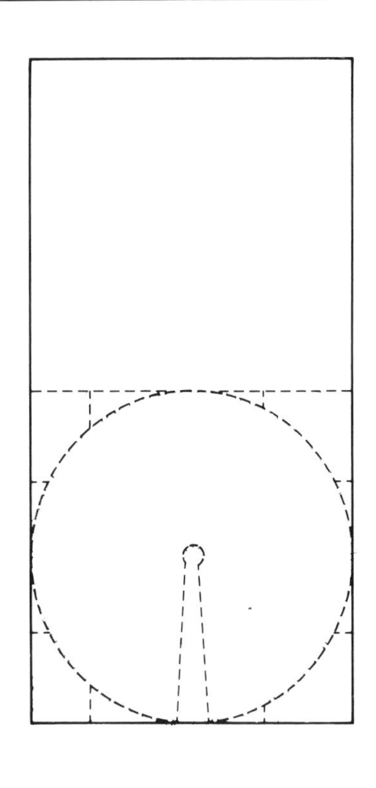

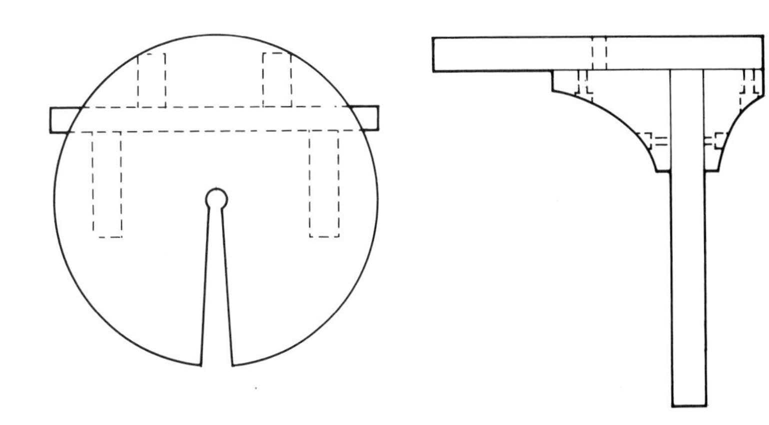

78. A design for a marquetry sawing table. This may be made as follows.
i. Take a piece of clear, hard stuff (eg beech) 18″×9″×$\frac{7}{8}$″ and cut it in half across its width.
ii. From one half cut a 9″ diameter disc, saving the off cuts.
iii. Drill a $\frac{3}{8}$″ hole in the centre of the disc then cut a slot which tapers from $\frac{1}{4}$″ at the centre to $\frac{5}{8}$″ at the edge.
iv. Assemble, using the off cuts as brackets, with countersunk screws. Position the upright section approximately halfway between the edge and the centre, allowing adequate clearance for the hand to grip the saw.

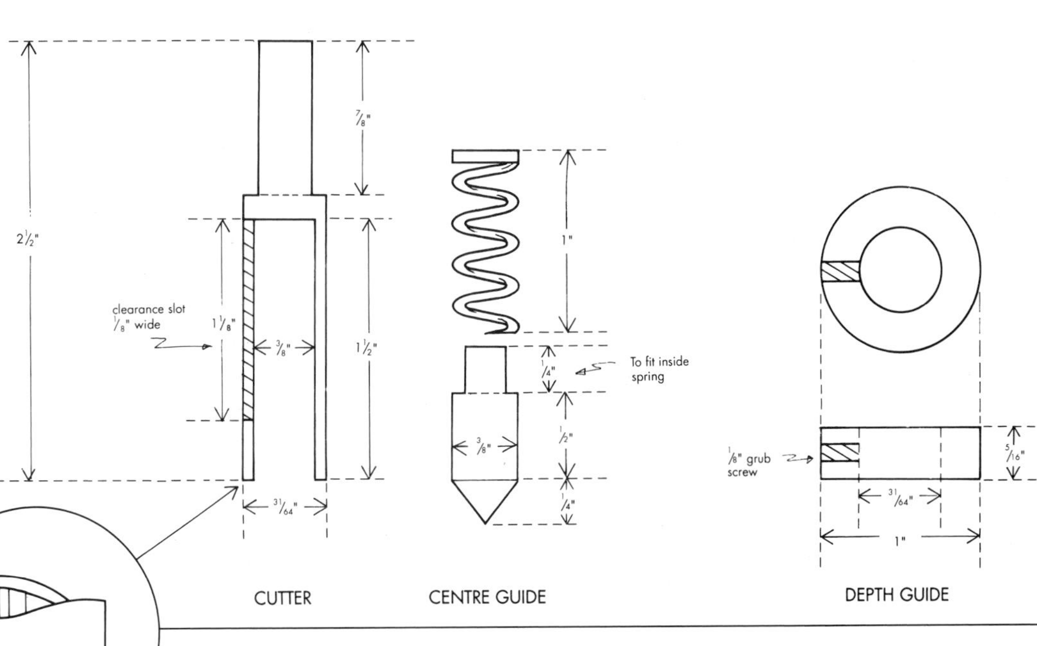

79. Drawing for the manufacture of a holzer drill ($\frac{1}{2}$″ version). Note that the diameter of the drill is fractionally smaller than its corresponding plug cutting bit (see Fig. 89, page 58).

The cutter and centre guide are machined from EN 24 steel alloy (or similar). The centreguide spring is 20 gauge, $\frac{1}{8}$″ pitch.

The depth guide is made from heat-resistant plastic.

80. Holzer drills, $\frac{1}{2}$″ and $\frac{3}{8}$″ sizes, with accessories.

The wood

Recognition of the types of wood which make up the piece of furniture you are working on is an essential first step towards its successful restoration. Some of the more exotic timbers have features which can only be identified by microscopic examination, but most furniture woods you are likely to find in English antique furniture are fairly easy to recognize, usually with the naked eye or sometimes with the assistance of a 6× magnifying glass. These features, together with the type of furniture or decoration in which you are likely to find the woods used, are briefly described in the Appendices, p. 147. There is, however, no substitute for handling timber specimens to learn their characteristics and the effects which various cuts bring out. Your local museum might well have a crateful hidden away and it is such old samples which you need to seek out, for many of the species used in furniture manufacture today have no relevance to antique furniture. Of course, all this is about identifying the features of freshly-worked wood: the real problem starts when you are inspecting a wood with a finish on it. Matters are further complicated when both wood and finish have been mellowed by years of sunlight and burnishing with a polishing cloth. The eight woods shown in Fig. 81 demonstrate the similarity in colour, and often in grain and figure, in aged wood, against the features of the natural halves, which are quite distinctive.

The extent of your stock of woods, in solid or veneer forms, will depend on the amount of restoration work you are intending to do. Except for furniture made from English hardwoods, of which there is a plentiful supply of well-seasoned stuff about, you will have to obtain much of your wood from 'breakers' – pieces of furniture which are too far gone to be economically

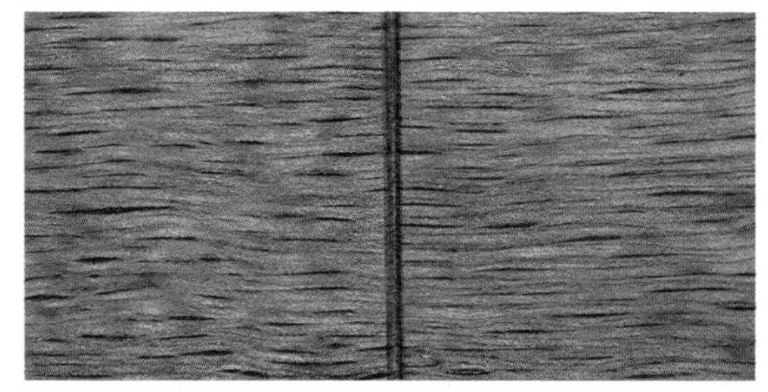

a. Oak

b. Elm

c. Cherry

d. Walnut

e. Yew

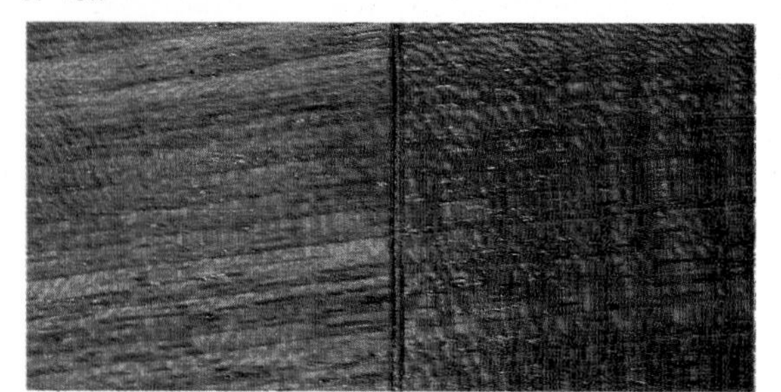

f. Mahogany

g. Satinwood

h. Rosewood

81. Eight furniture woods, half of each showing its natural colour and the other half treated to reproduce the effects of the aging and mellowing processes.

restored. Obviously such pieces will have to be absolute wrecks to justify breaking them up but even then you will surely feel a twinge of regret as you set about it. A favourite source of breakers is the local auction room. Go for old case furniture; a chest of drawers may be obtained for a sum which is often insignificant in relation to the value of the material which you recover from it. Don't discard anything. When you have taken the piece apart, using a rubber-headed mallet to open the joints, a few minutes spent removing and sorting nails, screws, handles, escutcheons, locks, mouldings and even glue blocks, will be well rewarded. You will be left with case panels, drawer fronts, linings and back boards to store away for future use. Store veneered panels separately from those in solid wood to reduce sorting time when it comes to selecting a piece for a repair.

One trick of the trade for removing old veneer from its ground wood is to leave the veneered panels in a damp cellar for a couple of months. This certainly removes the veneer but it doesn't do much for its shape or finish. A more satisfactory result is achieved by the use of a heat gun, two large, old table knives and a pan of boiling water (Fig. 83). Immerse the blades of the knives in the boiling water and leave them to heat up while you cramp the panel to your bench. Only secure one half, leaving the other half free to work on. Get the heat gun to its working temperature, then aim it at one corner of the veneer, keeping it close enough to soften the glue beneath the veneer but far enough away to prevent scorching of the surface (with practice you will be able to remove an entire sheet of veneer without so much as blistering the finish). After a few seconds of warming the veneer, try to slip a heated knife blade beneath it. When the glue is soft enough the blade will go under easily; as soon as this start is made point the heat gun at the next bit, warming an area of about the length of the knife blade and twice its width. Remove the blade frequently and immerse it in the hot water again to reheat it and to remove accumulated glue, carrying on with the other which has been standing in the water. Keep moving the heat gun and working the hot knife blade under the veneer until you are approaching the

82. Repair patches in mahogany. Three patches have been let into this piece. One of them (lower centre) is deliberately misaligned; the grain does not match that of the ground, lines of figure go nowhere and reflectivity has not been taken into account. Can you find the other two (the glue line around one of them has been disguised with pigments)?

83. Removing veneer from a drawer front.

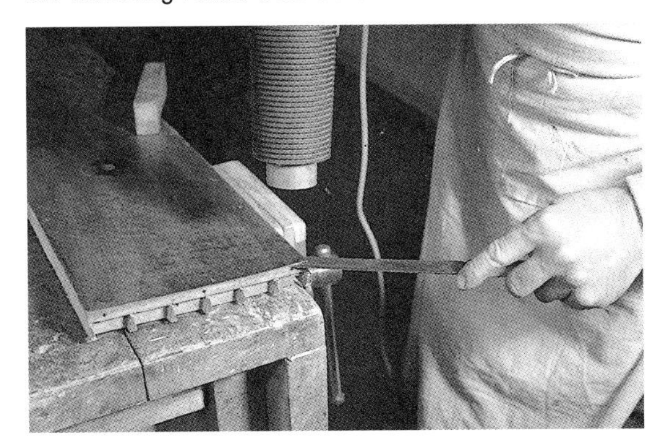

a. Starting a corner.

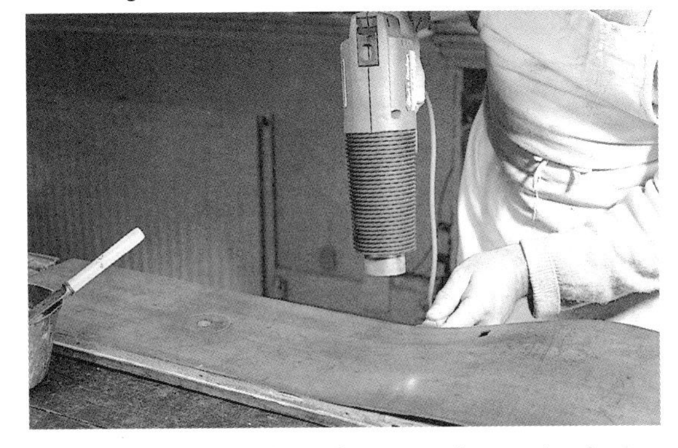

b. Steady progress, with no damage to the wood or finish.

c. All traces of glue removed from veneer and ground wood.

d. Under weights until completely dry.

cramped part. Then remove the cramps and put them on the end you have been working on, securing the ground wood only and leaving the veneer loose. Renew the hot water in the pan if necessary and finish off the removal of the veneer. As soon as the sheet of veneer is free, wash the rest of the old glue off, dry both sides of the veneer thoroughly with rag, then place it on a flat surface between several sheets of newspaper with a board on top (the veneer's ground wood will often serve this purpose). Place some heavy weights on the board and leave them in place until the veneer has dried completely, after which you should be able to store it flat on a shelf without it distorting too much.

The restorer does have a storage problem which is peculiar to his branch of woodworking, for every scrap and off cut of those precious old woods and veneers must be segregated and put away against the day when they will be needed to make the perfectly-matched repair. 'I know I've got a piece somewhere' is a familiar moan in most workshops, but is no substitute for a well-labelled storage system. In an ideal workshop – which few of us ever manage to achieve – veneers and solid woods would not only be stored by species, but to take account of those characteristics which are so very important when it comes to matching the repair to its surroundings:

Colour

Grain and figure patterns

Reflectivity

It will help enormously if you can find a piece of wood with an old, mellow colour to match the area being repaired. You will, of course, have the task of fitting it and levelling it (from the back of the patch) so as not to disturb the old surface but the effort is always rewarded by the reduction in finishing time. You may come across a piece of wood which, in its natural, unfinished state, is a good match – check with a wipe of meths to see what the colour is likely to be when the finish is applied. Your principal concern should not really be to match the colour of the wood but to see if you can duplicate the direction, size and texture of the grain and details of the figure. If all these *can* be matched you will be well on the way to making that repair invisible. But no matter how painstaking you have been in the matching process so far, if you get the repair patch in the wrong way round, it will show up like a beacon. This has to do with the way light is reflected from the fibres of the wood and, therefore, the orientation of those fibres in relation to the surface of the wood will determine the amount of reflection and its brightness. Try standing at one end of a table top made from a highly-figured mahogany, looking along the direction of the grain. Note the colour and brightness of a light area and an adjacent dark area, then go round to the other end and look at those same areas again – the effect will have reversed. Some woods are more of a problem than others. Apart from the mahoganies, satinwood and well-faded rosewood can take on a translucent quality that makes reflectivity all the more difficult to cope with. If you can see which way the grain is lying from the side of the area being repaired and match this in the piece which you are putting in, then you stand a fair chance of getting it right. Of course, this is extremely difficult when you are working with veneers, when you will have to use a magnifying glass. Whatever checks you have made and whatever decision you come to, when you think you have got things right, give the repair patch a wipe with the polishing rubber (Chapter 9), lay it in place and walk round it a couple of times, viewing it from all directions, with and against the light. Figure 82 illustrates the importance of matching reflectivity.

The glue

For centuries furniture makers have used only one sort of glue: animal glue made from hide and hoof, now generally known as Scotch glue. Advocates of modern adhesives will tell you that animal glue is not the perfect adhesive, being susceptible to heat and moisture. This is absolutely true, which in fact makes it the most desirable adhesive for the restorer to use. Scotch glue, properly prepared and applied, will endure for hundreds of years, but should the need arise to undo a joint or previous repair to facilitate further restoration it will always, with a little patient work, soften and allow the parts to be taken apart. (The opening of joints secured with animal glue is described on p. 56.) If there is any doubt in your mind, this will be dispelled when you have to repair something which has been glued before with one (or more) of the hard – or at the other extreme, rubbery – modern adhesives. The join will either be locked solid or it will have fallen apart leaving deposits which won't respond to the simple washing operation that can be used on animal glue. At best you will have to spend hours picking and scratching at the stuff before you can be satisfied that the surfaces are clean enough to be reglued.

Thorough cleaning to remove old glue, of whatever sort, and accumulated dust and wax polish which have worked their way into open joints and poor previous repairs, is an essential operation before gluing again. The strongest bond is formed between two surfaces which have the smallest possible space separating them, so one overlooked lump of old glue or dirt can prevent a perfect join, throw the surfaces out of alignment and leave an ugly gap. Sometimes old animal glue in a joint will have perished to the state where it can be scraped off with a chisel without causing damage. Generally, though, hot water and a stiff brush (a 1″ paint brush with its bristles reduced to about half their length is ideal for most jobs) will be safest and will take dirt and wax away with the dissolving glue. Keep the glued area well wetted but surrounding surfaces, whether polished or not, must be kept as dry as possible and care must be taken not to allow water to seep beneath any surrounding veneer or inlay.

Scotch glue was originally produced in large slabs which had to be broken up before use. This form has now been superseded in general use by pearl glue which, as its name suggests, comes as small beads, making it easier to handle and prepare. This type of animal glue has to be soaked in water before you can use it (Fig. 84). It is advisable to prepare only enough for a day's work, for while the soaked glue will keep for a day or two covered and stored in a cool place, mould and bacteria soon take a hold in the warmth and make it useless. You will soon get used to estimating the amount of glue you will need to prepare – usually a couple of handfuls of pearls will be enough. Put these in a small plastic tub and cover them with cold water, to about half an inch above them. In a couple of hours, or less, depending on how quickly the glue absorbs all the water, you will be ready to heat it.

Which brings us to the gluepot. An old-fashioned cast-iron pot certainly lends atmosphere to the restorer's workshop, but you will probably be served just as well by an enamelled steamer pan which has been pensioned off from the kitchen. (You can even heat glue in a jam jar in a saucepan of water, providing you keep the jar well clear of the bottom of the pan.) Whatever you use, fill the water container about three-quarters full (with hot water if you need to save time) and bring it to the boil. A thermostatically-controlled electric hotplate is best for this purpose; you don't want naked flames about the workshop. When the water is boiling, turn the heat

84. Pearl glue before, during and after soaking in water prior to heating it. The ideal consistency of heated glue will be produced if the soaked pearls remain in one firm but flexible piece, as shown. If it feels dry and breaks up easily, the hot glue will be too thick; if it is pale and sloppy, the glue will be too thin, perhaps even for veneering.

85. This was not set up for the benefit of the photographer!

86. Carefully made, close-fitting formers will ensure accurate alignment of the pieces when glue is applied and the cramps tightened.

down to a simmer and fit the glue container with as much soaked glue as you think you will need for the job.

While the glue is coming to working temperature, check to see that everything is prepared for the gluing operation: all the pieces to be glued laid out in the proper order and all necessary cramps and other means of fastening available. This is the clever part, about which, unfortunately, no specific rules can be laid down. Most jobs can be secured with G-cramps or sash cramps but when there are awkward shapes involved, or when cramps cannot be positioned to apply pressure at right angles to the face of the join, then it is essential to make softwood formers. These may be used for the one job only but the time spent making them will be as nothing compared to the frustration and wasted time in attempting to work accurately without them. Sometimes cramps and formers alone will not be able to hold the work securely. This is where your ingenuity comes in, using toggle cramps, hand-screws, masking tape, pins, webbing cramps, weights, wedges – the list is endless, and only you can devise the combination and layout appropriate to the job (Figs. 85 and 86).

When the cramping requirements are anything but the simplest, it is a good idea to have a practice set-up before glue is applied, so that you can assess the effects of the various devices and adjust the layout accordingly. Bear in mind that the hot glue is going to reduce the friction between the pieces, so make allowances for possible movement. Note, however, that it is *not* essential to tighten all the cramps, or whatever, as much as possible, but just enough to make sure that the join is in position and closed up. Over-tightening will cause misalignment and distortion. And when using metal or hardwood cramps without formers, don't forget to place softwood blocks between their jaws and the work. Apart from protecting the antique wood, these softening blocks spread the pressure of the cramps evenly over the area of the join, so make them large enough. Those to be used on areas where there is likely to be squeezed-out glue about should have their work faces rubbed with paraffin wax or covered with heavy-duty polythene to stop them sticking to the repair.

In the meantime, the glue is heating.

Scotch glue needs to be good and hot (but not boiling) before it will do its job properly. It usually takes about half an hour for the brew to get to the right temperature, when wisps of steam will come from the glue as you stir it. Before you do that, though, check to see if there is a scum on top of the glue. There nearly always will be and it must be removed as this thick stuff could prevent the close join you are striving for. Cut round the edge of the scum with a thin, flat piece of scrap wood and try to lift it out in one lump. Then you can put the glue brush in and give the glue a stir. As a conclusive test as to the readiness of the glue you might like to try a trick of the old-timers – dab a little on the back of your finger and if it hurts, it's hot enough!

Before you start work, there is one more check to carry out and that is to make sure the glue has the proper consistency for the job. Raise the glue brush a few inches above the pot and watch the glue as it runs off (Fig. 87). For most jobs the hot glue should flow in a steady, even stream with the consistency of cream. If it is too thick to use it runs unevenly, with lumps like hot toffee, in which case it must be diluted with hot water, given a stir and left for a few minutes for the temperature to settle. If the glue is too thin, it breaks up into drops as it comes off the brush and you will need to top up the pot with more soaked pearls. When gluing veneer, particularly large areas, glue of a somewhat thinner consistency is needed than that used for general work, but never so thin that it breaks up into drops when poured from the brush.

It will be advantageous to warm the surfaces which you are about to glue to give you a bit more working time. If this is not practicable, then at least make sure you do the job in a warm place. Even with all conditions in your favour, you will have to work quickly to get the pieces together and the cramps in place before the glue cools to the point where it starts to gel. So, if there are lots of bits and pieces to glue up, don't try to get too many together in one go, because you will probably end up with none of the joints closed up or properly aligned and have to wash the lot clean and start again when they are dry.

Now, are all those cramps to hand, opened to just over the required span, and the formers and softening ready? Right. Apply a dab of glue to both surfaces, put them firmly together and get the cramps on, in rapid succession. With everything aligned and secure, wash off as much of the excess glue as you can while it is still soft, using hot water and the washing-out brush, and drying up with a clean rag as you go along. You may not be able to reach all the glue behind cramps and formers so this will have to wait until the join is set. The glue often separates from a well-polished surface as it dries; even if it doesn't, it will not be too difficult to wash off, but extra care must be taken to ensure that the surrounding finish is not scrubbed off. Don't be tempted to take off the cramps after a couple of hours to see if you have made a neat job: leave it until next day at least. And when you have removed the cramps and cleaned off any remaining glue don't be in too much of a hurry to start levelling patches and finishing. Put the piece of furniture away in a warm, well-ventilated place for a few days to let things settle down.

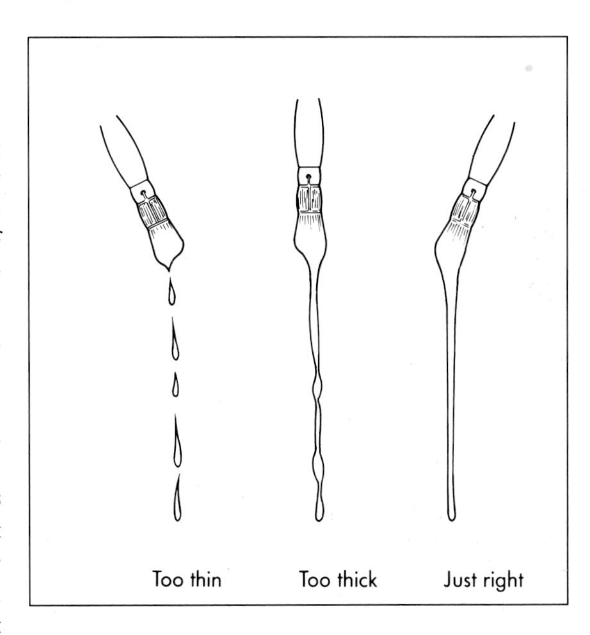

87. Consistency of hot animal glue.

CHAPTER 5
Structural repairs

Loose and broken joints

A loose joint will not be magically cured by pouring in adhesive or driving in a nail or two. A statement of the obvious maybe, but people do it, or worse pay someone else to do it for them, as illustrated in Fig 4, p. 17, and in Fig. 93. If you are going to repair anything with joints, be thorough and rebuild each joint as it was originally made. Don't use screws and nails 'to give it strength', as they tend to do just the opposite. Don't use any adhesive other than animal glue (see Chapter 4), for someone may need to get into that joint one day and will be faced with enormous difficulties if he has to undo modern glues.

Taking joints apart

Most joints which have been previously glued with animal glue will present little problem in opening them. Often a joint will be loose simply because the original glue has perished with age, in which case a gentle tap with a rubber-headed mallet, or a hammer against a softwood block, will be all that is needed to get the bits apart. Sometimes, though, it will be necessary for you to undo a joint which is perfectly secure in order to facilitate work on some other part (usually another joint). This is most common when working on chairs. The procedure for getting such a joint open is straightforward if somewhat time consuming. First, check the location of the interfaces of the

a

b

88. Opening a firm mortice and tenon joint.
a. Fine holes are drilled at the interfaces of the sides of the tenon with the mortice.
b. Several injections of hot water will be necessary before any movement is felt.
c. The joint is eased apart.
d. The softened glue takes little time to wash off.
e. The joint ready for reassembly.

parts of the joint, estimating their positions from gauge marks if these are evident. Drill small holes ($\frac{1}{16}$" or so diameter) into each interface and inject hot water with a hypodermic syringe, holding a rag beneath the joint to prevent excess water spreading onto surrounding surfaces. It may take several dozen injections, spread over an hour or more, but eventually the glue will soften enough to allow you to ease the joint apart (Fig. 88).

Embedded screws and nails

Before you attempt to open a joint, though, even if it is very loose (in fact, particularly if it's very loose, for if it has not fallen apart by itself there's something else holding it), have a good, close look at the surfaces around it. If there is so much as the tiniest bit of stopping showing, or a plug, then there may be a screw, nail or panel pin concealed beneath (see Fig. 3, p. 16). And even if you cannot see anything, a check over with the metal detector is advisable. Such concealed bits of metal must be removed if the wood is not to be severely damaged in attempting to open the joint.

The removal of embedded nails and broken screws is almost impossible to accomplish with conventional tools without some damage to the wood and finish. A precise job will be done with the specially-made drill bit illustrated in Fig. 89. This device is not available at the tool shop but will have to be made for you by a precision engineer (the specification is given on p. 49). The price you are quoted for its manufacture may seem high but when you are faced with a chair with a dozen little panel pins driven into the joints you may well think the expense justified. As you will see when you read the specification, the bit is used in a two-speed electric drill, and requires a standard plug cutting bit as an accessory.

If the nail or screw is found to be deeply embedded, unnecessary destruction of sound wood will be avoided if the thing can be removed without taking the drill in beyond it. This is particularly important when removing screws and nails which have been driven through joints. When the cut is $\frac{3}{4}$" to 1" deep (or at the first interface you come to in a joint), remove the drill from the hole, break out the wood of the core with a bradawl and

c

d

e

a

b

c

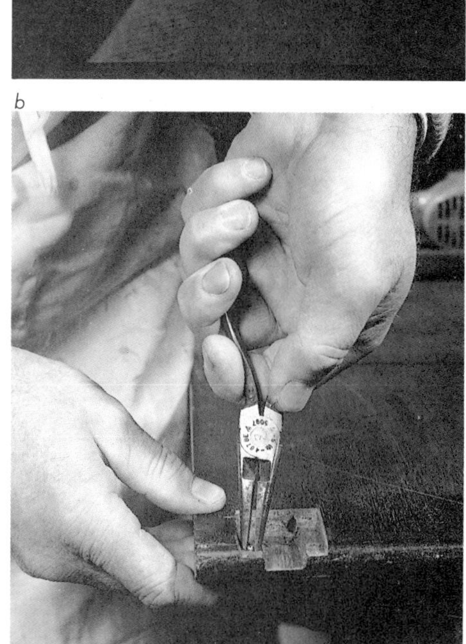

d

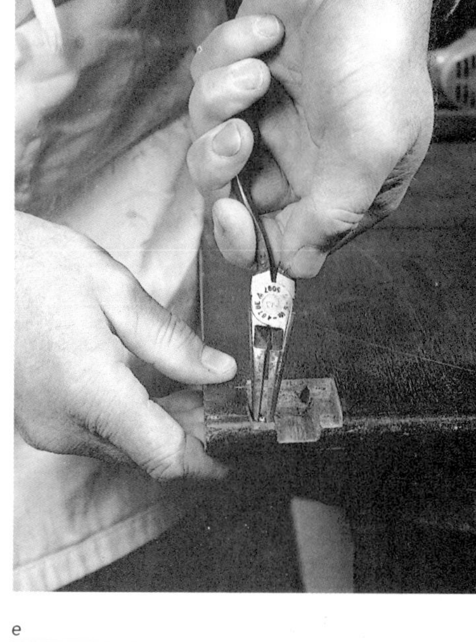

e

f

g

89. Using the holzer drill.
a. A screw has broken during the removal of a table fork housing. The sheared end of the part remaining in the wood is marked with a centre punch.
b. The holzer bit is fitted into the drill chuck, speed set at low, centring guide inserted and its point located in the punch mark.
c. Applying steady pressure, the bit is driven into the wood. The spring on the centring guide compresses to permit an initial cut of $\frac{1}{4}$″ depth.
d. With the centring guide removed the cut is completed. Some woods will cut quicker if pressure on the drill is eased every few seconds. If there is any danger of the bit penetrating too far and breaking through the other side then the depth guide should be fitted, as here.
e. The remains of the screw may be removed with snipe-nosed pliers, or if the core remains intact around a small screw or pin this can be loosened with a fine screwdriver, taking care not to damage the edge of the hole. Sometimes the core will come out with the drill bit, in which case it is easily removed with a nail inserted through the clearance slot.
f. A plug is cut with a standard plug cutting bit. The holzer bit is designed to be fractionally smaller in diameter than plugs produced with the corresponding plug cutter to ensure a perfect fit.
g. The plug is glued in, ready for the fitting to be replaced.

try to ease the object out with snipe-nosed pliers. If it won't budge, carefully reinsert the drill, cut another $\frac{1}{4}''$ or so and try again. This procedure applies also when it is suspected that the path of the nail, or whatever, strays from the direction it entered the wood, for while the steel alloy specified for the drill bit will enable it to cope with quite severe contact with iron, prolonged contact is not recommended.

Mortice and tenon joints

When a loose mortice and tenon joint has been taken apart, the cause of its particular problem will be evident. It may well simply be the perished animal glue mentioned before, in which case it is the most straightforward of jobs to wash out the joint and reglue it. If, having cleaned out the old adhesive, the tenon is found to be intact but loose in its mortice, never be tempted to reassemble it reinforced by fox wedging (Fig. 90). Whilst this method does produce a very strong joint, it is impossible to take the thing apart again without causing considerable damage. Better to build up the faces of the tenon which are lacking and recut it to fit the mortice – the joint might not be quite as strong as the original but at least future restorers won't be muttering dreadful imprecations over your workmanship.

It may be that a small part of the tenon has broken off and stayed inside the mortice. If the piece can be removed from the mortice intact and without doing any other damage, all well and good, because it can be glued back to the tenon with very little loss of strength to the joint. More often than not, though, the detached piece will have to be chiselled out of the mortice and the tenon repaired with new wood. Make sure that you cut out the damaged area squarely to provide ample gluing surfaces. Tenons that have had to be drilled through in the process of removing embedded metal, as described above, may be plugged, again with little loss of strength.

If the tenon is extensively damaged then the only way to ensure a strong repair will be to fit a replacement (Fig. 91). This problem is most frequent in chairs.

The procedure for fitting a replacement tenon is as follows (capital letters refer to the diagram on the following page):

i Carefully clean old glue and bits of tenon out of the mortice.

ii Secure the rail upside down in a vice (you may need to remove the rail from the rest of the chair to give you the necessary access), placing softening blocks to protect polished surfaces. Cut off any remaining fragments of the tenon.

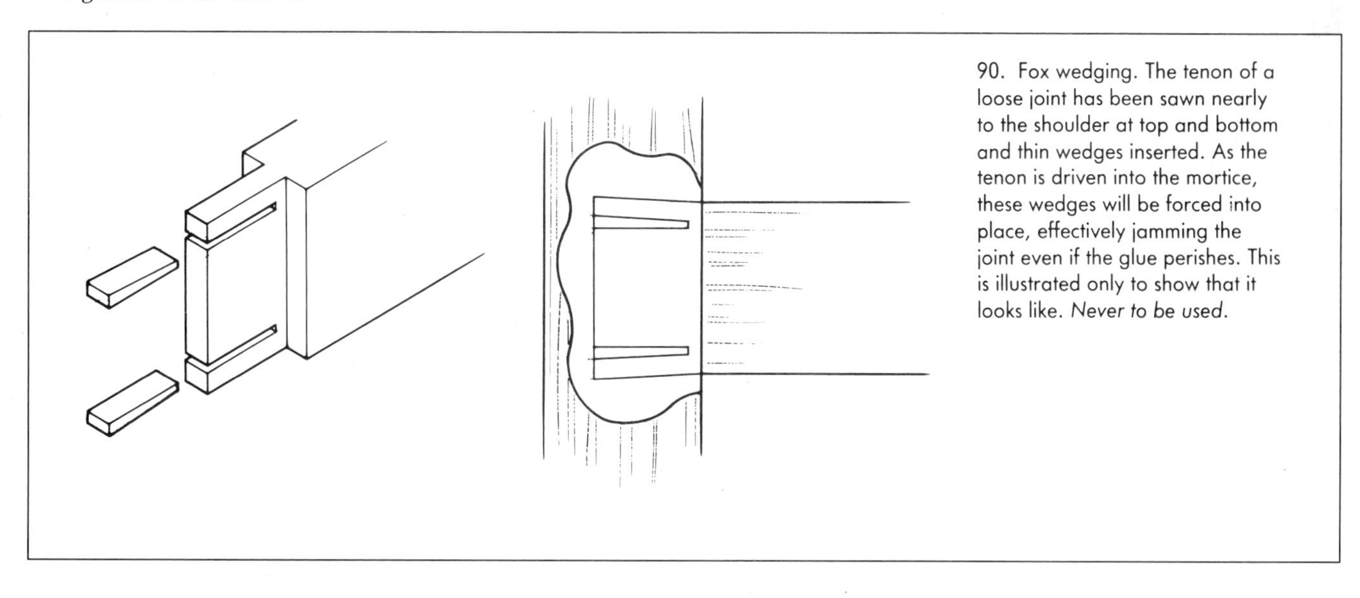

90. Fox wedging. The tenon of a loose joint has been sawn nearly to the shoulder at top and bottom and thin wedges inserted. As the tenon is driven into the mortice, these wedges will be forced into place, effectively jamming the joint even if the glue perishes. This is illustrated only to show that it looks like. *Never to be used.*

91. Critical dimensions to work to when fitting a replacement tenon.

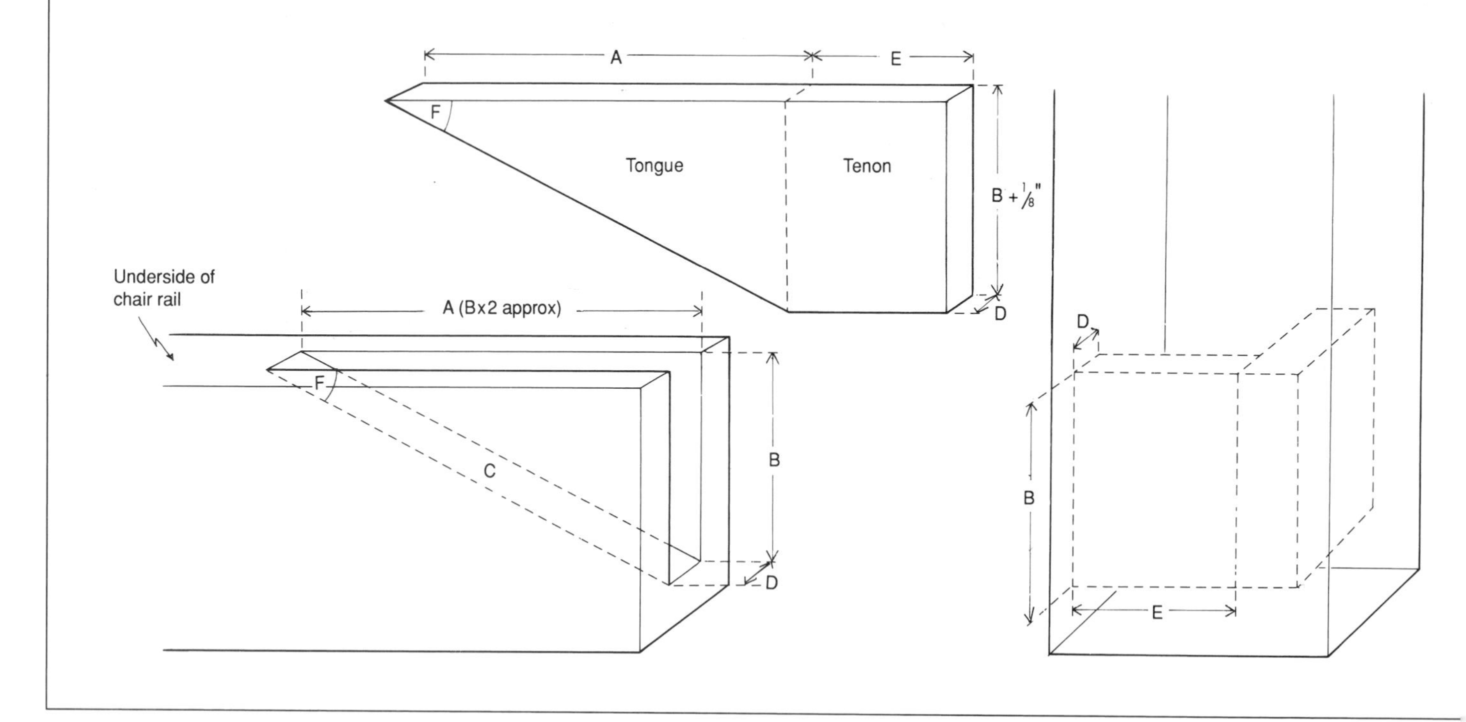

iii Score lines with a marking knife to define the area of the tenon, checking its width, height and location on the rail with the dimensions and location of the mortice. To assist, you are likely to find the maker's gauge marks on the rail.

iv Extend the marks for the sides of the tenon (A) back along the underside of the rail a distance which is approximately twice the height of the mortice (B).

v Saw down to the full length of your marked lines on the underside of the rail and to the position of what will be the top of the new tenon, keeping the cuts inside the lines.

vi Remove the waste with chisel and mallet (watch out for embedded tacks). Make sure that the slope (C) for the tongue of the replacement tenon is absolutely true, or a perfect fit will be impossible.

vii Cut a piece of beech to the thickness of the required tenon (D), long enough to cover the depth of the mortice plus the length of the tongue (E + A) and wide enough to cover the height of the mortice (B) plus about $\frac{1}{8}$" waste. Beech is chosen for most seat rail repairs of this nature for its straightness of grain and strength. For repairs to joints where it is necessary to fit the tongue of the new tenon into a visible surface, such as at the join of a chair's upright to its cresting rail, matching wood will have to be used.

viii With an adjustable bevel, copy the angle of slope (F) of the section cut out of the rail, mark this on the piece of beech, then cut off the waste.

ix Plane the saw marks off the long edge of the tongue and check its fit in the rail. After any minor adjustments, the tongue may be glued into the rail, cramping with a G-cramp across the rail to be on the safe side.

x When the glue has dried, plane off the waste from the tongue and fit the new tenon in the mortice. All being well, you are now ready to reassemble the piece.

a

b

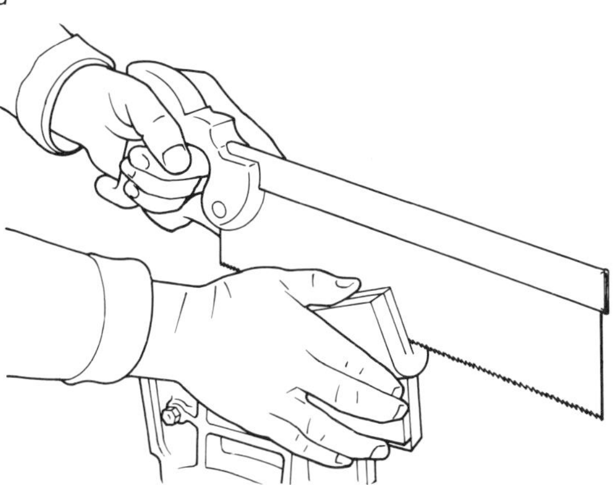

c

d

e

f

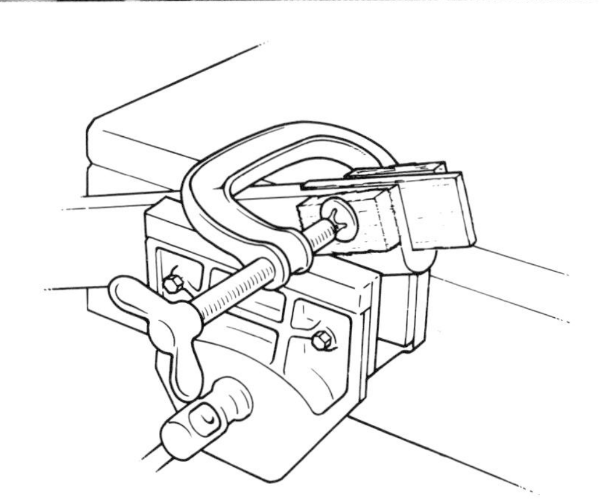

g

h

92. Fitting a replacement tenon to a chair rail.
a. The seat rail with part of the damaged tenon remaining.
b. The damaged wood is removed and the chair-maker's gauge marks extended to define the position of the new tenon.
c. The housing is sawn for the tail of the tenon.
d. The waste is chiselled out (having first checked for hidden tacks).
e. Gauging the angle of the slope . . .
f. . . . to transfer it onto the repair piece.
g. The repair piece cut to size and glued in place.
h. With the waste removed, the joint is ready for gluing.

a

b

c

d

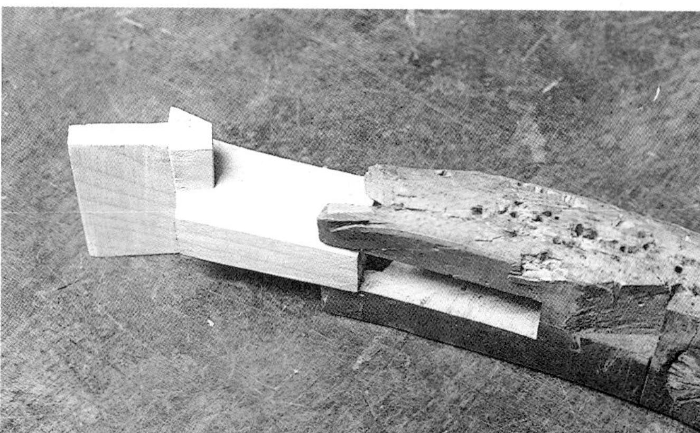

e

93. Making good the botcher's handiwork.
a. Signs of things to come. Four patches of stopping are broken up to reveal large screws.
b. Worst fears confirmed. The purpose of those four screws – to support the tenonless end of the front seat rail – is revealed. The crude repairs have left little for the restorer to work with.
c. A hand-forged 3″ nail, driven through the other front leg into the end of the tenon, suggests that the botcher is not a breed peculiar to the twentieth century!
d. The angle and position of the major break in the leg make it essential to build a snug former. Here the layout is being checked to ensure that there will be no misalignment of the pieces when the glue is put on and pressure applied.
e. The woodworm-damaged seat rail has to be cut back to sound wood before designing a replacement section, which will include the new tenon. A piece of beech is spliced into the rail in such a way as to provide the maximum gluing surface with no possible movement in any direction.
f. The joint remade, botched patches replaced, screw holes plugged and covered, and the detail recarved.
g. The repair to the leg is finished.

f

g

One day you will come across a joint so badly damaged that a straightforward tenon replacement will not suffice. Such a case is illustrated in Fig. 93. The leg, as the chair's owner said, was 'just a bit wobbly'. Suspicions that things would not be so simple to deal with, aroused by the sight of crude patching of the wood and large blobs of filler, were amply confirmed as work progressed. Woodworm had obviously been the original cause of the problem. Starting their journey at the front seat rail tenon, the larvae had eaten away so much wood that the joint gave way. The resulting stress on the legs caused at least one fracture at its weakest point, where it is joined to the seat rails, and subsequent attempts to repair the damage succeeded only in weakening the wood further. The structural problems to be overcome in such circumstances vary so much from case to case that general rules cannot be formulated; the repair must be made as strong as possible whilst retaining as much of the original material as possible.

Wedged through-tenons

Many of the tables of the tilt-top variety develop a wobble about the joints at the top and bottom of the pedestal column. Sometimes the pedestal is held together by a long bolt, in which case a couple of turns on the nut can effect a cure. If it is a mortice and tenon joint problem, you could well have a struggle to get the tenons out, for they are nearly always wedged as well as glued. This is not the sort of problem you would have with fox wedged tenons, for these will be through-tenons, usually two on each end of the pedestal column. To do the repair properly, you will have to start by cutting the wedges out of the tenons. Provided you are the first to perform this operation, you won't have much work to do – a little careful chiselling will leave you with complete tenons and the joint can be undone, washed out and reglued with new wedges in place. So often, though, someone has had a go at tightening the joint without taking it apart, by the simple expedient of splitting the ends of the tenons in a few more places and driving in additional wedges, a short-term solution which inevitably leads to a staggering amount of restoration work. When you do eventually get inside such a botched joint, you are likely to find that the tenons are virtually useless as gluing surfaces, in which case there will be no alternative but to fit new tenons (Fig. 94). A few hours work with chisels and mallet will be required to create mortices in the ends of the column, of sufficient depth to take strong new tenons, for you will have to go in to a depth at least equal to the height of the required tenons.

Wedges are also frequently used to secure the back of a Windsor chair to its seat. In the event of the back loosening, these can often be removed intact, washed and reglued. Do remember, though, that when tapping the wedges back, the top of the chair back must be as well supported as the seat, or you may find youself with the seat on the workbench and your feet surrounded by the back hoop and a pile of spindles!

Dovetails

Broken dovetails will be found most often at the join between the sides of a drawer and its back. There isn't much point in trying to avoid the ultimate solution, to make a new back from old wood of the same type. While waiting to find the right piece of wood, you can, as a short term measure, glue the back in place and fit fine hardwood pegs through the dovetails. Don't overload the drawer.

94. Wedged through-tenons holding the pivot block of a tilt-top breakfast table.
a. Several attempts have been made to secure these loosened joints by putting in more wedges, with the inevitable consequences shown here.

b. The completed repair ready for gluing. (The wedges are not the conventional shape but that is how the original ones were.)

Dowelled joints

According to the purist, dowelled joints and antique furniture don't go together, since dowels were not in general use for furniture-making until well after the bench-mark date of 1830. However, the school which defines antique as anything over a hundred years old will debate this point, so for the sake of argument, dowelled joints are included here. In some respects they can be more difficult to repair than mortice and tenon joints. Dowels can be fickle things, changing shape when a joint is taken apart to such an extent that it may be impossible to line them up with their holes when the time comes to reglue them. When a dowel is broken, it is most important to remove the remains in such a way as to ensure that the replacement dowel fits perfectly, at the correct angle, so try this method:

- i Saw or chisel off the remains of the broken dowel and mark its centre with a punch.
- ii Drill out the dowel, starting with a fine bit and repeating the operation with progressively larger bits, finishing with one which leaves just a fraction of the dowel remaining.
- iii Remove the remaining 'shell' of the dowel with the appropriate size of scribing gouge and wash out the old glue.
- iv Cut a length of dowel (since the metrication of our system of measurement, you might have to search around to find a supplier of dowel of the correct diameter to match the imperial size which was used originally), slightly shorter than the sum of the depths of its two holes.
- v Plane a flat along the piece of dowel (e.g., $\frac{1}{8}$" wide on a $\frac{3}{8}$" diameter dowel), or cut a shallow groove with your tenon saw, to prevent glue building up in front of it as it is driven into place.
- vi Glue the dowel into one of its holes, wash off the surplus glue and allow to dry.
- vii Check the fit of the joint before finally gluing it together, in case the dowel is too long and needs trimming.

Pegged joints

By their nature, pegged joints are inclined to work loose as changes in temperature and humidity affect the wood. For practical reasons, these joints may have been reinforced with glue by some previous restorer, although with a little more time and patience a perfectly sound 'dry' joint may be achieved. The first step is to remove the existing pegs, which can usually be accomplished by tapping from the inside of the joint, always providing that they are through pegs. If they are not, or if they have been glued in place, then you will have to drill them out in the same way described for removing the remains of a dowel (but remember that pegs are tapered, so drill cautiously). Sort through the pegs you have removed and discard any which are broken or badly bent (see Fig. 27, p. 26). It is likely that the tenons may also have suffered damage due to the stresses which bent those pegs, so you might have to repair them as described above. Loose tenons can be built up, and it will probably be necessary to plug the original peg holes and redrill them a fraction closer to the shoulders of the tenons than the original ones to compensate for shrinkage of the legs. Make any new pegs required to the dimensions of the existing ones, and when tapping them home leave them slightly proud of the surface, as would natural shrinkage of the rails.

Rubbed joints

The shrinkage of boards used in the construction of panels and table tops causes them to part company from each other, leaving unsightly gaps. Unless the item is a relatively small one, it can be a two-man job to reassemble and is therefore probably best left to the professional restorer. Assuming that the number and size of boards is manageable, the procedure is as follows. Remove any framework, separate the loose boards and wash off the old glue. You will also nearly always have to remove filler and assorted strips of veneer used in previous attempts at filling the gap. Now try the boards together. One or both of a pair will seldom be true and will require the attention of the jointer plane (hopefully not too much on circular or oval tops, for this can produce misalignment of the edges). Even when you have succeeded in producing a hairline join, you will probably find that movement of the wood has also created differences in levels in the boards which change from side to side of the join along its length.

The next stage is to determine whether or not some sort of jig or layout of cramps is going to be required to hold the work while the glue is drying. With small pieces which have true joins in level boards you will almost certainly not need them: apply the hot glue to the edges of both boards (held close together to avoid taking too long to get the glue on) and bring them together immediately, rubbing one board firmly against the other to squeeze out surplus glue. As the glue begins to gel, make sure that the two boards are correctly aligned, then secure them on edge with the join horizontal. You should then be able to start washing the glue from surrounding surfaces straight away but if the boards are very thin don't try to remove too much or you may disturb the join – leave the final cleaning up until next day.

You may have several boards to assemble and unless you are prepared to rub the joints one at a time over a number of days you will need to invent some means of support and/or a system of cramps, formers and weights. Again it must be said that there can be no set pattern for a particular sort of job. However, no matter what layout of cramps you come up with there is one basic rule you will need to follow when securing boards – apply pressure to the edges from both sides of the assembled boards or the work will buckle (Fig. 95).

The rubbed joint method is extensively employed to secure glue blocks in carcase-work and in the assembly of bracket feet (see p. 70). It will be obvious that it is essential that the faces to be glued must meet perfectly for this method to work successfully, so check the angle into which each block is to be placed (many pieces of antique furniture haven't got a true right-angle in them) and plane the gluing edges accordingly. As with board joints, apply the glue to both surfaces, bring them together immediately and rub the block back and forth half an inch or so a few times with sufficient pressure to force out surplus glue, which can be washed off straight away.

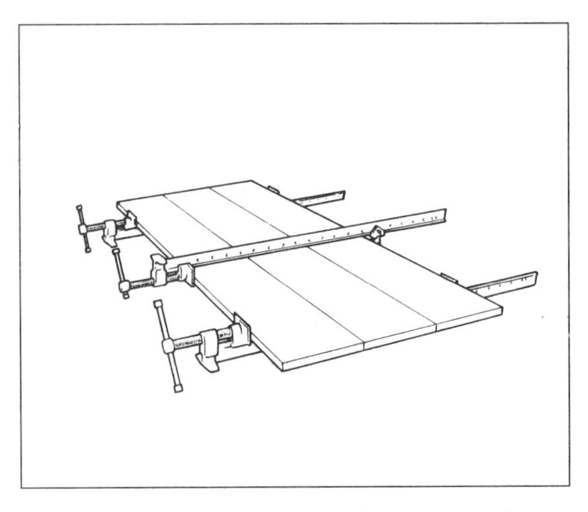

95. The method of cramping a board top to ensure that it does not buckle.

Hinge joints

There are a couple of problems with hinge joints which occur so frequently that they are often overlooked. That sagging leaf on the drop-leaf table is usually the result of the knuckle joints of the brackets which support the leaf wearing round their pins. The solution to this problem is *not* to put a tapered packing piece on the underneath of the leaf for the offending bracket to bear on. Remove the table top (usually secured with a half dozen screws) to give you access to both the top and bottom of the knuckle joint.

96. Perfect cabinetwork. The almost engineering precision with which this knuckle joint was cut some one hundred and fifty years ago (in the workshops of Titter & Co., Norwich; see Fig. 1) ensures that it will seldom need the attention of a restorer.

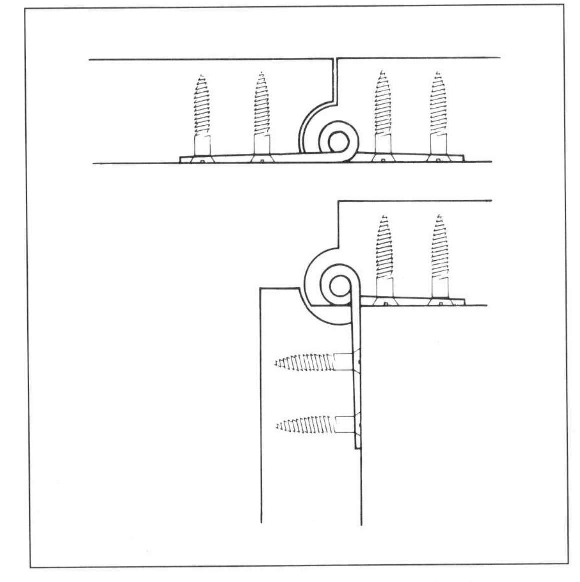

97. Cross-section through a rule joint. Note the thin section of wood above the knuckle of the hinge, which is an area prone to damage.

Cramp the bracket in the closed position, with its top edge absolutely level with the side frame. Remove the old pin and drill through to accommodate a slightly thicker pin made from mild-steel rod or a piece of a round nail. You must drill with great precision – just a fraction off course and the joint will not only bind but the bracket will not be horizontal when opened. This is a defensible repair, rather than restoration, in view of the amount of work involved in removing, remaking and replacing the rail, bracket and knuckle joint.

It is not unusual to see drop-leaf tables with unsightly gaps in the rule joints above the hinges (Fig. 98). Such damage is a bit tricky to repair because of the thin section of the wood. You must have unrestricted access to the damaged areas, which means that the hinges must be removed from the centre leaf, often necessitating the removal of the top before you can get to the hinge screws there. As you remove the screws, check to see if they are all the same. Eighteenth- and early nineteenth-century screws are often variable in both size and shape (as illustrated in Fig. 40, page 29), so taping each by its hole or, in the case of hinge screws, putting them back in their holes, will save a lot of fiddling about when it comes to reassembly. The damaged wood must now be cut away. Before attempting to chisel it out, saw through the quarter-round section on each side of the damaged area, or you might very well extend it. Having cleared away the damaged wood, the next task is to cut a rebate into the edge to take the repair patch. To give the repair maximum strength, you will need to take this rebate at least as far as the outer two hinge screw holes, preferably making the patch dovetailed. When the repair patch has been glued in and dried thoroughly, you will face the trickiest part of the operation – cutting the recess for the hinge knuckle

98. Repairing a rule joint.

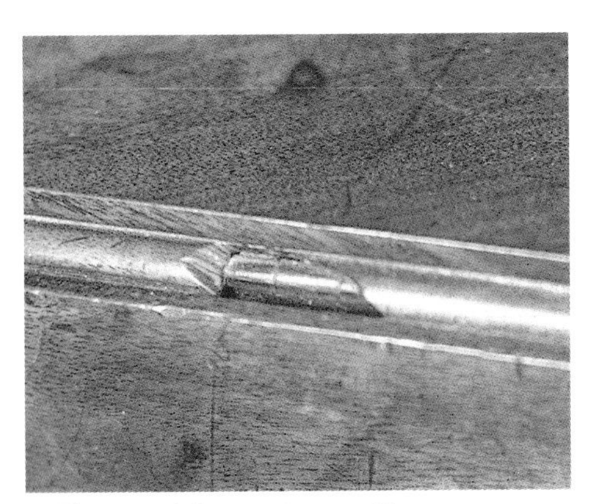

a. This typical damage is caused by pressure on the thin section of wood above the hinge, probably aggravated by accumulated dust.

b. The damaged area ready to work on.

c. All the damaged wood is removed and a dovetailed repair piece prepared.

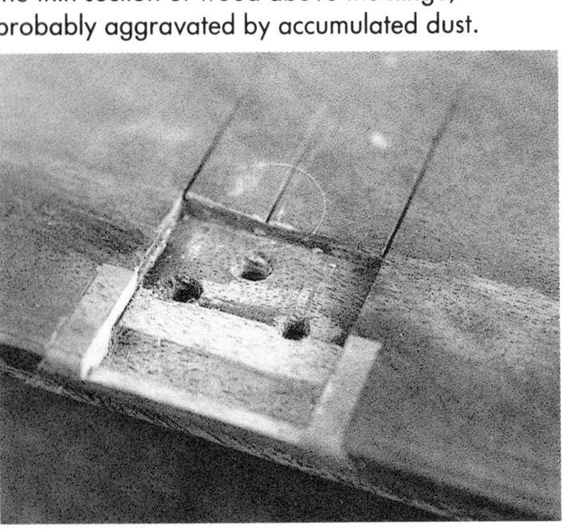

d. With the new wood in place, the hinge recess is cut out . . .

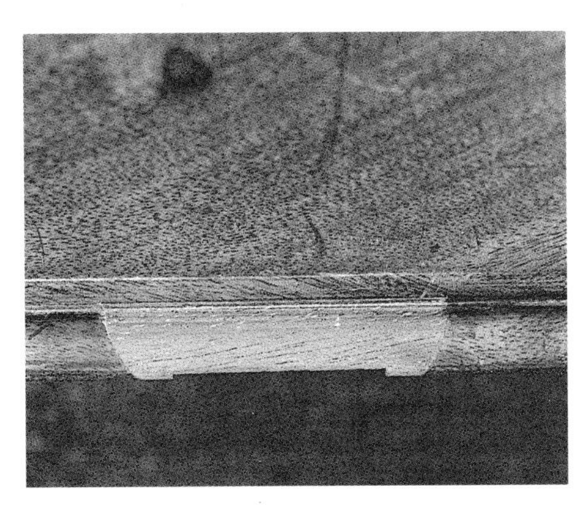

e. . . . and the radius shaped.

f. The completed repair.

and shaping the quarter-round section. You will often find gauge marks along the underside of the top to indicate the position of the recess but its depth must be governed only by the size of the knuckle. Don't be guided by the depth of the recesses for the other hinges or you may find that there's too little wood left when it comes to cutting the outer radius to shape. When you think you have it right, it is best to reassemble the whole top to check the free movement of the leaves, then take it apart for finishing. This will not seem like a waste of time after you have experienced a binding rule joint on which you have just spent an hour to get the colour and patina matched. And while you have those leaves off, clean out the dust and fluff which has accumulated round the knuckles of the hinges, which probably contributed to the damage in the first place.

Splits and warps

There is no miracle cure for misshapen timber. The effects of warpage and shrinkage of woods used in the construction of antique furniture are frequently distressingly obvious, as illustrated in Figs. 7 and 8 on p. 18, and here in Fig. 99*a*. Opened joints, described at the beginning of this chapter, are simple to repair. At the other end of the scale, distorted and cracked table tops and the movement of the ground wood beneath marquetry and other delicate veneers and finishes, is damage which, if not irreparable, is likely to take many hours and much expertise to stabilize or restore – and even then cannot be guaranteed to stay put for ever (Fig. 99*b*). At the root of the problem are three factors: first, the way in which timber used to be seasoned; second, the effects of changes in temperature and humidity; and third, the way in which timber is cut up.

Until recent times, all timber was seasoned by 'air-drying', that is, it was allowed to dry naturally either in log form or after primary sawing, depending on the type of wood. Drying from its 'green' condition, with its full capacity of moisture as in its growing state, wood will retain its original dimensions until the moisture content falls to round about 30%, from which point it will shrink as it dries. (The moisture content is expressed as a percentage of the dry weight of the wood; a piece which is half dry wood fibre and half moisture therefore has a moisture content of 100%.) With thorough air-seasoning, the moisture content of most types of wood will fall to between 23% and 17%, at which level it will be in balance with the moisture content of the air about it and would, in those pre-central heating days, be stable enough to be cut up and made into furniture.

Humidity, properly described as relative humidity, is the amount of moisture held in the air expressed as a percentage of the maximum amount which it can hold at the same temperature. When air is heated, its capacity for moisture increases. So a room at a temperature of 50°F with the air at 100% relative humidity could contain a pint of water vapour but increase the temperature to 70°F and the capacity of the air for moisture will double.

Moderate levels of heating in houses with a reasonable amount of air movement (draughts to most of us) will not usually have any adverse effects on antique furniture. However, today's acceptable comfort level of 70°F or more, in houses sealed by double glazing, can reduce relative humidity to 20–30%, which is detrimental to even some modern furniture, the wood of which has been kiln-dried to a moisture content of 10–12%. The effect of such an environment on air-dried wood is often disastrous. The greatly increased capacity of the air to hold moisture has to be filled from somewhere. Not only furniture but fabrics, books, plants, and you will give up

a

b

99. Irreversible warpage. This pair of card tables have tops of satinwood veneered on oak. Both have considerable warps. A previous attempt to correct the warp by the accepted technique of relieving the tension with grooves (although the clamping strips should perhaps have been treated separately) has clearly not effected a permanent cure. Short of removing the veneers and relaying them on a new ground, which would be a prohibitively lengthy and costly operation, there is little that can be done. (The shrinkage damage, visible at the left front of the left-hand table, is described on page 18.)

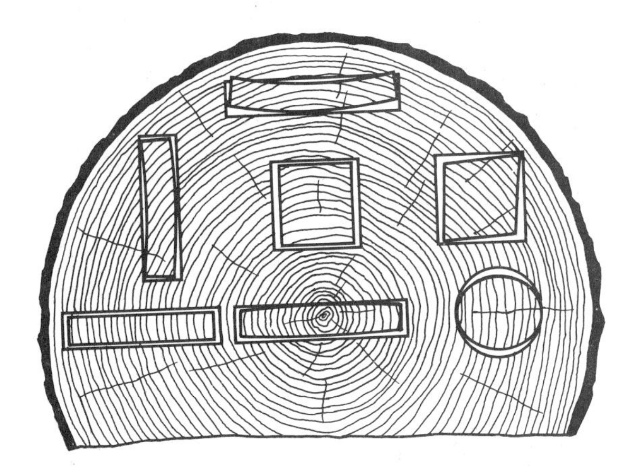

100. Characteristic shrinkage and warpage of various cuts of timber. Shrinkage along the grain is minimal whilst that at right angles to the radius of the log is as much as three times that in the direction of the radius, producing the effects shown here.

moisture to the air. When the changes in temperature and, therefore, in relative humidity are sudden, as when the heating system is turned on in autumn and off in spring, the effects are likely to be the most severe, for it seems that it is when the wood has to give up or re-absorb moisture rapidly that it is most prone to damage. Much depends on how the wood used in the furniture was cut from the log.

You will have noticed that much antique oak furniture has not suffered from warping or any other distortion, whilst mahogany furniture seems to have more than its fair share of such problems. The principal reason for this is that much of the wood used for oak furniture was quarter-sawn or riven (split) to produce boards the width of which followed the radius of the log along the medullary rays, at right angles to the growth rings (see Fig. 100). This cut produces a board which is still liable to shrink but not distort. When a panel was made from quarter-sawn boards, it would be fitted in a rebate without glue so that it was free to move with seasonal changes in relative humidity. If such a panel has split it is probably because movement has been inhibited by accumulations of dust and grit.

In the case of mahogany furniture, it seems that demand was for the widest boards possible, which often meant taking a piece from the full thickness of the log. Such a board will cut through the growth rings of the tree at varying angles across its width, thus exposing it to problems of distortion. Maximum shrinkage takes place at right angles to the radius, so that while the quarter-sawn board loses a bit of its thickness, a tangentially cut board will tend to warp, the edges moving outwards towards the bark with loss of moisture and inwards towards the heart when re-absorbing it.

Vast arrays of houseplants and pots of water will do little to build up and maintain the moisture level in air depleted by overheating. A relative humidity of 50–55% is ideally required for the stability of wood in antique furniture, and for many other antiques. The only way in which you can get anywhere near this level in most centrally-heated homes is by the installation of purpose-built humidifiers. The cost of these may seem to be high in relation to the amount of engineering which goes into them, but it is insignificant against the expense of rectifying warped or shrunken pieces of furniture. In the meantime, don't turn your heating on full blast in autumn, but rather raise the temperature a little at a time over a number of days and leave it on a little longer each day; don't set the thermostat too high and make sure that the air can circulate about the house. Similarly, gradually reduce the heat and the time the system is switched on in the spring. And if something untoward does happen, heed not such advice as placing the offending piece on damp grass with a pile of bricks on top – consult a well-qualified restorer.

101. There will be little difficulty in correctly positioning a new drawer stop here.

Drawer stops, runners and rails

There are not many chests of drawers or bureaux without a couple of drawer stops missing. It is a simple job to replace them if the marks left by the original ones, or the cabinet-maker's gauge marks, are clearly visible (Fig. 101). If there are no clues as to the original positions, don't rely on the distance of other stops from the front of the drawer rails, but measure the thickness of the drawer fronts (allowing for moulding or cockbeading) at the position of each missing stop and place the new ones accordingly. When gluing the new stops in place, don't be tempted to nail them as well. Panel pins may be driven in half way to secure the stops while the glue dries, but permanent nails eventually protrude from the wood as it wears, causing considerable damage. (Fig. 102).

The replacement of worn runners on the bottom of a drawer is straightforward, particularly when they are separate strips of wood which are glued on, but do remove the old ones carefully as they are usually fixed to fairly thin bottom boards which will not take kindly to a vigorous bashing. As with drawer stops, by all means secure new runners with temporary pins while the glue is drying but don't nail them on, although this is evidently what many cabinet-makers did. The resulting damage is even more catastrophic than that evident in Fig. 104, made by an un-nailed runner.

Carcase drawer runners are not so easy to replace but if they are badly worn there may be no alternative, for patching them is often more difficult and is not a long-term solution. When the runners are housed into the sides of a piece of case furniture it will usually be necessary to remove the back boards to get at them. If the runners are loose, don't try to pull them out without checking how they are fitted, as they are likely to be secured in mortices in the front rail. Try to ease them out without disturbing that front rail – which is probably fitted into the case sides from the front with the joints veneered over, just to complicate matters. Once internal runners are out it is a fairly simple operation to copy them and glue the new ones in place (Fig. 104).

It is not uncommon to see drawer rails $\frac{1}{8}''$ or more proud of the side of the carcase, with the veneer covering the joint cracked or missing (Fig. 105*a*). This is caused by shrinkage of the side panel across the grain leaving the runners in place and probably supported by the back boards, forcing the

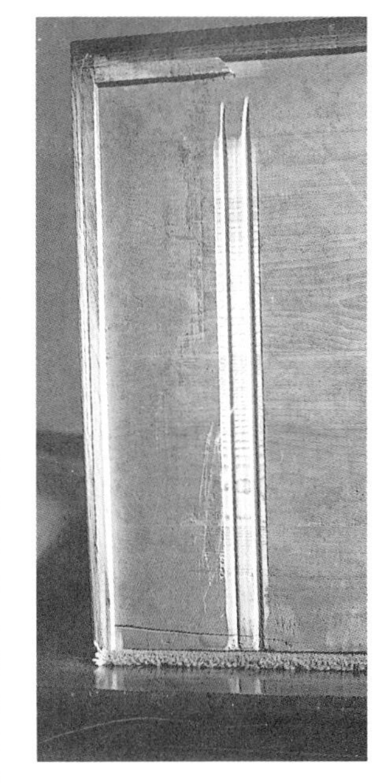

102. The results of nailing a drawer stop. Whether or not the drawer was heavily laden, friction has worn the wood of the stop to the point where the nail heads were exposed (*above*), to cause considerable damage to the drawer bottom (*left*).

103. The angle of this drawer front indicates that there are major problems with the runners.

104. Repairs to carcase drawer runners. The removal of this well-worn runner presented no problem.

The new runner was made slightly shorter to allow for shrinkage of the side panel of the chest, which caused the old rail, supported by the back boards, to push the drawer rail forward (see Fig. 105*a*).

a

105. A close-up of the joint of the drawer rail, before and after repair.

b

drawer rail forwards. Again, the cure usually involves access from the back of the piece, to remove and relocate (and sometimes to shorten) the internal runners. Sometimes the drawer rail joints will be loose enough to be reglued in the correct position without more ado, but they may be locked solid and require the injection of hot water into the interface before relocation is possible.

Feet of case furniture

No part of a piece of furniture is more vulnerable, or neglected, than its feet. At least tops and fronts get an occasional polish, but damp floors and woodworm take their toll of feet over the years and a carelessly-handled vacuum cleaner finishes them off. Many pieces of furniture which started their existence with bun feet have had them replaced by bracket feet, albeit more than two hundred years ago! It doesn't seem right to remove such venerable repairs, or evidence of changes of fashion, to replace them with turned buns of the period, but if the existing bracket feet are in really terrible condition and the original blocks for the bun feet are intact, then by all means, do your research and get busy on the lathe.

Most pieces of case furniture with either plain flat or ogee curved bracket feet have common problems. A frequent problem is that the blocks behind the feet are worm-eaten or missing altogether, the case then being supported by the brackets alone. If, by some miracle, the brackets have remained firm, then it is a simple job to clean out the rubbish and fit new blocks. However, if a bracket has had to take the weight of a well-filled piece of heavy furniture for a long time it may well have given up and parted company from its mate or broken in half. In either case it must be taken off, repaired and the whole assembly rebuilt.

Even the re-creation of an entire set of feet, with no pattern from which to copy the replacements, need not be too great a problem, for reference books will doubtless provide you with exactly the right style for the period of the piece, and the method of construction of bracket feet is common to nearly all types of case furniture. However, the complexity of the job is entirely dependent on the accuracy of the workmanship of the fellow who built the piece. You'll soon get accustomed to recognizing old cabinet-work made 'be 'and 'n' be eye', in which the bottom of a carcase is seldom absolutely level, nor the corners absolutely right-angled. On such a piece, you will have to do some careful measuring, cutting and planing to make the replacement feet fit perfectly.

Whether you have an existing foot to work from or are designing from scratch, your first job is to make a template from heavy card or hardboard. If you have taken a design from a book, try the template against the piece of furniture to make sure that it looks right. Now turn the piece upside down on to a blanket or a piece of carpet, on a trestle or not, depending on what working height you prefer. Pieces without large, flat tops, such as bureaux, will be awkward in this position and require propping, but it is the only satisfactory way to work on the feet. The next operation is to remove all damaged and loose bits, and any glue blocks which are not actually supporting a foot, and then wash off the old glue from the case and any parts you are going to save.

Next, measure up and select the materials you need for the job. If the piece you are working on is made from oak, the feet will be of solid wood with the grain running horizontally, in which case producing a plank of suitable dimensions should be no problem. With walnut, mahogany and much veneered furniture you will often find that the feet are veneered on a ground of the same wood as the carcase, with the grain of the ground wood running horizontally and that of the veneer vertically. In this case it will be easiest to cross-veneer a board of the ground wood before cutting out the brackets. Since this involves the application of pieces of veneer which are probably no larger than 6″ square, it should not be too difficult a job (see p. 78). Ogee bracket feet are invariably cut from solid wood, grain horizontal, the ogee shape being planed into the length of wood before the brackets are shaped.

When the piece for the brackets is ready, use the template to mark out the required number, making sure that the template is turned over for brackets of the opposite hand and that there is adequate waste to allow a decent clearance for the saw blade. In the case of brackets for the front feet, it is best to cut the mitre before working the shaped part – if subsequent adjustments to the mitre are required, a bracket might end up noticeably shorter than others. Check the angle of each corner, halve it, and mark and cut the mitre accordingly. Plane the mitre faces to fit precisely, then mark each bracket blank and the case bottom at that corner with a number to avoid confusion when it comes to assembly. The construction of the back bracket foot is somewhat different to that at the front. The side part is shaped as the front brackets but instead of a mitre, a rebate of half the thickness of the wood is cut into it, into which the plain, usually pine, back part is fitted.

When all the brackets have been cut and tried on the base, make up the corner and edge blocks. The corner blocks are not merely to keep the two brackets together, but are the main support for the piece of furniture. You must make sure that these are sturdy (of square pine at least twice as thick as the stuff from which the brackets are cut, wherever possible) and, most important, are planed to fit the angle of the brackets precisely. They must be butted squarely up to the bottom board or rail (whatever the feet are mounted on) and be $\frac{1}{8}$″ longer than the foot is high, so that the corner blocks take the weight, not the brackets. The edge blocks should be of 1″ square pine and about three-quarters the length of the bracket. It doesn't matter if the edge blocks overlap the shaped part of the bracket as they can be cut to conform to it after everything is glued together.

Once you have all the parts tried and fitting perfectly, assembly is straightforward (Fig. 106). First, glue on the brackets, rub-joining them to the bottom of the case and making sure that their outer faces are parallel to the case and the mitres of front brackets properly aligned. In the case of back feet, secure the rebated join with two panel pins (punched in – the holes filled with matching beeswax stopping) through the side bracket into the end of the back bracket. Clean up surplus glue as you go. When all the brackets are in place, fit the pine blocks, starting with the foot which you

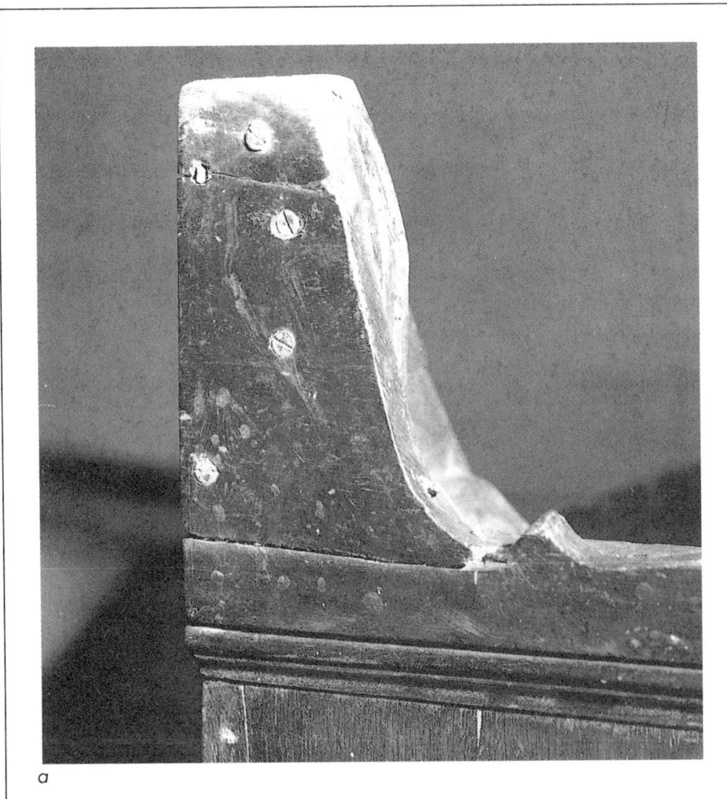

a

b

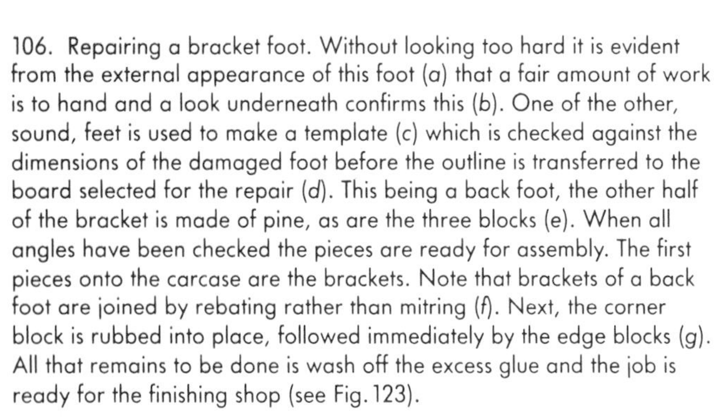

106. Repairing a bracket foot. Without looking too hard it is evident from the external appearance of this foot (*a*) that a fair amount of work is to hand and a look underneath confirms this (*b*). One of the other, sound, feet is used to make a template (*c*) which is checked against the dimensions of the damaged foot before the outline is transferred to the board selected for the repair (*d*). This being a back foot, the other half of the bracket is made of pine, as are the three blocks (*e*). When all angles have been checked the pieces are ready for assembly. The first pieces onto the carcase are the brackets. Note that brackets of a back foot are joined by rebating rather than mitring (*f*). Next, the corner block is rubbed into place, followed immediately by the edge blocks (*g*). All that remains to be done is wash off the excess glue and the job is ready for the finishing shop (see Fig. 123).

c

glued first and proceeding in the same order. Rub-join the corner block first, following immediately with the edge blocks, butting these right up to the corner block, and again clean off excess glue before moving on to the next foot. When all is done, leave the job overnight, then shape the edge blocks to the profile of the feet, if necessary, chamfer the inside corner of each corner block by about half an inch and take the sharp corners off the protruding $\frac{1}{8}$". The new wood is now ready for finishing.

e

g

CHAPTER 6

Repairs to surfaces and decorative features

Chips, blisters and dents

Patching solid wood and veneer

Edges and corners of furniture are the most prone to accidental damage. The duster catches a loose bit and off comes a sliver of veneer, which is put away in a safe place 'to be glued on later', never to be seen again. There is then no alternative but to put in a patch. Apart from those considerations of colour, grain, etc., which have been discussed at length already, the thickness of the stuff you select for the repair is important. You won't want to waste wood by using a piece which is much thicker than you actually need, so that you are cutting off lots of waste, but this will sometimes be inevitable if you are to match those features perfectly. By the same token, if you have some veneer which is a perfect match but is too thin, then it is legitimate to pack the patching piece up to the correct height with veneer or a shaving. When you are dealing with a wood with random grain and figure patterns, such as burr walnut, the matching and orientation of repair patches to conform to their surroundings is relatively easy to achieve but where the straighter-grained woods are concerned much more care will be required to ensure a perfect repair. The shape of the patch which you set into straight-grained wood will depend on the location of the damage. Fig. 107 shows some ideal shapes.

In most cases it is not advisable to cut out the damaged wood and then try to fit a patch to the hole you've made – it will take far too long and the fit is unlikely to be perfect. Greater accuracy will be possible by cutting the repair patch first.

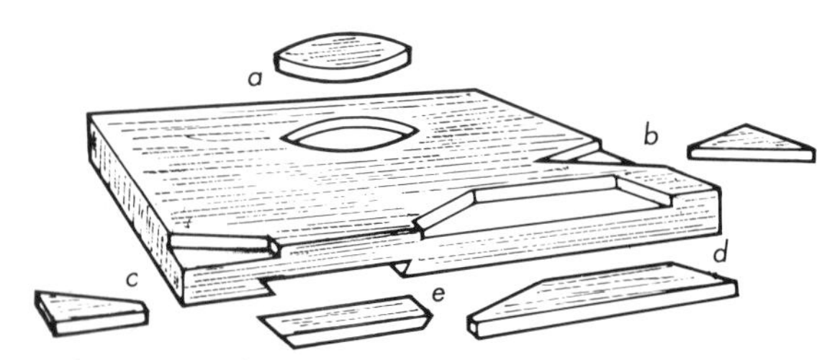

107. Shapes of patches
a. Boat-shaped, for any part of a surface away from the edges.
b. Triangular, for patching into end-grain.
c. Triangular, for corners. Note that the patch does not have an acute angle for a duster to catch – $\frac{1}{8}''$ straight in from the edge will do.
d. Wedge, for long edge repairs. Squared-off points for acute angles also.
e. Dovetailed, for repairing areas which will be under strain, as at the position of hinges (see rule joint repairs on p. 66).

Having chosen the perfect piece for the repair, draw the appropriate shape on the area which you have selected to be used for the patch, of sufficient size to cover the damage and, in the case of an edge repair, with $\frac{1}{4}''$ or so to overlap the edge to allow for handling and adjustments when fitting it. Cut the patch. If it is a boat-shaped piece you are producing, angle the cut inwards underneath the patch very slightly; a degree or two is all that is necessary. Place the patch in position, check that it is the correct way round, to match the reflectivity, and mark round it with the tip of your scalpel (10A blade) or marking knife. If the patch is small and difficult to handle, double-sided tape will help to keep it in position while you do this. Cut out the damaged area and try the patch. With accurate cutting, the patch will fit neatly in the hole with no space beneath. The bevel you put on the boat-shaped patch will help to ensure that the fit is such that the glue line will be almost invisible, but it does mean that you are likely to spend more time on trimming and checking the fit than on other shapes.

Judging when a patch is perfectly fitted is difficult but crucial, for the final assessment can only be made when it has been glued in and the glue has dried completely. If the patch is slightly proud of the surface (a minute amount which is more felt than seen – a fingertip might just detect the step) when you have put the glue on and pressed the piece down firmly, then that is likely to be perfect, for the glue will draw the patch down as it dries. But if you misjudge it you are in trouble. If you have taken a lot of time and care to select a beautifully matched piece, with colour, grain and figure perfect and finish intact, all this can be lost if that patch ends up even a fraction proud of the surface. Bringing the level down will not only destroy the finish and the mellow colour but even the grain and figure patterns may be different to those which show on the surface of the patch. So take your time and get it right. When working with solid wood, you can make the necessary adjustments by deepening the hole or taking a little off the back of the patch, but if it is a veneer repair you strictly only have the latter choice. If your luck runs out and the repair does end up proud, all is not lost, for you can rely on the finishing techniques described later to rectify the appearance. Whatever you do, you must avoid ending up with a patch which is below the surrounding surface – you might think you will get away with a repair which feels slightly depressed but as soon as the finish goes on it will be an eyesore and have to be taken out.

When there is a chip out of crossbanding, you can patch it in the same way as ordinary veneer, using a triangular repair, but a more satisfactory result will be achieved by patching it right across, particularly when the banding is of a highly decorative and reflective straight-grained veneer.

Repairing blistered veneer

A fairly frequent problem with veneer is blistering. Some blisters, particularly in highly-figured wood, are caused by moisture invading minute fissures in the veneer. Once a crack has started, more moisture, followed by dust and wax polish, will raise and extend the blister until it will become difficult to cure without some trace being left, usually in the form of a rippled surface. So the sooner a split blister is treated, the better (Fig. 109). The essential first step is to remove all dirt, wax and old glue from beneath the veneer, first by scraping with a scalpel or other fine blade and then by washing out with warm water and a suitable flat brush – not too much water at once, swabbed out with rag folded over a fine knife blade – and then allow it to dry completely before gluing the blister down. If the veneer is

108. Patching a mahogany table leaf. One of the screws securing a hinge has penetrated the leaf and broken wood away (a). The hole is too large to fill with stopping so a patch of matching wood must be fitted (b). The bevel on the patch ensures that only the finest of glue lines will be seen when the repair is completed (c).

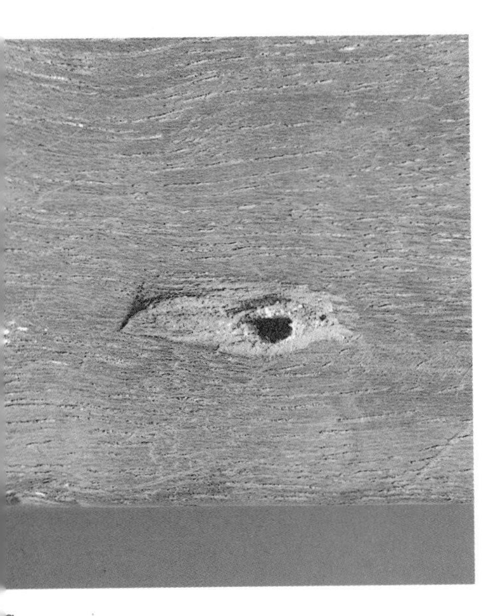

a

b

c

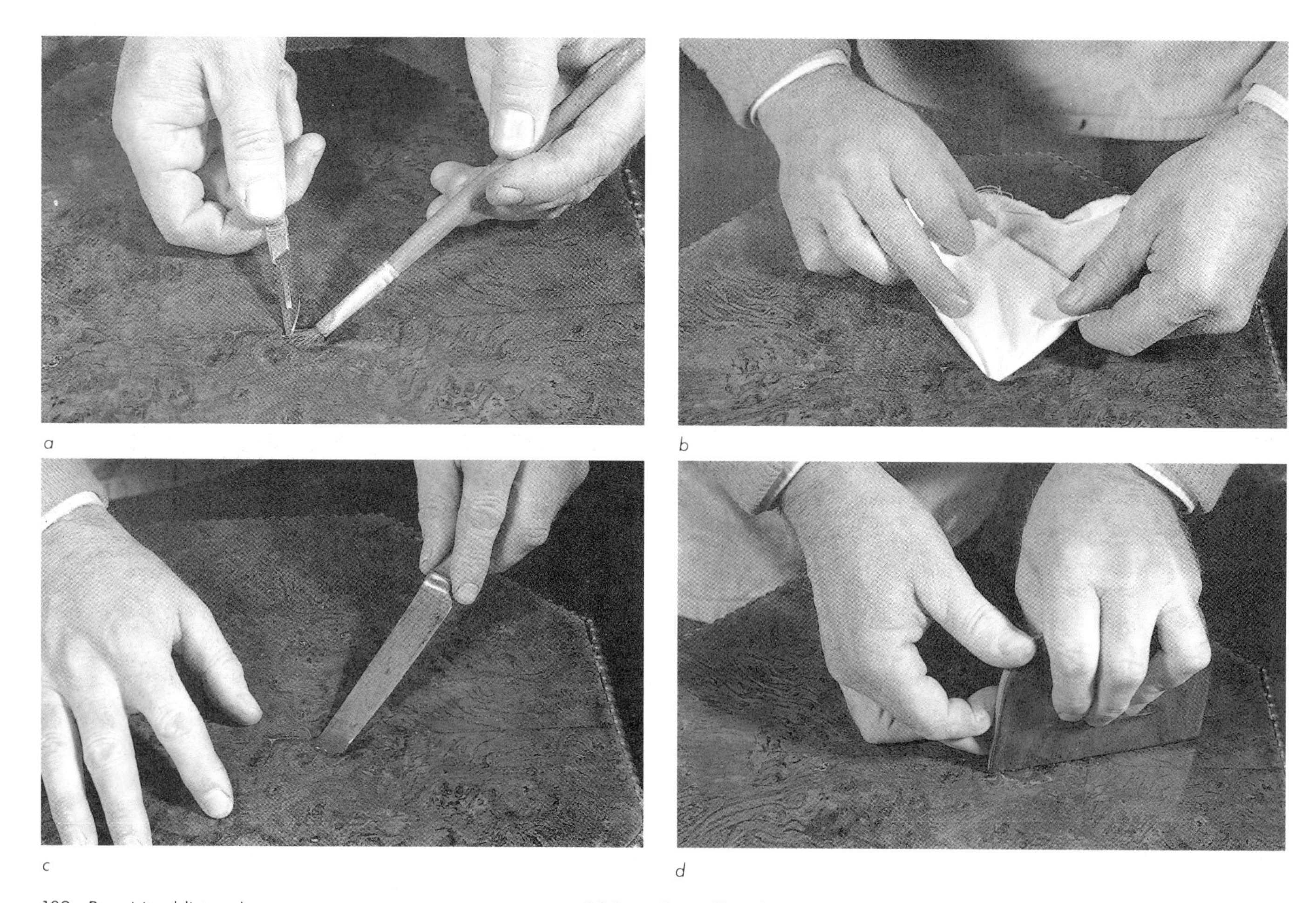

109. Repairing blistered veneer.
a. Cleaning out the dust and old glue from beneath the veneer with a small, stiff brush and hot water.
b. Drying out with linen over the tip of a knife blade.
c. Working in animal glue with a hot knife blade.
d. Pressing out excess glue with a veneer hammer.

thick or the split a short, narrow one, it may be difficult to get in to perform the cleaning operation. In this case it will be necessary to break out a piece of the veneer from one side of the split or extend the split with the scalpel. Which method you choose to do will depend on the thickness of the veneer and its grain. If you think a piece will break out cleanly, as many of the highly-figured woods tend to, then this will give you the best access. If the veneer is straight-grained, then a clean cut along the grain will probably be best. If you opt for the removal of a piece, wash off the glue and, while it is still damp, put it between a few layers of newspaper under a weight to keep flat until you are ready to do the gluing.

The method of gluing again depends on ease of access. The hypodermic syringe filled with a thin mix of glue is best for small or brittle areas of veneer (if there are several blisters to attend to, keep the syringe immersed in hot water while you are not using it), whilst a hot knife blade will spread glue beneath large areas.

Blisters which are neither split nor too high usually respond to the application of a warm flat-iron, providing the glue beneath has not perished. Get the flat-iron as hot as you can just bear to touch, place a piece of clean, dry white linen over the blistered area, and apply the iron with plenty of pressure for a few seconds – the thicker the veneer, the longer you will need to keep the iron on to allow for the warmth to penetrate and soften the glue. If the iron scorches the cloth, it is too hot for this operation (and you have asbestos hands if you can stand it) and will not only damage the finish unnecessarily, but may also cause the glue to dry out to the point where the veneer will not adhere any more. When the hot iron has been in place for a few seconds, remove it and the cloth and check to find out if the glue is responding; it may stay down or pop up again, in which case press the blister with your thumb to feel how tacky the glue is. If it is good and tacky, cramp or weight it down for half an hour or so until the glue resets.

Another method to try on small blisters is to press the tip of one of your old table knives onto the blister and hold the hot soldering iron to this for just a few seconds. When you take the soldering iron away, keep the knife in place for a few seconds more until the glue resets. There is an obvious danger with this method: if the iron is too hot or left on one spot too long, both finish and veneer may be scorched.

A word of caution: don't use a hot iron on faded rosewood, as the heat will most likely change its colour back to the original dark purple-brown. To be on the safe side, clean out, glue and secure all rosewood blisters.

Blisters which persist in popping up again obviously haven't enough adhesive beneath them. In the case of split blisters, you'll just have to repeat the cleaning and gluing operation. For small, unsplit blisters there is a simple solution – drill a fine hole in the blister and inject a thin mix of glue, squeeze out surplus glue and smooth the blister down with a veneer hammer or the pein of a Warrington pattern hammer (make sure this is clean and smooth beforehand), wash off the glue and secure.

If an unsplit blister is judged to be too high to respond to treatment without the veneer buckling, you will have to cut the veneer and proceed as if it were a split blister. In this case, and also when blisters have been caused by shrinkage of the ground wood beneath, it may be necessary to cut a sliver out of its centre (along the grain, of course) to ensure that there is no overlap when the veneer is reglued.

Some of the more conventional ways of securing repairs are not always much use in repairing veneer, particularly when working in the middle of large panels. A useful method of securing splits and blisters while the glue is drying is illustrated in Fig. 110. Cut some strips of softwood (2″ × ½″ × ¼″ is a good size), rub a little paraffin wax on the faces which are going to be in contact with the veneer and put a couple of veneer pins (⅝″, 22 gauge) part way through each. Place one of these blocks over each split or blister as soon as the excess glue has been washed off and the surface dried, drive the pins in until about ¼″ still shows then bend them over and hammer them flat to ensure a good grip on the block. The fine holes left in the veneer are easily filled with matching stopping (see p. 102).

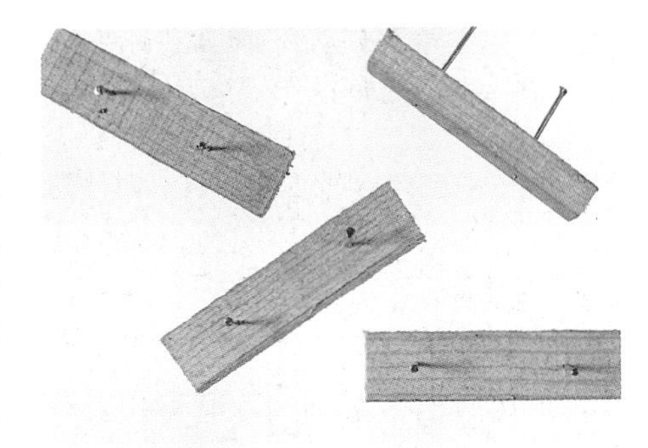

a

b

110. Securing repaired veneer.
a. Pin blocks ready for use.
b. The blister repaired in Fig. 109, held down securely while the glue dries.

Removal of dents

A dent in solid wood or thick veneer may often be successfully removed, or at least considerably reduced, provided that the fibres of the wood are intact. If the fibres are broken, as with a scratch across the grain, then the method described here will not be effective, for it depends on being able to swell the crushed fibres so that they return to their original positions, which torn fibres cannot do. The success of the operation also depends on how recently the dent was made and on the hardness of the wood. A recent dent in soft, open-grained wood will usually come out completely, but if it is an old dent in hard, close-grained wood, don't expect much response. The method involves applying heat to a moistened cloth to force steam into the damaged wood. The means of applying the heat depends on the extent of the damage: several closely-spaced dents can be treated at one time with a flat-iron, whilst small, isolated ones are best tackled with the soldering iron (Fig. 111). Whichever method is used the iron must be so hot that a good loud hiss results from applying it to a damp cloth.

a

b

c

111. Removing dents.
a. Two depressions in solid mahogany, made with the pein of a hammer.
b. The hot soldering iron placed firmly on well-dampened linen over the dents.
c. The result of a few minutes' work. The faint marks which remain will all but disappear when filled with shellac polish.

Lay a well-dampened piece of clean, white linen over the dented area and apply the iron. When the cloth has dried out beneath the iron, put another dampened area over the spot and replace the iron, and continue with this routine until it is evident that you are getting no further movement from the wood. If it seems that the treatment is going very slowly, it will help to make a few fine cuts in the dent, with the grain, to assist the penetration of the steam. If you use the electric soldering iron for this job, do switch off and unplug it before use. You will undoubtedly have to plug it in again several times to heat up, which will be inconvenient but a lot safer. When you are satisfied that no benefit will result from further work, put the piece aside for a day or two to dry before setting about finishing. The refinishing necessitated by this process may be considerable but is usually preferable to patching. Or you might decide to live with that dent!

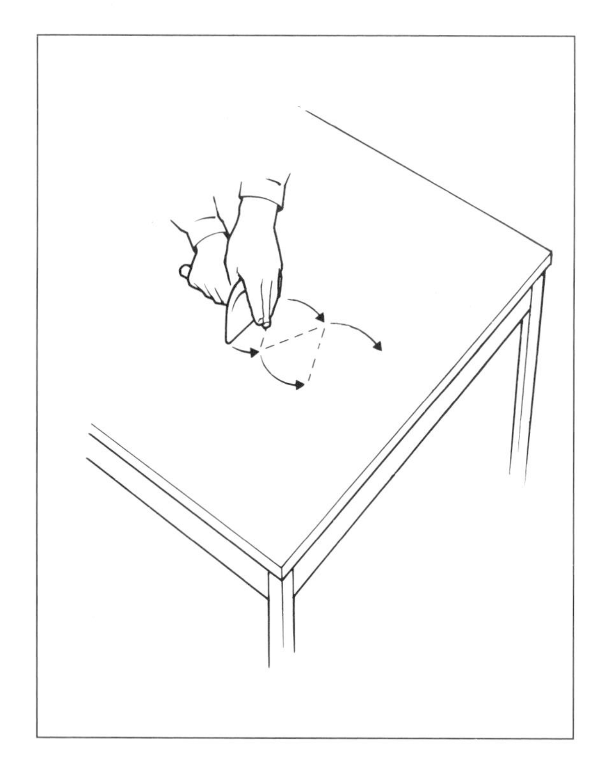

112. Using a veneer hammer. Keep the blade upright and press it forward with a zigzag movement working from the centre of the veneer outwards.

Reveneering

If veneer is very badly damaged, to the extent that patching would be excessive and you are contemplating reveneering, you are strongly recommended to put the job in the hands of a restorer who is well versed in the art. Veneering large areas in a way which is compatible with antique furniture really is a specialized business which only the most experienced craftsman should be allowed to undertake. Small areas, such as the faces of bracket feet (see p. 71), may reasonably be undertaken in the home workshop. Warm the veneer and the ground wood with a few passes of the heat gun, apply a thin mix of animal glue to both and bring them together immediately. Work the veneer hammer from the centre of the veneer out towards the edges quickly and firmly, pressing the blade forward with a zigzag movement (Fig. 112). This will squeeze out the excess glue and should result in the veneer staying down without the need for cramps. If, however, the odd spot does pop up, secure it with a pin block or two, as when treating blistered veneer. Wash off excess glue with a cloth which has been soaked in hot water and then well rung out, dry the surface and let the work settle down for a few days before doing anything else to it.

Mouldings and beads

Mouldings

If you find you have some mouldings to replace but no mouldings planes with which to produce them, despair not, for some fairly large and complex mouldings can be struck with a scratch stock, the construction of which is described on p. 48 (Figs. 74 and 75).

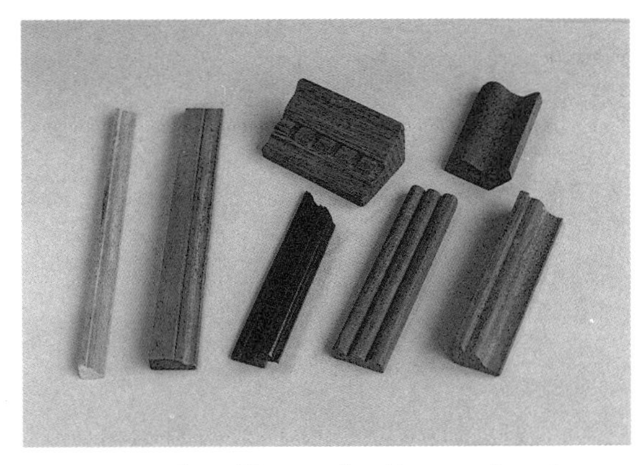

113. A group of mouldings made with a scratch stock.

Then you have to make your blade. The best material for scratch stock blades is the thin, tempered steel of cabinet scrapers. Most tool suppliers sell $3 \times 1\frac{1}{2}''$, 20-gauge scrapers for a few pence and one of these will make several blades. The only tools you will need to make a blade are a hacksaw and a variety of fine files. Saw a strip of cabinet scraper steel of sufficient width to accommodate the moulding, clean it with steel wool and meths, then coat the area to be worked with black pigment mixed with a little shellac. When this is dry, hold the steel against one end of the moulding to be repaired and copy its profile onto the painted surface with a fine point. Saw off as much of the waste as you can then set to work with the files, trying the developing profile against the moulding as you progress. Don't be surprised if the profile which you are cutting matches the moulding in some places and not in others, for few antique mouldings are exactly the same right along their length (and if the profile *is* exactly the same it is likely to be a later machine-made replacement). When you are satisfied that your scratch stock blade will produce the right profile, make sure its cutting edge is absolutely square to the faces of the blade or it will not work with optimum efficiency. Clean off the paint and secure the blade in the scratch stock with its longest edge held in the side fence.

114. A selection of scratch stock blades.

Now comes the selection of a board of wood from which to make the moulding. Ideally, this will be as long as the longest piece of moulding you need for the repair, plus a couple of inches for the blade to run off at each end. Its thickness should be a fraction greater than the height of the moulding and it should be wide enough to be held securely in the vice whilst allowing for the required number of mouldings to be struck and sawn off.

Put your selected board in the vice, checking that you are leaving sufficient of it clear of the bench top for the side fence of the scratch stock to run unobstructed. Place the blade against each end of the board and trace round it with a sharp pencil. Mark the area of waste along the length and remove this waste with a plane. Start working with the scratch stock about 3″ from the end nearest to you and draw it towards you to begin the cut. Then work forwards a few inches at a time – don't try to run the blade down the full length at this stage. You will have to hold the fence firmly against the side of the board and you must keep the scratch stock perfectly upright and square to the work. Having worked your way along and made some impression, come back to the beginning and start again, gradually removing waste until the moulding takes shape. You may find it necessary to clear compacted waste from the angles between scratch stock and blade from time to time, some woods being more troublesome than others. When you have worked down to the point where the whole cutting edge of the blade is in

a

b

115. Working a straight-grained moulding with a scratch stock.
a. The waste removed and the cutting started.
b. The completed moulding.

contact with the wood, the moulding will be almost complete. Now run the blade back and forth along the full length a few times and you should have a moulding which will need little or no sanding, save perhaps for raising the grain preparatory to applying the finish (see p. 93).

Cross-grained mouldings are really very little more complicated to make than long-grained ones, although this doesn't seem to be common knowledge. Why else do you see so many pieces of long-grained stuff used to patch cross-grained mouldings? The larger and more complex patterns will have to be struck with well-sharpened moulding planes but many small ones, such as those commonly found on the edges of tops and fronts of case furniture, are simple to make. From a board of matching wood which is slightly thicker than the moulding is deep, cut some strips which are wide enough to allow for trimming the edges once the moulding has been struck. If a long length is required, try to cut the strips from a board which is as wide as the average length of the pieces which make up the moulding you are copying. Find a board of scrap pine about 3″ wide, as long as the moulding required and as thick as the strips are wide. Plane one edge absolutely square, glue onto the planed edge a couple of strips of newspaper and then glue on the strips of cross-grained wood, securing every piece with a 'butterfly' of masking tape at each end. Allow a day for the glue to set. Remove the tape, then plane and scratch the moulding to shape as described above. Raise the grain and sand the moulding before removing it from the base board. Removal is easily accomplished with a thin knife blade which has been dipped in hot water, and with careful handling the entire length may be taken off without it breaking at the joins.

The size, shape and location of mouldings generally preclude their being cramped in position when you are glueing them on. Pre-drill holes in an inconspicuous part of each length of moulding and secure it with panel pins until the glue has set, or hold fine mouldings and beads in place with masking tape 'butterflies'. As with other applied decoration, you may find it more convenient to do the majority of finishing before gluing them on.

a

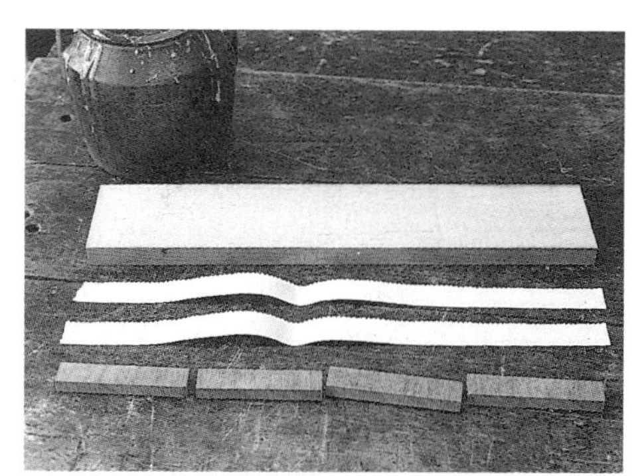

b

c

d

e

116. Working a cross-grained moulding with a scratch stock.
a. Some strips of walnut cut from the end of a board.
b. The strips ready to glue onto the backing board with pieces of newspaper interleaved.
c. The strips held with masking tape 'butterflies' while the glue sets.
d. The completed moulding.
e. The moulding (now with grain filled and two coats of shellac polish on) being removed from the backing board.

Cockbeading

Compared to that of mouldings, the repair of cockbeading is straightforward, but there are one or two points worth noting. When cutting out damaged cockbeading, don't try to chisel through it without first sawing through the lip with a fine saw (Fig. 117*b*). If you don't do this you are likely to find that as the chisel cuts to the inside of the beading the unsupported edge breaks away, extending the damage even further (and do look out for concealed panel pins). Even with the greatest care, damage will sometimes be done to sound beading, so this is one of the few instances where the repair piece is not cut before the damaged area is successfully removed. It may be a bit awkward to measure and match the angle of the mitre (necessary to hold the repair securely and to help make the repair less conspicuous) but you will save time, and beading, by doing it this way. When you have cut the new cockbeading to width, round off the edge which will form the inner side of the lip before gluing it on, which is much easier than rounding it after it is in place and avoids the risk of damage to the drawer front. The outer face can be planed to thickness and the rounding of the lip completed once the glue has dried. If you need to secure a piece of cockbeading during gluing, you may pin it with veneer or panel pins (Fig. 117*c*), predrilling with a fine (archimedean) bit to prevent it splitting, but do take the pins out afterwards so that some future restorer is not cursing over his bruised chisel. Sometimes you will come across cockbeading which is secured with thin hardwood pegs as well as glue, and this should be copied when you are repairing it. You might find it easier, in doing this, to cheat a little by temporary pinning as above, and then when the glue has dried, drill the holes a little deeper and wider to accommodate the wooden pins.

a

b

c

117. Repairing cockbeading.
a. How not to patch cockbeading. Even if this previous repair had been level with its surroundings, that join at a right angle to the grain would be difficult to disguise. Note also the scratches on the drawer front next to the piece of beading used to repair the end section; these were obviously caused when the inside of the beading was rounded after it had been glued on.
b. Sawing through the lip of the beading to avoid damage when the waste is cut out.
c. The new beading secured by temporary pins. The final shaping will be done when the glue is dried and the pins removed.

Decorative inlay and veneers

Marquetry and inlay

The replacement of pieces of marquetry and inlay wood is an uncomplicated procedure when you have single, isolated pieces to replace. Whether a repair is simple or complicated, however, the first job is to clean old glue, accumulated wax and grime from the hole, taking care not to damage its edges. If a piece has been missing for a long time, the edges may already have become rounded and chipped, in which case it will be necessary to trim back beyond the damage to produce clean, square edges which will be level with the pieces to be inserted. Now place a piece of thin paper over the hole, securing it with small pieces of masking tape if necessary (and if the surrounding finish and/or veneer will take it without suffering damage). Gently rub the paper in the area over the edges of the hole with heelball (melt beeswax, add a little vegetable black pigment and allow to cool), to and fro, side to side, until a clear image of the edge of the hole appears. If the outline is a simple one, this rubbing may be used for the cutting operation; otherwise you had better copy it onto good-quality tracing paper and check it against the actual outline of the hole to make sure it is perfect. Attach the pattern to the selected piece of veneer with double-sided tape, then cut with a few strokes of the scalpel (10A blade) and it is ready to glue in.

The re-creation of complex pieces and large tracts of marquetry is an entirely different matter, not least because it is possible that you won't have much to go on. An essential first step is to study those bits which are left around the damaged area, noting the types of wood used and the variations in direction of grain. The latter is surprisingly important. Marquetry

118. The base of a late seventeenth-century clock case. Woodworm and damp have taken their toll of both the holly and pear marquetry and the pine ground, presenting a formidable task for the restorer.

119. Tracings and designs. Many hours of patient work will be necessary to re-create the design for large tracts of missing marquetry, particularly when there are no two parts of the original which are the same.

120. The final design is ready to be glued onto the veneer sandwich.

pictures are not only characterized by the types and colours of the woods (many different colours of stained wood were probably used to make the picture you are looking at, now all faded to an ochre or honey colour) and by the use of shading, but also by the variations in reflectivity created by changing the grain direction in adjacent pieces. In the case illustrated in Fig. 118 there are horizontal, vertical and diagonal grain directions in the surrounding areas of marquetry, all of which have to be taken into account if the repair is to blend in successfully.

It is to be hoped that there is sufficient of the original design left for you to get an idea of the pattern, if not actual outlines (many of the late seventeenth-century marquetry patterns had hardly any repeats). Whatever there is, you are faced with several hours of trial and error with pencil and tracing paper until you produce a design which fills the gap and is entirely in keeping with its surroundings. The resulting tracing (Fig. 119) is a very valuable item, so get a couple of photocopies made straight away (make sure that the machine does actually do size for size copies – some can distort the image slightly, which will be enough to affect the accuracy of the repair).

If you have a major job on your hands, such as the one illustrated, it is a good idea to colour in one of the photocopies, shading each piece of the pattern in the intended direction of its grain. This will give you a rough idea of the effect of the finished picture and tell you how many veneers are going to be needed for the cutting operation which follows. Obviously, it would be a soul-destroying business to cut each of those intricate pieces individually in order to get the grain lying the way you want it – there may be many yards of saw cuts to make anyway, without adding to the burden. All the pieces for a section of marquetry are cut together, the area which you can cut at one time being limited by the capacity of your piercing saw. You can use a fret saw to deal with really large sections, but it is unwieldly and tiring in comparison to the piercing saw. It is better to divide the work up (along simple saw lines) into manageable pieces, and so ensure accurate cutting (Fig. 121*a*).

Having selected the veneers required to make up the marquetry picture –

the one in Fig. 119 needed four: three pale (holly) and one dark (stained pear wood) – they are cut into pieces of a predetermined, manageable size and glued together, their grain direction orientated to suit the plan and with a sheet of newspaper between each. The glue should be of very thin veneering consistency, as described on p. 54. If the veneer is thin, or brittle, one more veneer should be glued on the bottom of the pile to support it whilst sawing. The veneer and newspaper sandwich should be left cramped between boards for a day or two before the next stage, which is to fix the cutting pattern to it. A good, sharp photocopy is secured to the top veneer (Fig. 120), again with thin glue, and left overnight. It is not advisable to try to save time by gluing the pattern on at the same time as the sandwich is made up, as the pressure of the cramps can distort the paper and press glue into it, leaving an indistinct sawing line.

When all is ready, fit the sawing table (see p. 49) and put a blade in the piercing saw (getting the teeth pointed towards the handle can be a bit tricky when you are using the finest ones). The size of blade does, in theory, depend on the thickness of the work, but the finer the blade you can actually use without the teeth clogging with glue and dust, the better. Theory also has it that the thickness of the blade should be compensated for by tilting the saw slightly towards the edge of the work, so that upper pieces will fit into lower ones without any glue line showing when the picture is assembled. In practice, though, it is virtually impossible to maintain an angle to the cut through all the contortions of some patterns; a fine blade and careful sawing will produce excellent results. The most awkward parts of complex marquetry are the sharp turns which are so often necessary. Unfortunately, the fretwork method of doing a loop into the waste and returning to the point at the correct angle is not possible, for there usually is no waste. So you will need to acquire the art of sawing backwards when you come to a sharp turn, adjusting the position of the work on the table with your free hand until the new direction is in line with the saw. This is, naturally, where the saw blade will tend to break. Ensure an adequate supply of blades and also something to calm that nervous twitch which will surely develop as the day proceeds.

a

b

121. Sawing in progress.
a. A detail from the marquetry picture on the sawing table. The grooved block supports the saw when cramped fingers need to be rested in the middle of a cut.
b. The sawing of one small area is complete.

As the pieces are sawn away from the rest, reassemble them well out of the way. When everything is cut and assembled, you must patiently take those tiny pieces of the sandwich apart and make up the picture. Get a tub of hand-hot water and float each piece in it. This is where that interleaved newspaper comes into its own, as it absorbs the water much quicker than the glue would by itself, and the layers soon separate. When you've had a bit of practice, you will be able to manage several pieces of sandwich in the water at the same time, but to start with try just one and that, preferably, a large piece of background veneer into which the smaller pieces can be fitted as you go along. As each layer separates, make sure the pieces of veneer are free of glue, dry them and assemble them again in layer order, ie, all grain running in the same direction, unless you have a relatively simple picture, for trying to assemble the pieces to take account of the desired reflectivity can be difficult at this stage. An aid to assembly at both this and the final stage is the use of gummed paper secured to a board, particularly when you have lots of small pieces to manage.

122. Preliminary assembly. All the layers from which the veneers will be selected are laid out on gummed paper. The selection of the grain direction will be done according to the plan which was determined from a study of the remaining original marquetry.

The next stage is a two-part operation: selecting the pieces for the picture and shading them if necessary. If you have done your planning, the selection of pieces according to their grain direction will be straightforward. The determining of which pieces should be shaded depends on the extent of shading on what remains of the original marquetry. To judge the effect on

123. Sand scorching to give a shaded effect to parts of the marquetry picture.

124. Final assembly. The finished section will now be put in its place in the marquetry picture, which then has a heavy paper glued to the front before being secured to the ground wood.

125. The result of many weeks of work (*a*). This restorer did not count the number of pieces he cut, nor the length of the saw cuts!

Note: Before embarking upon a project of this magnitude it is as well to have a bit of practice. (*b*). Such a test piece is useful for perfecting the sawing technique and for seeing how glue and finishing processes react.

the new marquetry, the photocopy which you previously used to mark out grain direction can be shaded. The actual shading may be done at a later stage in the repair by the use of vandyke stain (see p. 118), but it's much more satisfying to do it as the original would have been, by scorching the veneer in hot sand. Fill a shallow tin or baking tray with clean, fine sand and put it on the hotplate, setting the thermostat to about the middle of its range, and leave it to reach working temperature. While this is going on, start to make up the marquetry picture. Assemble the pieces on a board and make any final decisions about grain direction before selecting those pieces which are to be shaded. Before you go to work on these, practice with off cuts of various sizes to make sure you get the expected results. The speed with which the veneer is scorched and the degree of scorching will only be determined by trial and error; plunge each piece into the sand to the level at which you want the shading to finish and check it after a minute (Fig. 123). Small pieces may require longer to achieve the desired effect; larger ones, less time. When you are confident about the heat setting and the time required in the sand, take the pieces to be shaded out of the assembled picture, scorch them and return them to their positions.

Now you can proceed with the final assembly. Get the whole picture built up on gummed paper, making sure that the pieces are well secured and everything dry before the next stage. This is your last chance to make any changes without difficulty, so check grain direction and shading, and try to visualize the marquetry in place and the same colour as that surrounding the repaired area. When you are completely satisfied, brush a light application of thin glue all over the face of the assembled section and immediately place a piece of heavy brown paper over it, put the whole thing between flat boards with a layer or two of newspaper to prevent the work sticking to them, weight the boards and leave until the next day. Then remove the gummed paper from the back of the marquetry, dampening it only just enough to allow the paper to be peeled away. If any glue has seeped through the saw cuts, it should be removed with a rag dampened with warm water, again keeping the amount of moisture to a minimum. When it is dry, the marquetry with its supporting paper on the front should be quite strong enough to handle. Trim off the surplus paper around the edge of the section and – the moment of truth – try it in its place on the piece of furniture. There will usually be one or two areas to trim to make the perfect fit, but leave these adjustments until you are ready to glue it – and meanwhile keep it between those weighted boards. As with all repairs to veneer, once the piece is glued in, no attempt should be made to do any more work on it for a while. A day or so after gluing, the cramps may be removed and the brown paper and glue washed off, but then the job must be left alone for several days to settle down.

Boulle

The procedures for the repair of boulle are, in many respects, similar to those described for marquetry, and are often much easier because the materials used are less fragile. Sheet brass of the appropriate gauge will be available from a local supplier but tortoiseshell (actually turtleshell) is a bit more difficult to obtain. You will perhaps be able to pick up a damaged card case or hand mirror from an auction for a nominal sum (sometimes they throw out absolute wrecks as unsaleable, so do ask) and such an item will provide sufficient shell to do many minor repairs.

126. Making up a simple mosaic banding.
a. Black and white stringing is cut to length and a stop pinned to a piece of scrap. The stop is set at approximately the angle of the required pattern to avoid waste. Paper glued onto the scrap first will facilitate the removal of the completed banding.

b. The lengths of stringing glued in place.

c. Strips cut from the ends of the cleaned up stringing block can be made into a variety of simple mosaic bandings.

127. A selection of mosaic bandings made up from veneers and stringing.

The marquetry processes of taking rubbings, making tracings and cutting with piercing saw apply to making individual pieces of brass or shell, as does cutting both together (except that cutting patterns are best attached with double-sided tape and, therefore, the saw blade size generally needs to be larger to avoid clogging its teeth). A backing veneer of wood should always be used when cutting boulle. When applying brass and tortoiseshell, a normal mix of Scotch glue is used. (Some say that when preparing glue for securing metal veneer and inlay a clove of garlic in the gluepot will give it extra holding power. This little gem of information is offered without comment.)

It comes as something of a surprise to the newcomer to boulle repairing that references to red boulle indicate not the colour of the shell itself but the pigmentation of its background. To achieve a match a little whiting is mixed with the glue as a basic colour, to which is added orange chrome pigment with traces of vermilionette and rose pink. Other colours of tortoiseshell you might come across – green, yellow and blue – are similarly treated by adding whiting and the appropriate pigments to the glue.

Both boulle- and marquetry-work result in considerable quantities of 'spare' bits being produced. The maker of the piece you are working on would have used these to veneer another piece of furniture but, although the *première-partie* and *contre-partie* pieces do sometimes turn up as a pair, it is most unlikely that you will find a ready use for yours, although you will undoubtedly keep them, just in case!

128. A boulle 'apprentice piece'. The cutting of the brass and tortoiseshell together produces two veneer pictures, the *première-partie* and the *contre-partie*, both of which are shown in this example.

Stringing and mosaic banding

Other uses of decorative woods range from simple stringing to some fairly complex mosaic bandings. If you are faced with the replacement of a lot of stringing, it will be worthwhile obtaining a few lengths from one of the specialist suppliers (see p. 152), but if there are only a few small pieces to deal with, it won't be too laborious a job to cut them from the solid. A small but useful tip when fitting patches into stringing, is not to cut the joins straight across but angle them at about 45°, and the repair will be much less noticeable (Fig. 129). When you come to repair mosiac inlaid banding you are likely to find things a bit more complicated. Some of the bandings which you will come across are still produced today and are available from the aforementioned suppliers but there are many patterns which you will have to make yourself. Don't be put off by the apparent complexity of some of these bandings, for close inspection will reveal their method of construction to be fairly simple, if time-consuming. The example shown in Fig. 126 is made by gluing lengths of various stringings onto a newspaper-lined board, butting them up to a stop to keep them parallel. When the glue has dried the stop is removed and the surface cleaned up. Strips cut from the end, across the lines of stringing, are then glued between the bordering stringing, either before making the repair, if a long length is needed, or as the repair is being done. Quite complex mosaics can be made up in stages by following this basic procedure (Fig. 127).

129. Repairing stringing. The joins are cut at an angle to help blend in the repair.

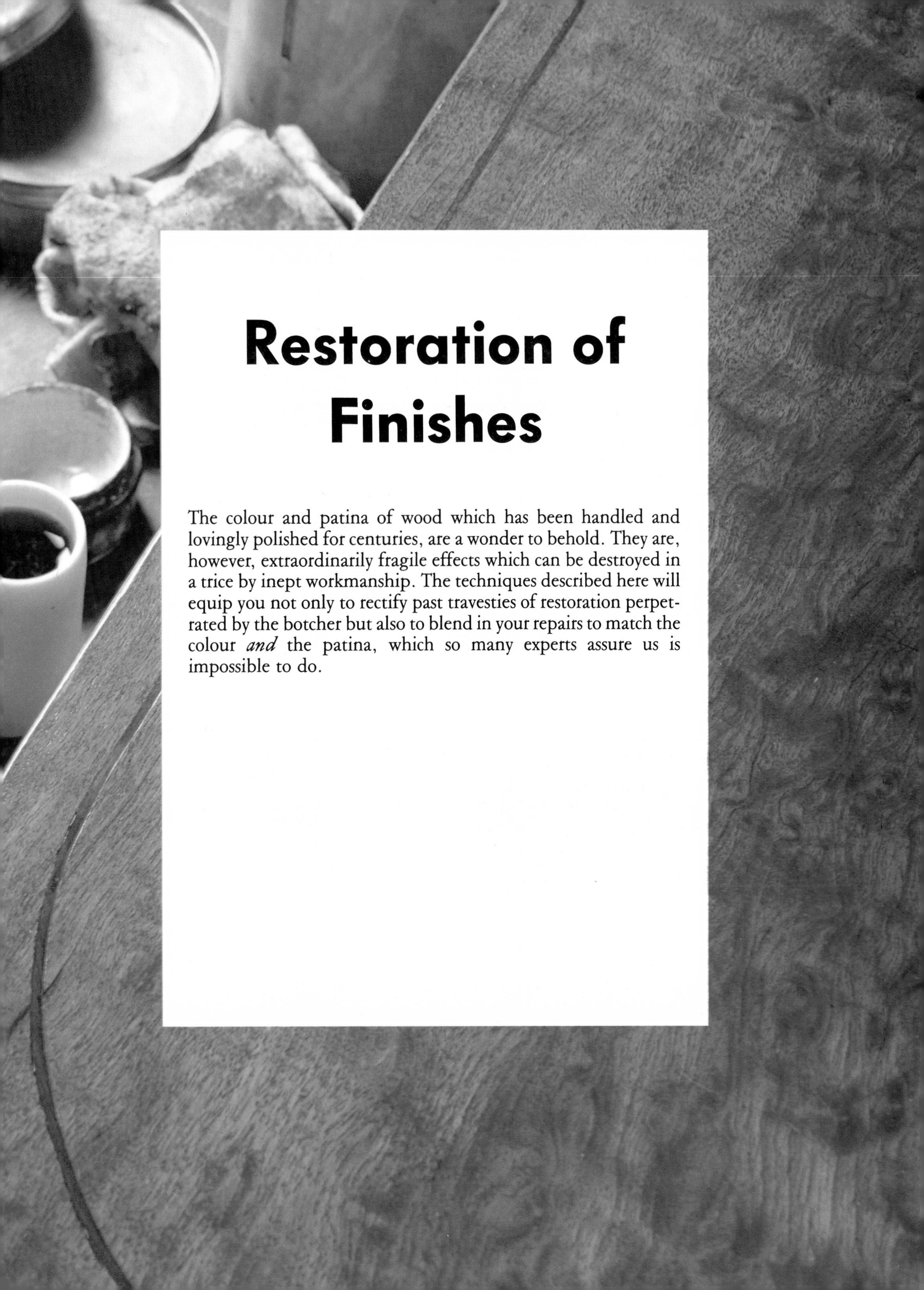

Restoration of Finishes

The colour and patina of wood which has been handled and lovingly polished for centuries, are a wonder to behold. They are, however, extraordinarily fragile effects which can be destroyed in a trice by inept workmanship. The techniques described here will equip you not only to rectify past travesties of restoration perpetrated by the botcher but also to blend in your repairs to match the colour *and* the patina, which so many experts assure us is impossible to do.

CHAPTER 7

Reviving a tired finish

You will be most fortunate if all you have to do in the way of restoration is cleaning and waxing. However, the processes described in this chapter are the most frequently used, hence their position here at the beginning of the section on finishing.

Washing

Most light films of dirt and grime, whether on shellac or wax finishes, will respond to a gentle wash with kitchen soap and warm water. Obviously, the water must not be applied too liberally, nor must too large an area be washed without rinsing and drying. Do a small area at a time and make sure that it is dried thoroughly with a soft cloth. When completely dry, all that should be necessary is a buffing with mutton-cloth (if you buy the genuine article from the butcher, make sure that it is well washed in several changes of hot, soapy water and is free from chunks of bone) or, if the surface has been left too dull, waxing with a good polish.

Revivers and cleaners

If there is too much dirt on a surface to respond to the washing method, you will have to try a cleaner. There must be dozens of concoctions which have been devised for cleaning and reviving finishes and some are indeed good cleaning agents, particularly those which contain a high proportion of solvents, but they must be treated with caution to avoid possible damage to the finish beneath the grime. Those which claim to be revivers or 'scratch removers' should not be used, for they will usually contain an oil (often linseed) which, while giving the appearance of making the scratches vanish and reviving the finish, will have merely penetrated faults in it and filled up the minute air spaces which make scratches show. As the oil dries out, or worse, finds its way into the wood, the faults will reappear. Damaged finishes can only be cured by the techniques described in the following chapters.

The following recipe is for a genuine cleaner which works wonders on varnish and shellac finishes which are in good condition. It will sometimes revive oxidized finishes and will do no harm to the wood if it doesn't work for this purpose.

	IMPERIAL	METRIC
Pure turpentine	8 fl oz	200 ml
Methylated spirit	4 fl oz	100 ml
Acetic acid B.P. (33%)	2 fl oz	50 ml
Teepol (liquid soap)	1 fl oz	25 ml
Brasso (metal polish)	1 fl oz	25 ml
Ammonia .880	½ a 5 ml medicine spoon	

130. Removing dirt and burnishing the finish. The cleaner described in the text has been used to remove accumulated grime from the right hand part of this rosewood panel.

Pour the ingredients into a one-pint (Imperial), or half-litre, bottle in the order in which they are shown above, secure the top and shake the bottle vigorously until all are blended into an emulsion. It may take a couple of goes before a good thick emulsion forms, particularly in cold weather, when you will probably have to stand the bottle of mixture in a warm place for a while before it will emulsify.

Shake the bottle before use and apply this cleaner with a soft cloth, changing to a clean part of the cloth frequently. It will remove as much, or as little, of the grime as you want, after which an application of wax polish will give you a shine to be proud of.

Wax polish

There are several brands of polish sold nowadays, many of them excellent products based on old, well-tried recipes. There is, however, a drawback to these commercial polishes, for they are made to be applied easily and therefore do not contain a high proportion of those hard waxes which produce a durable shine. The polish described below may be a bit more difficult to apply than the mass-produced products, but you may be sure that the results will be worth the effort of making it and using it on your furniture.

	IMPERIAL	METRIC	
Carnauba wax	1 fl oz	30 ml	Melted volume (see below)
Paraffin wax	1 fl oz	30 ml	
Beeswax	½ fl oz	15 ml	
Mansion Wax polish*	½ fl oz	15 ml	
Pure turpentine	4 fl oz	120 ml	

*This commercial polish, or similar, will contain those ingredients which prevent the solvent from evaporating too quickly whilst the wax is in the tin.

If you use unpurified carnauba wax (the dark grey-green variety), yellow beeswax and a dark commercial polish, the resulting polish will be suitable for all but the lightest-coloured furniture. If you require a pale polish it will be necessary to use purified carnauba, bleached beeswax and a white commercial polish.

To prepare the polish you will need a graduated pan, failing which, mark the appropriate levels inside an old saucepan. Blend the waxes together in the pan on a thermostatically-controlled electric hotplate which is set only just sufficiently high to melt them without bubbling or smoking. Under no circumstances should waxes be melted over a naked flame and, even with the hotplate, you must keep an eye on what is going on. To be on the safe side, keep the workshop fire extinguisher (see p. 47) to hand.

The waxes should be put into the pan one at a time, starting with the carnauba, melting sufficient of each sort to bring the level to the appropriate mark. The proportions do not have to be exactly as in the recipe, but try to get them as near as possible. When all the waxes have melted and blended together, *remove the pan from the heat* and immediately pour in the turpentine, stirring as you do so. Then decant the liquid polish into suitable tins (which have well-fitting lids) and allow it to cool slowly. Sealed well, this polish will remain usable for months. If it does get too firm to be used with reasonable ease, simply melt it again and add a little more turpentine.

On flat surfaces, the polish is best applied with a cloth. On mouldings, carvings and other uneven surfaces it will be easier to apply it with a brush. For this purpose, the most suitable implement is a 2″ paint brush with its bristles cut down to about half their length to stiffen them. As soon as the polish has been applied, remove the excess with a soft cloth (and a shoe brush on uneven surfaces, using cloth and brush alternately), turning the cloth to a fresh surface frequently. Don't try to treat too large an area at one go – if you wax more than a couple of square feet before removing the excess you may find it difficult to work. Don't try to produce a high shine at this stage. When you have waxed the whole surface, buff it gently with mutton-cloth and leave it overnight. The next day, a further buffing with mutton-cloth and a soft brush on mouldings and carving will complete the production of a shine which will last for months. After a few days a further application of this wax, or a commercial one if you prefer, will add to the patina, but don't overdo it, for waxing too frequently can build up a sticky surface which attracts grime and defeats the object of the exercise.

CHAPTER 8

Preparation for finishing with shellac

What you decide needs to be done to a finish does, of course, depend on how much work has had to be done to the woodwork, on the state of the existing finish and on the condition of the unrepaired wood. The cardinal rule is that fine, old finishes must be left undisturbed. Even original finishes which appear to be in poor condition can, in exceptional cases, be brought back to life: some crackly old varnishes will revive with a wash over with solvent; some overlaying finishes will respond to gentle pressure with the wax scraper and flake off to reveal the original finish beneath. Usually, though, heavily oxidized finishes and those which have been covered with paint or stained varnish will need to be removed completely. Naturally, if you are contemplating such disasters on a multi-thousand pound piece of Chippendale then you hesitate before slopping on the paint stripper and, hopefully, consult a professional restorer. However, the art restorer's cotton swabs are inappropriate to the restoration of finishes on the vast majority of pieces of functional antique furniture, many of which have accumulated more than their fair share of stains, sun-bleached patches, wear and scratches.

Sometimes, surfaces which appear to be dreadfully stained will miraculously recover when stripped of the finish, but an equal number will not and the decision then has to be made to either live with the stains or bleach them out. Stripping and bleaching do involve an enormous amount of work to bring back good colour and patina, so if the piece has a nice, original finish, think long and hard before using these techniques and if in doubt, consult a professional.

Raising the grain

Taking the best case first, let us assume that the existing finish is not too bad and it's just a question of blending in your superbly matched repair patches with their surroundings. First, the bare wood might need to be attended to, particularly if there are large areas and turned work, for the fibres of newly-worked wood, especially those woods with large, open grain, will usually be compressed and therefore react adversely if a finish is applied straight away. So to avoid wasting time, the grain must be raised and sanded. Go over all the bare wood with a well-dampened cloth and, when the wood has dried again, smooth it with 320 grit garnet paper. Then, for good measure, repeat the process.

Preparation of a sound existing finish

Now, that existing finish must be treated before any new finish can be put on, in order to blend in the repaired areas or, indeed, just to revive it. If you don't clean and prepare the surface you will almost certainly find that the new finish, although it may look well at first, soon shows marks where the new shellac is separating from the old. It must be emphasized that this preparation process is only effective when applied to an existing shellac finish and some varnishes. Most will be compatible with modern spirit-based shellacs but just check to make sure. Dampen a fingertip with meths and gently rub a small area of the existing finish, preferably in an out of sight place, and as it evaporates rub the spot with a dry finger. If it just drags but is not shiny and tacky, then you may be reasonably sure that new shellac will take to the surface. Varnishes which go very glossy and stay tacky for a while after the application of meths won't respond to the polishing rubber and will have to be removed, as will cellulose lacquer, polyurethane and other such incompatible finishes.

If the existing finish proves to be compatible, is sound and does not show obvious deposits of grime, start by giving it a wipe over with a soft cloth, well wetted with dewaxing solution, to remove what wax and grease there is. Follow this with one gentle wipe with a lint-free cloth dampened with meths and you should have a surface which will bond with new shellac polish. The degree of dampness of the cloth is crucial: too much meths and it may lift all the existing finish, too dry and it won't dissolve any, or worse, it will drag and damage the finish.

When there are heavy deposits of wax and grime obliterating the detail of the wood, the existing finish may require more severe treatment to prepare it. Start with the dewaxing solution again, but this time apply it with 2/0 steel wool, rubbing *very* gently. Follow this with the meths-dampened cloth or, if there are stubborn patches of grime, 2/0 steel wool may be used, just dampened with meths and applied to the surface with a very light touch. Follow this with a meths-dampened rag to clean up, and don't worry if white streaks appear as the meths evaporates; they are easily removed with dry steel wool, this time the finest, 4/0 grade, rubbing gently with the grain when the surface is completely dry. *Gently* is the operative word. Steel wool can go through to the wood almost instantly, particularly when used with meths or other solvents, and can go on through a nicely-faded surface to the raw wood beneath with little more effort. Don't try to clean all the grime off, either. Every piece of antique furniture which has been used at all has a little grime somewhere, in crevices, in carving and turning, in mouldings and all the places which the duster does not generally reach. So long as it is not excessive, leave it there, for a piece which is so clean that it could have just come out of the cabinet-maker's shop might be mistaken for a reproduction!

All things being equal, you are now ready to apply some shellac. If there have been minimal repairs to the woodwork and these have been nicely done with old, well-matched stuff with its finish intact, then you might get away with a couple of coats followed by wax polishing, but don't count on this often being the case.

Stripping

When you have been unable to revive the existing finish, there will be no way to make the surface presentable without stripping it and refinishing. Stripping off a finish is perfectly safe for even a well-faded surface, providing a few rules are followed. First, the fundamental rule: never remove a finish by sanding or scraping. The cabinet scraper, useful as it is to the cabinet-maker, has no part in the restoration of old, mellow surfaces. And the fellow who suggested that the best method of removing old varnish is a piece of broken glass needs drawing and quartering. Nor must stripping by means of

131. A chair which has been stripped in a caustic tank. This shows the damage which results from over-exposure to caustic solutions; the colour is completely removed and the wood is split and woolly.

a concentrated caustic solution (caustic soda, lye, potash) be even considered for antique furniture. Not only do these change the colour of the wood, but the hot and wet method of their application can cause an extraordinary amount of damage to the wood, lift veneer and inlay, and open up joints (Fig. 131). Be equally wary of the 'paste it on, peel it off' concoctions, which can cause severe and irreversible damage to many woods.

Often the removal of an old varnish finish may be accomplished by washing it with a meths-soaked rag, assisted if necessary by 4/0 steel wool (used very gently). Finishes which don't respond to this treatment will need the application of a paint-stripping solution. Use a thin, non-caustic stripper which is washable with solvent rather than water, but not one of the viscid ones, which are too thick to work the way which is best suited to the method described here. Prepare yourself well, for this is one of those procedures where you must have everything ready to hand (Fig. 132). Make sure that the piece to be stripped is standing on and surrounded by plenty of sheets of newspaper. Vertical surfaces which are not being stripped must be covered with a couple of layers of newspaper well secured with masking tape, and horizontal ones which are to be preserved covered with newspaper with a sheet of heavy plastic on top for good measure (you cannot rely on this for long-term protection though, as stripper goes through plastics as well as finishes). Keyholes, screw holes for fittings, etc., should be bunged up with paper. Plan the order in which you are going to tackle the surfaces. Do large surfaces one at a time and don't try to work on too many small ones all at

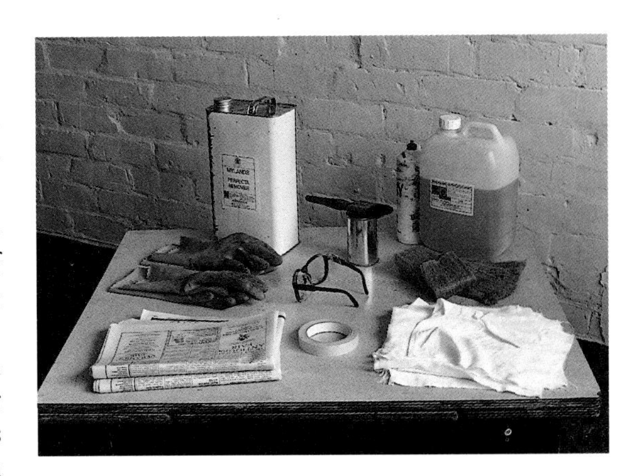

132. Make sure that you have everything to hand before you start stripping an old finish.

a

b

133. Stripping the top of a mahogany card table.
a. This stained top has already lost much of its finish.
b. With all but the top masked off, stripper is poured on and spread evenly over the surface.
c. The stripper is kept moving to make sure that no part of the surface is allowed to dry.
d. If the mixture of stripper and old finish gets too thick it is brushed off onto the surrounding newspaper.

c

d

When all the finish is softened, the stripper is wiped off with a rag . . .
. . . followed by 2/0 wire wool rubbing gently in the direction of the
ain.
The final stage is a wash with a meths-soaked rag followed by a dry
g, with the grain.
The stripped top, still showing many stains.

e

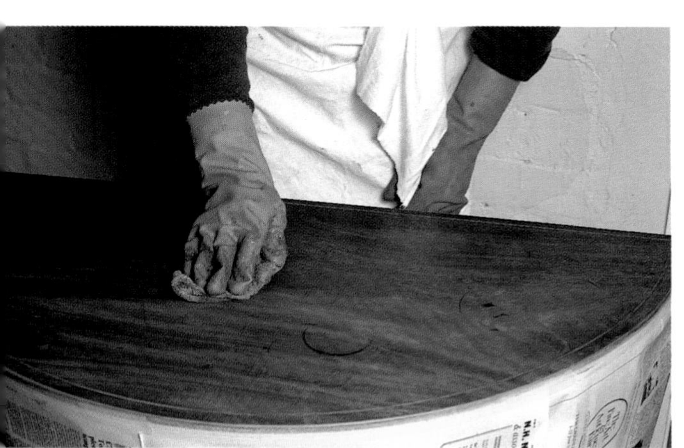

g

once, particularly when carving and turning is being stripped. Have ready plenty of good-sized pieces of rag and 2/0 steel wool, and make sure you have a 2- or 3-inch paint brush which is in good condition. If you are working indoors, make sure that the area is very well ventilated.

When you are ready to start, put on rubber gloves and a pair of safety goggles, preferably the type with side panels. Have a spare pair of gloves to hand, as there's always the risk of a glove splitting in the middle of the operation, which is exasperating if not dangerous. The stripper should not be poured onto the job straight from the container but decanted into a small can for ease of handling. Take care when removing the top from the stripper container, as temperature changes since the time when the top was last off may have caused a large difference in pressure between the gases in the container and the air outside, so cover the top with a rag while you unscrew it. If stripper does get on your skin, wipe it off with a meths-soaked rag fairly promptly.

The instructions on the container may tell you to leave the stripper on the offending surface for a few minutes and then remove it with a paint scraper. Don't do this unless you are dealing with multiple layers of paint on an absolutely flat surface. If you are taking off thin layers of finish, there is a danger of the scraper blade digging in and causing considerable damage to the wood. The most controllable and effective means of removing the majority of old varnish and shellac finishes is as follows (Fig. 133).

Put plenty on. On large, flat, horizontal surfaces (turn things on their sides or backs to present a horizontal surface whenever possible), pour the stripper on from the small can. Don't let it stand but spread it evenly over the whole surface with the paint brush and *keep it moving*. It must not dry out, so put on more stripper if it starts to. If the stripper and softened finish combine to form a mixture which is too thick to move about easily, it should be brushed off onto the surrounding wads of newspaper to make way for fresh stripper. Crevices in carving and mouldings should have the finish teased out with the bristles of the brush.

When this action has softened and lifted all the old finish, wipe off the stripper with rag and then immediately follow this with 2/0 steel wool, rubbing gently with the grain to ensure that no trace of the old finish remains. Wash the surface with a rag well soaked with meths, and finish with a clean, dry rag, again working with the grain. Note the colour of the wood before the meths dries out and also weigh up the effect of any stains which have not been removed by the stripping process.

If the surface has been left with a good, mellow colour and the stains and other marks are not excessive, then you will probably decide to go on with the refinishing. Sometimes, though, stains are an eyesore and surfaces have not undergone uniform fading (as, for example, the spare leaves of dining tables). In such circumstances you may decide to bleach. Whatever condition the stripped surface is in, it bears repeating to say *never* sand, scrape or otherwise remove that thin outer layer. If it looks too bad, take advice from a professional restorer. It is unwise to try to treat stains individually, especially when the existing finish is intact and acceptable, for many of the treatments which are so often recommended seldom leave the finish unaffected and can lead to a great deal of corrective work themselves. Whether refinishing or bleaching first, leave the piece alone for twenty-four hours before proceeding.

Bleaching

This, of all the processes described in this book, is the one which requires the greatest consideration and preparation. Consider that when you bleach to remove unwanted stains you will also be removing natural colour from the wood (although chemical treatments can restore it, as described later). When the decision is finally made to bleach, double check that you have everything ready, as follows.

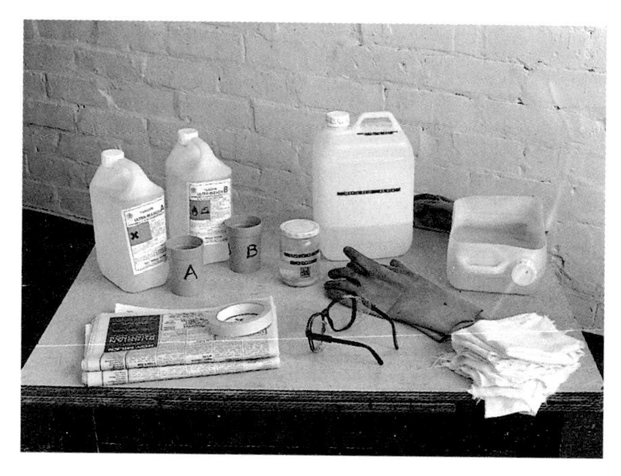

134. Bleaching materials ready for use.

a A two-part bleach pack. This will consist of two containers, one usually marked 'A' or '1', the other 'B' or '2'. The first is a caustic solution, the second a concentrated solution of hydrogen peroxide – they are to be treated with the utmost respect. Rubber gloves and goggles must be worn whenever these chemicals are handled. If 'A' solution finds its way onto your skin, swab the area with acetic acid (as c. below) and then rinse with plenty of water; if 'B' solution, swab with oxalic acid (as b. below) followed by lots of water.

b A saturated solution of oxalic acid. This is prepared by adding oxalic acid crystals to half a jar of cold water, stirring well (with a piece of scrap wood) and adding the crystals until no more will dissolve, then making up the contents of the jar with crystals to about $\frac{1}{3}$ undissolved crystals to $\frac{2}{3}$ water. Keep the jar topped up with more water or crystals to this proportion: make it up at the end of each bleaching session ready for next time. Since this chemical is described as dangerous, rubber gloves should be worn when handling it, even when making up the solution.

c Acetic acid B.P. (33% – see Appendices, p. 150). A weaker solution may be used if the smell is offensive but you will have to leave it on longer (see vii. below).

d Plenty of warm water. Make it a bit hotter than you need before you start – hotter than hand-hot but not boiling, and it should be about right when you need it.

e Plenty of colourfast rag. If you're not sure, use white to be on the safe side. Prepare at least ten pieces of handy size before you start.

f Two clean plastic (polypropylene) cups, clearly marked A (or 1) and B (or 2) respectively.

g Goggles and two pairs of rubber gloves – a split glove in this operation and you'll know all about it. Test the gloves before you start by blowing them up and listening for leaking air and have that spare pair ready in case of accident while you are working.

Having got everything prepared, and laid out to hand, you are ready to start. You are strongly recommended to read the following procedure a few times until you are sure that you can get through it without pausing. Then have a few practice goes on scrap wood before you set about the family heirlooms. The stages of colour changes you are likely to witness are illustrated in Fig. 135.

i Make sure that the area you are going to bleach has absolutely all traces of the old finish removed. Some finishes can be extremely stubborn and not respond to the first or even second application of stripper. Check by viewing the surface against the light, and if there are any patches which look a bit shinier than the rest give these a gentle rub with 2/0 steel wool dampened with a drop of meths, wipe the *whole* surface with a meths-dampened rag and allow it to dry completely. Make sure also that the grain of new wood has been raised and sanded.

a

b

c

d

135. Bleaching the top illustrated in Fig. 133. The colours shown are those which you might expect to see on completion of each of the stages:
a. 'A' solution.
b. 'B' solution.
c. Oxalic acid.
d. Acetic acid followed by warm water wash.

ii Cover all surfaces other than the one being treated with plastic sheeting, secured with masking tape.

iii Decant the 'A' and 'B' solutions into their cups (follow the manufacturer's instructions regarding the shaking of the containers). About half a cup (5 or 6 fluid ounces) of 'A' solution and a third of a cup of 'B' solution will usually be sufficient for an area of six square feet.

iv Pour on 'A' solution and immediately spread it over the whole surface with a piece of the rag. Keep that rag moving the whole time to ensure that no part of the wood dries out and put more 'A' solution on if necessary. The effect of the 'A' solution is usually immediate and quite dramatic. Most woods will darken straight away and the solution will take up the dark colour which appears on the surface. Depending on how quickly the wood gives up its colour and the amount of colour you want to remove, the 'A' solution will need to be left on for anything from a couple of minutes to quarter of an hour. Unfortunately, you will not be able to judge this timing accurately until you have had a considerable amount of experience. Unless you have an identical piece of wood spare on which to practise (and even then it might react differently), stop the application of the 'A' solution earlier rather than later, for you can always bleach again later. If you take too much colour out now you will have some complicated and not too predictable work ahead of you to restore it. When you have judged that the 'A' solution has done its work, mop off the excess with a clean piece of rag, finishing with strokes which follow the figure pattern, if any. Now put the cup of 'A' solution out of the way on a few sheets of newspaper, and the rags used with it (don't get them mixed up with rags used for following steps as you might want them again later).

v Before the surface starts to dry out, apply the 'B' solution, again spreading it quickly and evenly over the whole surface with a clean piece of rag. Now comes an important departure from the instructions on the manufacturer's label, which usually state that the 'B' solution should be left to dry. This will certainly bleach the wood but the result will not produce the mellow colour which is the basis of a good antique colour and patina (Fig. 136). The method described here requires that the 'B' solution be left on for a somewhat shorter time than the 'A' solution – somewhere between one third to half the time, but this is not critical – after which it is wiped off with clean rag, again working with figure patterns. Put the 'B' solution cup and rags out of the way when you have finished with them.

vi Don't allow the surface to dry out. As soon as the 'B' solution has been wiped off, pour on oxalic acid solution and spread it quickly over the whole surface with clean rag. This is another stage which shows immediate and spectacular results, for the colour changes as soon as the oxalic acid touches the wood, so move quickly, working with the figure and grain.

vii As soon as the oxalic acid has worked, wipe over the surface with a dry rag and then wash it with acetic acid. (Leave this on for five minutes or so if a weak solution is used.)

viii Wipe off the acetic acid and then wash the surface with a couple of changes of warm water, dry it thoroughly with lots of clean rag and leave it to dry for twenty-four hours (at least) in a warm, well-ventilated place.

ix When you have finished with the rags used in this process, wash them thoroughly in a few changes of water before disposing of them.

136. A demonstration of the effects of bleaching by the method usually recommended on the bleach container (top) against that described in the text (bottom).

x The colour which you see while the wood is still wet at the end of the bleaching process is not usually the final result. Only when the wood is completely dry will you be able to assess the true effect of your efforts. Do this by wetting the surface with a rag soaked with meths, wiping over the whole surface, in the direction of figure and grain.

If you have managed to produce a nice mellow colour, you will now be ready to make a start at re-creating the finish. If not, then you'll just have to bleach again, but if you do, remember to leave the 'A' solution on for only a couple of minutes at the most or you may take too much colour out.

Stopping and grain filling

Before any finish is applied, inspect all surfaces, repaired or unrepaired, to see if there is any open grain, or blemishes which require filling. Small holes and cracks which don't warrant having patches cut for them may be filled with hard (shellac) stopping or soft (beeswax) stopping, depending on their size and position on the piece of furniture – even minute blemishes in surfaces which are subject to considerable handling are likely to require a hard stopping. Open grain of small repair patches may be filled with the beeswax stopping, but large areas which need filling prior to polishing with shellac will require different treatment.

Shellac stopping

Shellac stopping can be obtained from the cabinet-makers' suppliers but the range of their colours won't be anything like that which you can easily make up for yourself. You will need shellac flakes, beeswax, various dry pigments (the umbers, ochres and siennas listed on page 150 will be the ones you use most frequently but make up a good range whilst you're about it) and some four-inch lengths of wood about $\frac{3}{16}''$ square. Melt together a little shellac flake and a sliver of beeswax in a shallow tin on the hotplate, keeping the heat low enough to melt them without bubbling. Take a small heap of pigment (the tip of a knife blade will hold sufficient to produce quite a

137. Some home-made shellac stopping sticks.

strong colour; if you use too much pigment the stopping will be too hard to use) and stir it into the melted shellac with one of the sticks. You will have to stir the mixture longer with some pigments than others to make sure that the colour is evenly dispersed. When it looks right, take the edge of the tin with pliers, tip it up and scrape the mixture together, then dip in the stick and twist it round to take up a ball of stopping. If the mixture is too runny, take it away from the heat while you do this. As the ball of stopping cools on its stick, roll it on a clean, flat surface to draw it out into a cylindrical shape, dipping it back into the melted mixture to collect more and rolling that out, until the stopping stick is the required size, then lay it aside to harden completely. Put more shellac and a little beeswax in the tin and start another stick, changing the colour of pigment as necessary.

To apply shellac stopping, you will need an electric soldering iron and, preferably, a current regulating plug to reduce the heat of the iron. Choose a stopping which is closest to the colour around the hole you are filling, and if in doubt use one which is a bit lighter to start with. Melt the shellac into the hole with the tip of the iron. If the shellac bubbles as you touch it with the iron, it is too hot and you will have to reduce the heat setting (or switch off, if you are not using a regulating plug) and let the iron cool before going on. Build the stopping up in the hole until it is just proud of the surface, let it cool, then pare off the excess with a sharp chisel. Finish off with a gentle rub over with 320 grit silicon carbide paper, apply a coat of shellac polish and, if your eye for colour is good, the blemish will have all but disappeared. Any further blending in of the repair can be done with pigments in shellac polish, as described on p. 115.

Beeswax stopping

This is prepared in much the same way as shellac stopping, except that only beeswax and dry pigments are used (but use separate tins for the two sorts). When the melted wax and pigment have been thoroughly mixed, pour the mixture into shallow moulds made from tinfoil, which are easily formed over the end of a chisel handle. Allow the stopping to cool completely before using it.

Beeswax stopping is particularly useful for tiny cracks and grain filling of small repair patches. First, give the area to be filled a couple of coats of shellac polish, allow it to dry completely and rub firmly with a lump of matching wax stopping (shellac polish and beeswax, properly used, are entirely compatible). The colour you will need to match will vary according to circumstances – either the colour of the filling in surrounding grain will

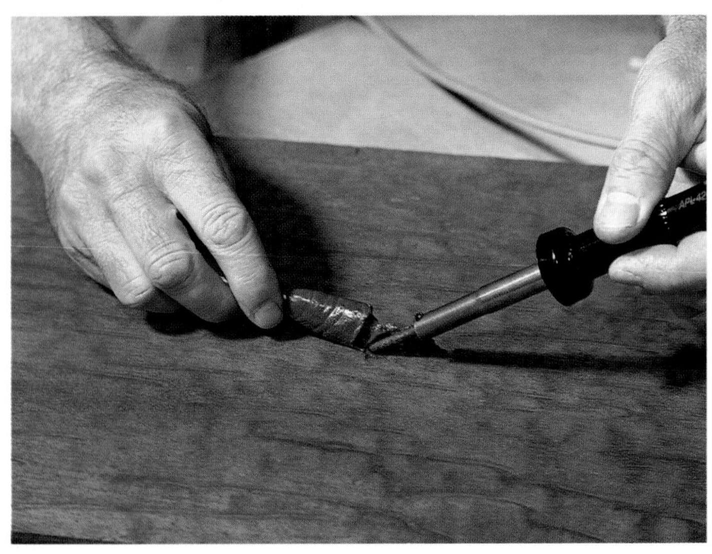

a

b

be most important or the colour of the wood itself if there is no distinct grain colour. Remove excess wax from the surface with a hardwood scraper (see p. 48), without using so much pressure that the wood is bruised. Rub the area firmly with the *back* of a piece of abrasive paper to distribute the wax and key it into the grain completely, follow this with another go with the scraper if there is any trace of wax on the surface, then go over *very* lightly with well-used 320 grit silicon carbide paper to remove invisible traces of wax – on a nicely faded surface there must be no risk of cutting through to unfaded wood. Finally, a coat of shellac will seal in the stopping and let you see the true result.

138. Beeswax stopping with tinfoil moulds.

Grain filling

Unfortunately, there is no known method of grain filling for large areas of wood which is not extremely laborious. Perhaps the simplest, and certainly one which produces a first-class result, involves the use of shellac sanding sealer. A full-bodied sealer of this sort will fill the grain of many woods with a couple of coats. Brush it on liberally with a 2″ paint brush, without working it more than is necessary to ensure that there are no great pools or streaks, leaving at least half an hour between coats, particularly in cool weather. Leave it until next day before going on to the next stage, which is to test a small area to see if the grain has been filled sufficiently. Choose an area which has got the most open grain and rub this gently with a pad of 320 grit silicon carbide paper (Fig. 139) using a circular motion. Rub until *either* there is no trace of open grain visible *or* the surface takes on an appearance which is a shade cloudier than the effect produced on the sealer, indicating that you have gone through the coats of sealer. And if any trace of colour appears on the silicon carbide paper in place of the white powder of the sealer, *stop immediately*, because you're abrading the wood. If there is still open grain in spite of cutting the sealer back to the wood, then you will obviously have to apply more sealer. If the open grain of the test area has been eliminated, you can start work in earnest. Be warned that you will get through a considerable quantity of silicon carbide paper, for the sealer is tough stuff. Get plenty made up into pads, don a dust mask and set to working over the whole surface methodically, wiping off the dust with a wad of soft cloth from time to time so that you can see where you're going. The result of lots of careful and patient work will be a surface perfectly prepared for the application of shellac polish. However, if you feel that there is the slightest chance of damaging the surface of the wood by this method, you will have to rely solely on the shellac polishing procedures to fill the grain.

139. Cutting back grain filler. The spread fingers will follow the slight undulations of an antique surface as no sanding block can.

140. Filling a hole with shellac stopping.
a. Melting stopping into a small hole with a warm soldering iron.
b. Smoothing the stopping.
c. Levelling the surface with a sharp chisel.

CHAPTER 9

Rebuilding a finish

Much plain wooden antique furniture – 'brown' furniture to the trade – which is described as having its original finish will, in fact, by now have some, if not most, of the original varnish finish rubbed away and replaced with wax polish. The basis of most finishes used on furniture made since the sixteenth century is known to be varnish in some form or other. Varnishes of linseed and other types of oil, in which a resin such as copal or lac was dissolved, were the first to be used, but these were largely superseded for the finishing of furniture by the spirit-based varnishes of the eighteenth century. The 'shell-lac' varnishes of those days are the forerunners of today's shellac polishes. These are often sold as 'French polish', which is not strictly correct – french polish*ing* is the technique of imparting a very high gloss using shellac polish. This became popular in the first quarter of the nineteenth century and is still frequently requested of the professional restorer, who has to spend much time, and patience, explaining why it is an inappropriate finish for English antique furniture: it may be fine for a piece of ormolu-mounted French furniture, but somewhat out of place on an oak bureau, for example.

Occasionally, pieces turn up which were originally finished with oil, but these are often so well polished that it is difficult to distinguish them from those with a varnish/wax combination. A burnished beeswax finish is most appropriate when repairing such pieces, as described at the end of this chapter. The majority of pieces you will come across will, however, be best dealt with by finishing with shellac followed by wax polishing.

Shellac polishing

For this process you are recommended to use a hard, dewaxed, clear shellac polish with little colour to it, so that the colour of the wood shows through unchanged. The suppliers shown in the Appendices, p. 152, sell a Special Pale Button Polish which is suitable for most work, but if you have a particular requirement they will be glad to advise. Whatever sort of shellac polish you use, its method of application will not need to differ from the procedure described below.

Making a polishing rubber

Shellac polish is most often applied with a rubber which is similar, in principle, to those you may have seen described for use in french polishing. You will, however, only need the one type of rubber, consisting of a square of fine wadding, which is folded, then wrapped in a square of lint-free white cloth such as sheeting or handkerchief linen.

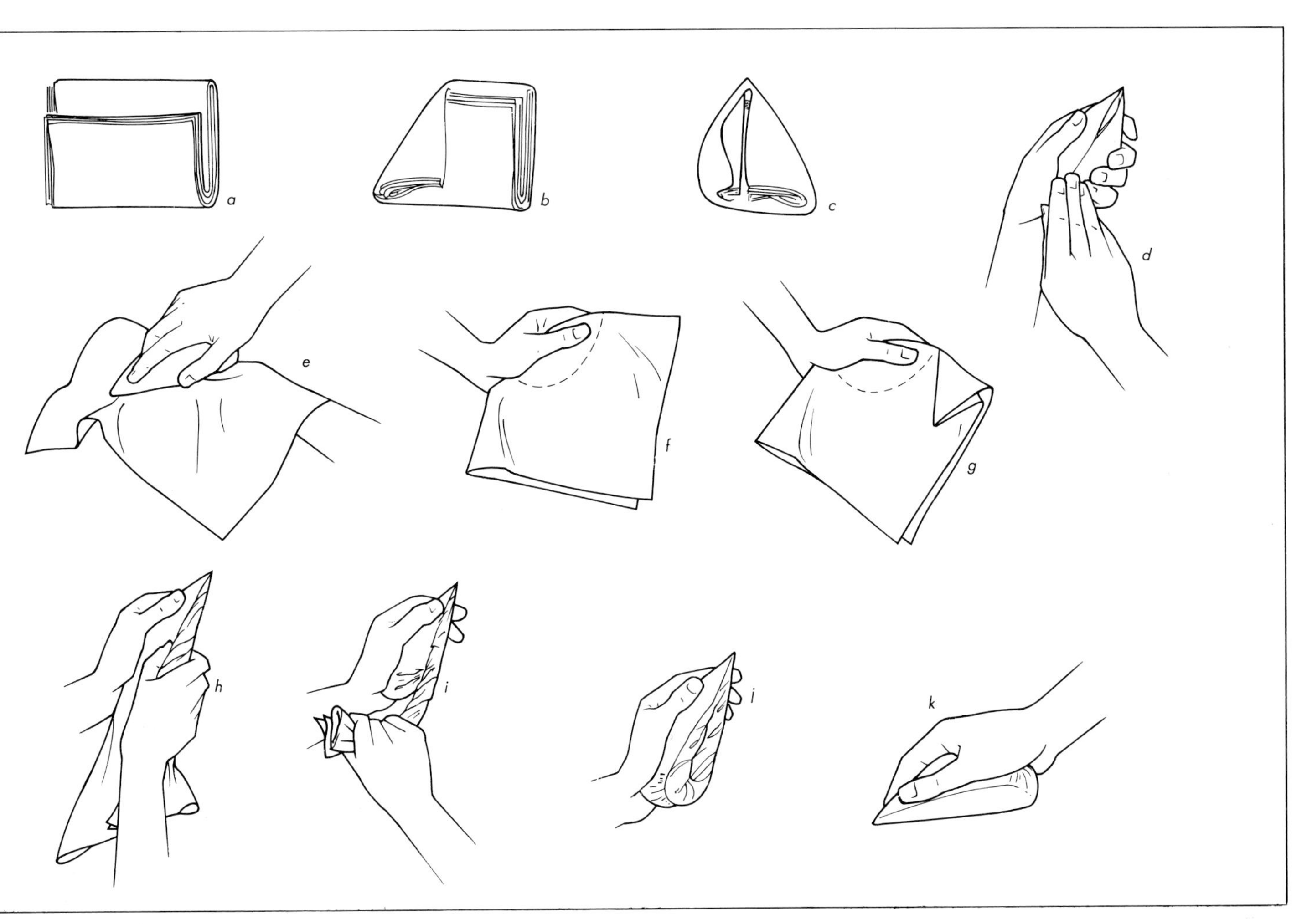

141. Making a polishing rubber. Cut a piece of wadding 10–12″ square (depending on the size of rubber which best suits your hand) and a square of linen the same size. Then:
a. Fold the wadding so that the covered edge protrudes $\frac{1}{2}$–$\frac{3}{4}$″ beyond and below the cut edge.
b. Fold the top corners inwards and back to form a point at the centre of the covered edge of the wadding.
c. Fold the bottom corners inwards.
d. Knead the wadding into a pear shape in the cup of your hand, retaining the point at the tip.
e. Put the square of linen onto the palm of one hand and place the shaped wadding on it (without letting go of the wadding), the point towards a corner and 3–4″ away from it, with the open part of the wadding uppermost.
f. Holding the wadding firmly through the linen, with the point between forefinger and thumb, turn your hand over to allow the linen to hang down around the wadding.
g. Fold the linen back to form a triangle, the apex of which is exactly at the point of the wadding inside.
h. Working from the very point, twist the linen to form a rope along the back of the rubber, taking up all the slack material round the wadding.
i. Double the rope of linen back on itself . . .
j. . . . and tuck the end into the back of the rubber.
k. The rubber is now perfectly formed, with a point to get polish into those awkward corners. Soak the completed rubber in meths and allow it to dry out. This will prevent the wadding unravelling when the rubber is opened to charge it.

Charging the rubber

To charge the rubber with shellac, rest it in the cupped hand, undo the linen and open up the wadding slightly. Pour in the polish a little at a time and squeeze it in with your thumb, until the wadding is well wetted with polish but not so wet that it drips out again. Remake the rubber and test it by pressing its working face firmly with your thumb. If polish just oozes through the linen round your thumb tip then the rubber is ready for use. Usually, though, there will be too much polish in the rubber for proper use: remove the surplus and complete the distribution of the polish by patting the rubber firmly on a clean, flat surface. It is only possible to judge with experience the amount of polish needed in the rubber for optimum working efficiency. Too much, and runs will be left on the surface; too little, and the rubber will drag and damage polish already applied. A few practice sessions on a prepared panel will be advisable before you set about your treasured furniture.

Storing the rubber and polishing materials

Before describing the polishing procedure, a word about storage of rubber, shellac and meths. Keep your rubber in an airtight plastic box when it is not in use, and it will remain in good condition for many months. Get into the routine of putting it into its box the second you stop actually polishing with it. The only time you will then need to make a new rubber is when the wadding has become so compacted that the polish will not flow properly – when the linen cover gets dirty or torn, just fit a new piece. If the rubber is not used very often, check it from time to time and sprinkle it with a few drops of meths if it is too dry, and if necessary seal its box with masking tape between polishing sessions. Store meths and shellac polish in plastic containers. The small quantities of each which you need for day-to-day use are best kept in one pint size squeezy bottles. Not only do these make for easier handling and more controllable pouring, but when the inevitable happens and one falls off your bench, little damage is done.

Ideal polishing conditions

The conditions in which shellac polish is applied are not too critical, but a successful job will be done, and done more quickly, if the optimum conditions prevail. Firstly, polishing should be done in good natural light, preferably northerly light; working in artificial light is not too bad providing it is well diffused, but bright overhead light tends to create shadows so that you cannot be sure how the work is going. The speed with which you can get the required amount of polish on depends on the time it takes each coat to dry. This, in turn, depends on a number of factors.

Ideal conditions for the polisher are a temperature of 60–70°F, with relative humidity in the region of 50% (see p. 67 for an explanation of 'relative' humidity). Cold and/or damp conditions will not hinder the application of shellac, but there may be a tendency for streaks of opaque 'bloom' to appear in the polish. If this does occur, stop polishing until the entire surface is clear again. Pass the back of your fingers lightly across the surface to make sure that it is dry enough to continue. If the polish feels cool and resists your fingers a bit, the solvents have not completely evaporated and further polishing will be prone to blooming. Wait until the surface feels smooth and warmer before you go on.

When you have a large area to polish, there will usually be no reason for you not to apply several coats of shellac one after the other, in one continuous operation, with a well-filled rubber. By the time you have worked your way across from one side to the other the surface should be dry enough to start again. If the rubber is felt to drag in spite of being properly charged, stop until the surface feels right, as described above. And never use linseed oil, or any other oil recommended for use in french polishing, in this process. There is no need for oil to lubricate a polishing rubber if it is kept moist with shellac and meths, as described in the following paragraphs, and its use can cause problems long after the polishing process has been completed.

Topping up the rubber may be accomplished in one of two ways, depending on what you are polishing: if you need a well-filled rubber for large areas, the quickest way is to open the rubber and pour shellac into the wadding, as described above. If you do it this way, take care that no strands of wadding get stuck to your fingers, as they are easily transferred onto the face of the rubber and from there to the work. This problem is avoided if you use the second method of recharging the rubber, which is to drip polish onto the face of the rubber without undoing it. As well as keeping the wadding in shape and intact, this is the best way when you only have a small area to polish, as just a little shellac in the rubber will reduce drying time between coats.

Other operations

If other operations are involved in the finishing of a surface, such as adding stains or pigments to blend in repairs (as described in the next Chapter), the shellac must be absolutely dry before you can proceed. Apart from sealing and fixing coats required in these other operations, it is not possible to predict how many coats of shellac a particular surface is going to need to produce a satisfactory result. Bear in mind that you are really only using shellac to seal in any stain and pigment, and to provide a base on which to build up a patina with wax polish, so use as few coats as you can – just enough to make sure that the dulling operation which concludes the shellac polishing process does not cut through and destroy all the hard work you have put in to match the repairs.

Bodying up

On absolutely bare wood (if grain filling is not required or you decide to fill open grain by the shellac polishing method), the initial coat should be applied with a well-filled rubber employing a firm, circular motion to seal the grain. The bodying up process then begins, building up the shellac until an even shine appears – not glossy, but with no dull streaks. This is accomplished by applying the rubber with firm but gentle strokes, working from the far side of a surface towards you, with the grain, in unbroken sweeps.

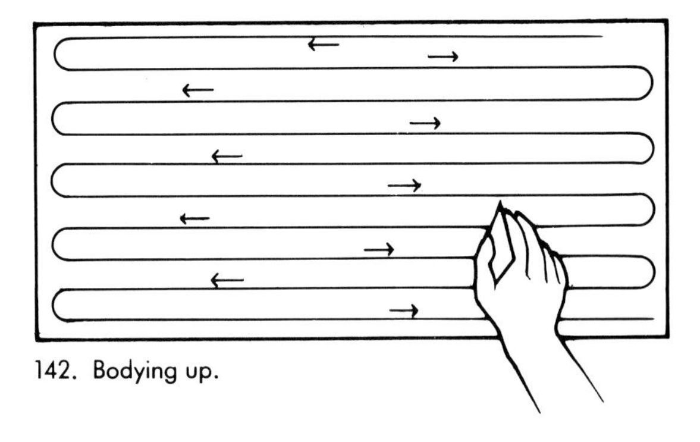
142. Bodying up.

The bodying up can continue without pause, other than to recharge the rubber, so long as there is no dragging or development of bloom, but do remember that staining and blending in of repair patches must be done at a reasonably early stage so that they are adequately protected by subsequent coats of shellac. If, during this operation or any other involving the use of shellac polish, something does go wrong – an unnoticed streak of polish, a bit of dust or wadding embedded in the surface – don't try to rectify it while the polish is soft. Wait a few hours until the polish is absolutely dry and reasonably hard (it will be several days before it is completely hard), then rub the offending part down very gently with 320 grit silicon carbide paper, before continuing with shellac.

When a satisfactory surface appears to have been built up, set the piece aside in a warm place and leave it overnight. Don't cover it with a dust sheet – the risk of someone then leaning on it is greater than that of dust affecting the new surface. The next day you will be able to determine what comes next. If the polish has not settled to reveal open grain or traces of pigment, and if there is absolutely no dust or streaks in the surface of the polish, then you could go on to dull and wax. If there are such problems, you'll have to level the surface gently with worn silicon carbide paper, then body up some more or, if the polish is free from blemishes other than showing the 'grain' of the rubber, pulling over will do the trick.

Pulling over

This operation is best done the same day as bodying up, but only experience will tell you that a surface is likely to need it by the time it has settled down. If you can do it the same day wait for half an hour or so after the last coat of shellac went on. If you do it the next day, prime the surface with two or three more coats of shellac, then wait a few minutes. Before you start, make sure that the rubber is in a fit state and not wet with polish. Squeeze out as much polish as you can by pressing the face of the rubber hard against your palm, wet it thoroughly with meths and squeeze it out again, so that when you pat the rubber it feels almost dry. When you are ready to start the pulling over, sprinkle a few drops of meths on the face of the rubber and pat it to make sure that the face is evenly dampened (Fig. 143).

Start with small circular movements and go over the whole surface, working from the edges towards the middle. Press just hard enough for a little spirit to pick up and spread a thin film of shellac, without leaving wet streaks or the rubber dragging. As the rubber dries out the pressure must be increased, but not to the point where resistance is felt. If there is any indication that the rubber is not running smoothly relieving the pressure will not help – only a few more drops of meths. Start and finish the series of strokes smoothly, approaching and leaving the surface at a shallow angle. Work quickly with a nice steady rhythm. Go over with the small circles twice then change the movement to figures of eight, the length of the eight in the direction of the grain, working towards you from the far side of the surface. The area covered by each band of figures of eight depends on the size of the surface. As a general rule, the first bands should cover a quarter of the surface, the second ones a third, the third ones half, the last the full length of it. When the series of figures of eight is complete, finish off immediately with one or two lots of straight strokes, working with the grain. There must be no pause during or between any stage of this process, except for the briefest moment to apply a few drops of meths to the face of the rubber when necessary.

It is unlikely that just one treatment will be sufficient to give you a completely smooth surface and another, and possibly a third, will be necessary, in quick succession. If, however, in spite of being properly lubri-

143. Pulling over.

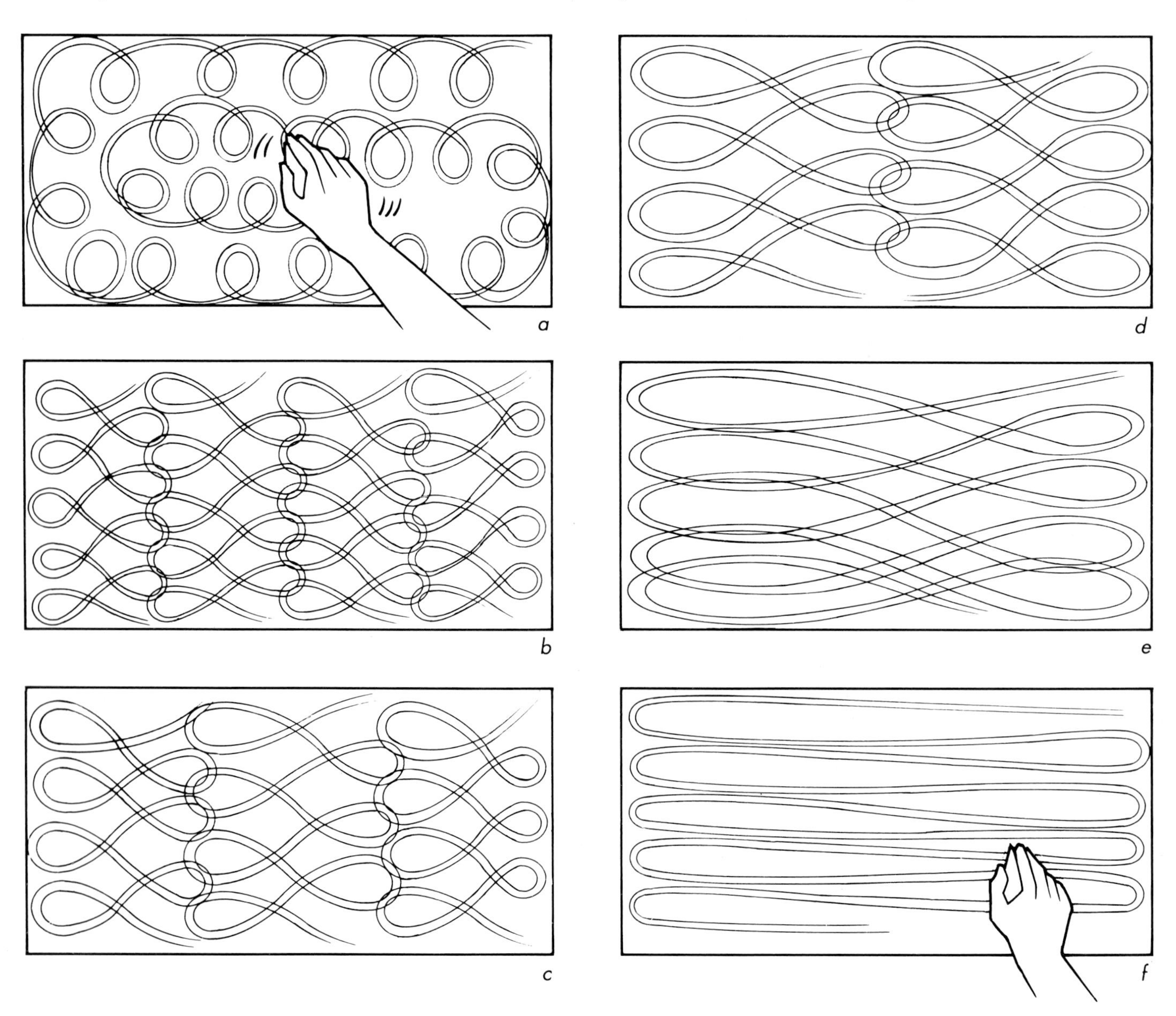

cated, the rubber should show any signs of dragging, stop immediately. If you are in the middle of a series of strokes just give the surface one rapid pass of straight strokes, then leave it to dry. You can always prime with another couple of coats later and continue with pulling over, but to go on when the rubber starts to drag will surely lead to disaster. The purpose of pulling over is to make sure that the shellac polish is spread evenly (and that any remaining open grain is filled), *not* to produce a high gloss. Surfaces of English antique furniture which have to be finished with shellac as part of the restoration process must have the hard shine which invariably results removed by dulling.

Polishing uneven surfaces

Carving, turning and other work which is too fine to be accessible to the point of your polishing rubber may have shellac polish applied to it with the aid of a polisher's mop (the type made from squirrel hair, for preference) or a sable brush. The polish should be diluted with about 25% meths and the mop or brush drained of any excess – several thin coats, each applied with just one pass over the surface, will avoid runs.

Dulling

Only when the shellac polish is absolutely dry, after a day or two, should the surface be dulled. If you are satisfied that the surface contains no particles of dust or other blemishes, the way to dull is by using pumice powder. It is worth buying a special dulling brush from the supplier of finishing materials, to ensure a perfect result. The procedure is simple: sprinkle fine pumice powder over the surface and brush lightly with the grain. You will find that the ends will need more attention than the rest, so start by treating these, then finish off with strokes the full length of the surface. If the surface does have embedded specks of dust, you will have to treat it with fine steel wool (4/0) grade. Cut about a foot of the stuff from the roll, fold it to make a four-inch pad, and rub the surface *very* gently. Start with a circular motion and go over the whole surface methodically. Don't press so hard that obvious scratches appear in the polish – the result should be smooth and evenly matt. To complete the job, go over the whole surface with light strokes along the grain. All being well, you are now ready to finish the job with a good waxing, as described in Chapter 7.

Burnished beeswax

This finish is particularly suited to large panels, table tops and other flat surfaces where the wood is in good condition but the original waxed (or oiled) finish is neglected. It may also be used on new wood provided that the grain is first sealed with one or two wipes of the shellac rubber. The process is very hard work but the deep patina which it is possible to produce is worth every bead of perspiration!

You will need to prepare the beeswax about a day before you need it. Shave fine flakes from a block of yellow beeswax, put them into a tin and just cover them with pure turpentine. Two ounces of beeswax will produce enough polish to do a large top, with some to spare. Leave the ingredients until they have completely blended together to the consistency of softened (not melted) butter. If after a day or so there are still bits of solid beeswax in the mixture, you will have to add a little more turpentine, stirring it in a few drops at a time or, if the mixture is thin and whitish, more shaved beeswax will have to be stirred in. In either case a further few hours will be needed for it to get to the proper consistency. While the polish is blending, prepare a rubber as for shellac polishing, except that the point is not so important.

The burnished beeswax process is as follows:

i Fold a piece of clean, coarse linen into a pad with no loose strands or frayed edges exposed, take up some of the beeswax polish and spread it with a circular motion. Apply plenty of pressure and work it until the cloth clings. Take up more polish and go over the next area, and so on, until all the surface has had an application of wax, all well rubbed until it's too difficult to work the cloth.

ii Take the new rubber, which should be absolutely dry before you start, and make sure that the wadding is well-compressed and its cover tight. Wet the face of the rubber with meths until it feels *just* damp when patted against the palm of your hand. Go over the beeswaxed surface with the damp rubber, again pressing firmly and working with a circular motion. This will level the wax and begin the burnishing process. If the cover gets clogged with wax, change the face to a clean part, put on a fresh cover when necessary, and sprinkle on a few drops of meths if it feels dry.

iii When you are satisfied that there is no excess wax on the surface, sprinkle on a little fine pumice powder from a shaker with fine wire-gauze cover, making sure that it is evenly distributed. Only the smallest amount of pumice needs to be applied, the object being to amalgamate it with the wax and fill any open grain. Continue with the burnishing process, keeping the face of the rubber covered with a clean part of the linen and just dampened with meths. If you have the amount of pumice on the surface judged correctly, the grain will start to fill up without a mass of abrasive collecting on the face of the rubber. If there *is* too much pumice on and in the wax it will build up on the rubber, doing the opposite of what is intended by dulling or removing the burnished wax. If the face of the rubber remains clean but the grain does not appear to be filling you probably haven't put on enough pumice, but do be careful to put on only the most minute amount more if you feel there is not enough already.

iv When an even lustre has been created it is time to assess progress. If there is still open grain about you will have to go through stages i. and ii. again, but you must leave it overnight for the new application of beeswax to harden a bit before going on the pumice stage (iii). In fact, you may have to put a further application of beeswax on after that and again wait until it has hardened before repeating the pumice stage.

v When you have eventually built up a satisfactory surface of wax, put a fresh cover on the rubber, dampen it with meths again and give the beeswax surface one final, light burnish, followed by a gentle buffing with clean mutton-cloth.

Leave the job alone now for a few days to give the wax a chance to harden properly. Thereafter, a monthly treatment with the polishing wax described on p 91 will build up the patina further.

CHAPTER 10
Matching colour and surface features

There are three principal ways of blending the colour and features of repaired areas into their surroundings:

Colouring: treating new wood chemically, altering the surface colour to imitate the natural processes which take place when wood mellows with age.

Pigmenting: disguising unsightly surface blemishes and minor damage which has been repaired with stopping, by the application of dry (earth) pigments in shellac polish.

Staining: adjusting the colour of already finished surfaces, or parts of them, by sealing in transparent stains.

A further process in the business of matching repairs involves the extension of acceptable marks, stains and minor blemishes from surrounding areas into and over the repaired parts. This is known as *distressing* and is an integral part of the staining operation, with which its description is included.

Colouring

Colouring by chemical means involves some smelly work (you certainly won't get away with doing it in the kitchen), but it does produce the most remarkable results. Combine the treatments described below with the bleaching process (see p. 99), and the range of colours and effects which can be produced will give you a perfect match to just about every old wooden surface you are likely to work on, finished or unfinished. The order in which you use these treatments depends on the effect you are trying to copy and the sort of wood you are working on. Even when you have become accustomed to the changes which are to be expected with different woods, developing exactly the right effect will still be largely a matter of trial and error. Practice, whenever possible, on a piece of planed and sanded wood taken from the same bit as you used for the repair and, when you think you have it right, leave it for at least a day to make sure that the result hasn't changed.

Most old surfaces are warm-coloured, with reds and browns predominant, although they also show cool green/grey tones in places, but it is the basic colour of the raw wood beneath that aged surface which will dictate the sort, number and order of the treatments. The darker woods will usually need to be bleached to get somewhere near the colour you are aiming for (it is the type and cut of wood you are principally concerned with when you select a piece from your stock and if the colour is right that's a bonus). If you are going to bleach, this should be done first, because the colouring treatments tend to darken the wood as well as change its colour. The four processes described below, used individually or in various combinations, are equally effective on surfaces which are to be finished with shellac polish or burnished beeswax, or left unfinished as, for example, the inside surfaces of new bracket feet and base or back boards of case furniture. On some pieces of furniture these have been protected by a matt, coloured size which is described on p. 123. Some of the effects it is possible to achieve by chemical colouring are illustrated in Fig. 145.

For all these processes wear old clothes which can take a burn and stain or two, and adequate protection for eyes and hands. Also, don't forget to raise and sand the grain very thoroughly before you start, as these hot and wet processes can play havoc with a less than perfect surface and lead to much unnecessary work.

Potassium bichromate

This is one of the simplest chemical treatments but its applications are somewhat limited when it is used on its own. Some woods darken quickly and others remain with an unnatural yellow tint; with some the colour change can be controlled by washing with water when the desired effect is achieved, but others won't co-operate.

Potassium bichromate solution (prepared as directed for oxalic acid solution on p. 99) may be applied to large areas with a rag and small areas with a fine, nylon brush. Put it on quickly and evenly, wipe off any surplus with a clean, dry rag, then set the piece in a sunny place for the quickest result. It should soon brown and darken, hopefully to the shade you require. When dry, wipe over with a rag dampened with warm water to remove any re-formed crystals, and allow the wood to dry naturally.

Nitric acid

For this process you will need:

- i Nitric acid (20–30%)
- ii Saturated salt solution (sodium chloride)
- iii Warm water
- iv A dozen 6″ × 6″ pieces of clean, colour fast rag
- v Heat gun (preheated to working temperature)

These items are for the treatment of large areas. For small areas, such as repair patches which are in, or close to finished or other heat-sensitive surfaces, replace the heat gun with the electric soldering iron (preheated) and add to the list a small, all-nylon brush.

144. The nitric acid colouring treatment demonstrated on a piece of beech. This colour is too bright to be the basis of an antique finish but is easily modified by the other processes described in the text, as illustrated in Fig. 145.

Apart from wearing rubber gloves and goggles (or other eye protection), you must work in a well-ventilated place, preferably with an extractor fan close to the work area. Protect all areas of the piece of furniture which don't require treatment with taped-on plastic sheeting.

For the treatment of large areas, apply nitric acid with a piece of rag, dampening one whole surface at a time thoroughly and evenly, without leaving it wet. Switch the heat gun on and hold the nozzle a couple of inches away from one end of the surface. Nothing will happen for a few seconds, then the transformation will be sudden and spectacular. As soon as the colour changes, move the nozzle along – you should be able to 'chase' the colour change across the surface in one unbroken sweep (Fig. 144). Heat-sensitive areas adjacent to the part being treated may be protected by holding a sheet of tinfoil over them while the heat gun does its job. Don't keep the nozzle at any one place so long that the wood scorches, and if you are working on veneer you'll have to make sure that there is no loosening or

145. Chemical colouring. The colours illustrated here were achieved by a combination of the processes described in the text, applied to a board of cherry wood. The right half of each has been sealed with shellac. The captions are coded to the key on the right.

A. Nitric acid – heated.
B. Acetic acid/iron solution – heated.
C. Potassium bichromate – air dried in sunlight.
D. Oxalic acid solution – air dried.
E. Sodium chloride wash plus warm water wash – air dried.

lifting (but have some of the pin blocks described on p. 77 to hand just in case). If the colour doesn't change fairly quickly you have probably missed it with the acid, so give the spot another wipe with the acid rag and heat it again. When you have changed the colour of the whole surface you can assess the results. If you are lucky you will have already come close to matching that mellow colour which shows through the finish on the rest of the piece – 'close to', because if the colour is a shade brighter than the surroundings it is ideal, for the next stage will correct the difference. This is a thorough wash with saturated salt solution, applied with a clean piece of the rag, followed immediately by a wash with warm water and drying with plenty of dry rag. Then leave things alone for twenty-four hours to dry.

In some cases, however, it will be apparent as soon as you have heated the nitric acid that the colour is going to be too bright, with an orange cast to it. An application of potassium bichromate after the completed nitric acid process, or of oxalic acid between the nitric acid and salt solution stages, might effect the desired change. Or, if a cooler look is required, follow the nitric acid heating with the acetic acid/iron solution treatment described below, leaving the salt solution and warm water washes until the end of the process.

For small areas, apply the nitric acid with the fine nylon brush and change the colour with the heated soldering iron, lightly brushing the bevel of the iron's bit across the surface, slowly enough to change the colour but not so slowly that the wood scorches. Needless to say, this calls for a steady hand, and practice.

Acetic acid/iron solution

The requirements list for this process is as for the nitric acid process, substituting acetic acid/iron solution for nitric acid. You will need to prepare this solution well in advance, as it takes a few days for it to reach a usable state.

Shred a handful of clean steel wool into a quart or litre bottle (you may as well make a decent quantity whilst you're about it) and cover it with acetic acid (about 30% – see Appendices, p. 150) until the bottle is nearly full. Secure the top and leave it to work. Check the bottle daily to see how things are going, giving it a shake for good measure. When the steel wool has dissolved, you will be left with a clear, dark red/brown solution. If there is any sediment, pour off the solution into a clean bottle and it's ready for use.

Apply the solution with a piece of clean rag (or nylon brush), again dampening the surface thoroughly, following immediately with the heat gun (or soldering iron) in the same way as for the nitric acid treatment. If the cooling/darkening effect is not pronounced enough, dampen again while the surface is still warm, and heat it again. The more applications you do in quick succession, the quicker and greater the effect. When the desired colour is achieved, wash the surface thoroughly with salt solution, followed by warm water, dry with plenty of rag and leave it to air dry completely.

Oxalic acid

The application of oxalic acid (made up as a saturated solution – see p. 99) can have a bleaching effect which is particularly useful for reversing the darkening effect of acetic acid/iron solution, if this has gone too far, and of other unexpected and undesirable results. The results of the nitric acid treatment are usually not affected. Wet the surface with the oxalic acid, leave it for a few minutes until the reaction is seen to be effective, then wash with salt solution, followed by warm water, wipe with dry rag and allow to dry.

Pigmenting

This process is, in essence, painting. The mixing of the dry pigments with shellac polish produces an opaque colouring medium which can be used to disguise unwanted details on the surface of wood that is finished with shellac or a compatible varnish. The decision as to when you use pigments to disguise blemishes, rather than replace these with matching wood, cannot be governed by any rules other than the basic one – preserve as much of the original wood and finish as you can, consistent with maintaining its attractive appearance (the ethical arguments having been exhausted – see p. 22).

The decision to use pigments must obviously be made at an early stage of restoration. The actual application should be done as soon as possible after making sure that grain is filled and the surface of the wood sealed, and before any overall staining is done, for the staining techniques are a further contribution to the business of blending in the repairs.

146. A guide to the choice of pigments for use on some common furniture woods.

Examples	BASIC COLOURS			TONING COLOURS			FIGURE PATTERNS
	Primary	Secondary	Trace	Primary	Secondary	Trace	
Pale oak, ash, beech, elm	YO	RU, FW	–	RS	–	FW	–
Warm oak, ash, beech, elm, fruitwood	RS	–	YO, RU	RS	BS, BU	OC	RS, BU
Faded walnut	YO	RU, FW	YC	RS	RU, FW	YC	BT, VB
Warm walnut	RS	YO	OC, YC	RS	BS	OC	BU, VB
Faded mahogany	RU	YO, RS	FW	RS	–	FW	–
Warm mahogany	RS	–	YO	RS	BS, BU	OC	BS, BU
Faded rosewood	YO	–	FW, BS	BU	VB	–	VB, BU
Warm rosewood	RS, BS	OC	–	BU	VB	–	VB, BU

KEY

BT:	Burnt Turkey Umber	BS:	Burnt Sienna
RU:	Raw Umber	OC:	Orange Chrome
YO:	Yellow Ochre	YC:	Yellow Chrome
RS:	Raw Sienna	FW:	Flake White
BU:	Brown Umber	VB:	Vegetable Black

Notes

Primary: The first pigment used, forming the basis for the colour build up.
Secondary: Subsequent additions of pigment to match the variations in primary colours.
Trace: Generally just the tip of the brush will pick up sufficient to influence the colour.

Where more than one pigment appears in a column the first one will usually be needed in greater quantity.

The range of pigments available from cabinet-makers' suppliers is vast but the number which you will actually need for regular use may be limited to the ten listed in Fig. 146. These will cope with all the effects you are likely to meet when finishing 'brown' furniture. Good-quality brushes are essential for this fine work. A set of sable brushes (0, 2, 6 and 8) and a rack to stand them in when not in use are the basic tools, plus a few odd pots.

The fundamental first step in the process is to identify the pigments you will need for the job. Close inspection (literally – a magnifying glass might well be necessary) will reveal the many flecks of colour that go to make up the overall effect of wood which, from a couple of feet away, appears to be warm brown with the odd cool greenish grey area. If at first you have difficulty in relating the colours in the wood to the pigments, the chart may help (and keep your pigments in clear jars so that you can compare colours without having to read labels or unscrew caps). Before you start selecting pigments, check that the light is right. This work *must* be carried out in good, natural light: not bright sunlight, but diffused daylight free from reflections. If you attempt to use any pigments or stains in ordinary artificial light, the odds are that the result will look completely different when viewed in daylight, and even lights which are supposed to give the effect of daylight are not likely to allow you to produce a perfect colour match.

To make up the mixture, you will only need the smallest amounts of the materials, so you don't need a jar to mix them in. Your used abrasive paper, so long as it is clean and uncrumpled, comes in handy here. The pads described on p. 47 will provide you with small containers which are perfect for the job. Tear off a square of the paper and fold it as shown in Fig. 148, get out your brushes, shellac polish, meths, polishing rubber and a small pot in which to put meths for washing the brushes. An eggcup, or something similar, is useful to stand the pigment cornet in when you're not using it.

To begin the pigmenting of a blemish, or whatever, put no more than half an inch of shellac polish into the cornet and add 20–30% meths. Identify the palest and coolest colour in the surface in the immediate area of the part you are working on. Dampen a brush (size 2 for average jobs) with the polish mixture, remove excess on the edge of the cornet (note the captions of Figs. 148f and g) and dip the brush into the pigment which is nearest to the colour you have identified. Mix the shellac and pigment together on a dry side of the cornet and check the colour against the wood. If it is too pale or too dark, adjust the colour with more of the same pigment – or with a different one? Again, you can use the chart as a guide but really it's your eye which must be the judge. When it looks right, test it on the surface, but not necessarily on the blemish itself, and adjust it until it blends in perfectly with the basic colour you are aiming for. When you are satisfied that you have got it right, test the thickness of the mixture. The addition of too much pigment can easily make the mixture too thick for proper application. It is most important to work with the thinnest possible mixture because, although a thick one will cover quickly, subsequent additions which are required to give the work variations will pile the layers up to form a lump which will show no matter how many coats of polish are put over it with the rubber. If you consider the mixture too thick, add more shellac and meths, and if this fills the cornet too much, give the mixture a stir and pour some out.

Apply the mixture with the smallest possible strokes, the size of the flecks of colour in the wood if you can, working from the centre of the blemish outwards along the direction of grain and figure markings, so that the thickness of the strokes tapers off to blend into the pale flecks of the wood. As the

147. The hub of the finishing shop.

148. Making a pigment cornet.
a. Tear off a third of a pad of used but clean abrasive paper.
b. Fold it in half with the abrasive on the outside.
c. Fold again.
d. Turn down the corners, . . .
e. . . . three on one side and two on the other, . . .
f. . . . to form the cornet. Make sure that there is an untorn edge . . .
g. . . . on which to drain excess mixture from your brush, or loose fibres may be transferred to the work.

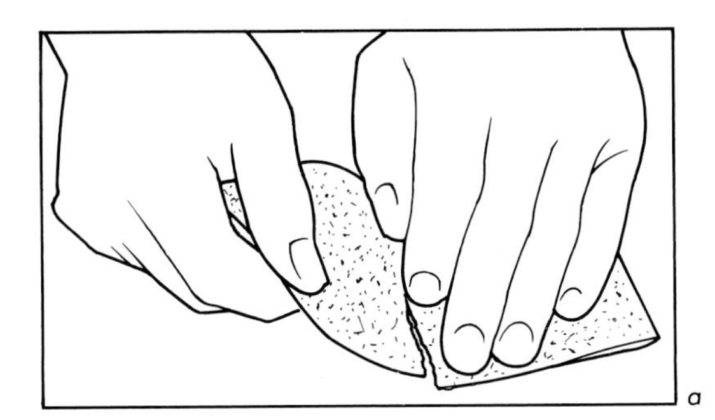

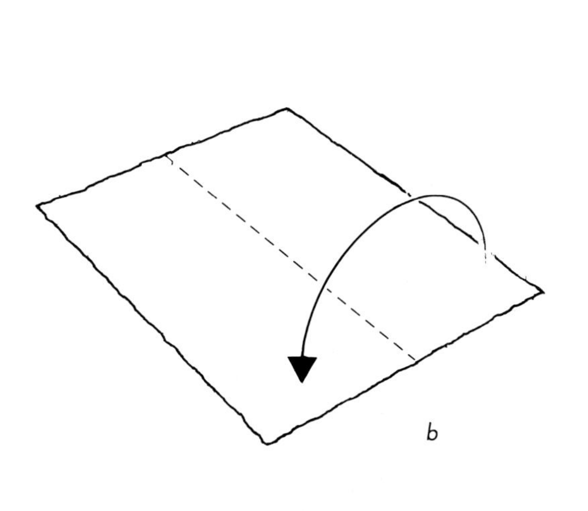

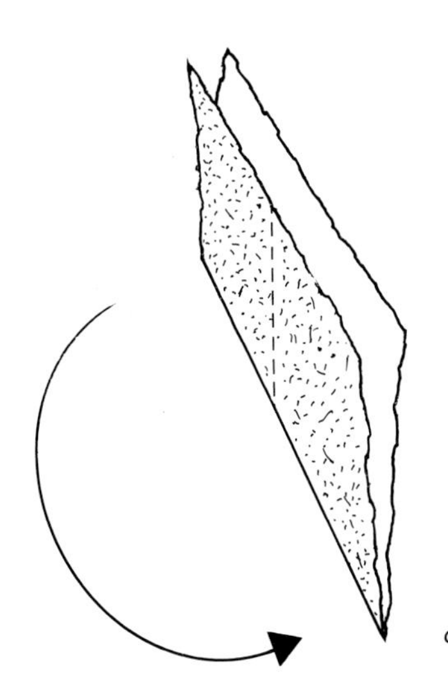

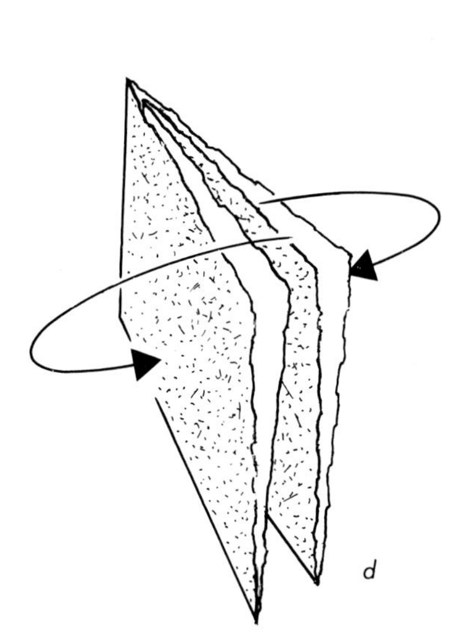

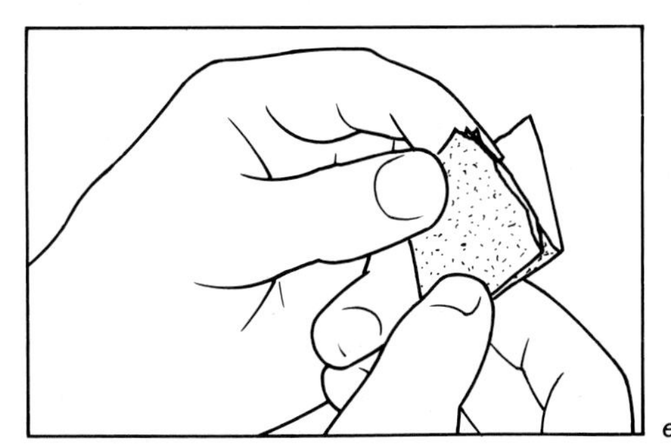

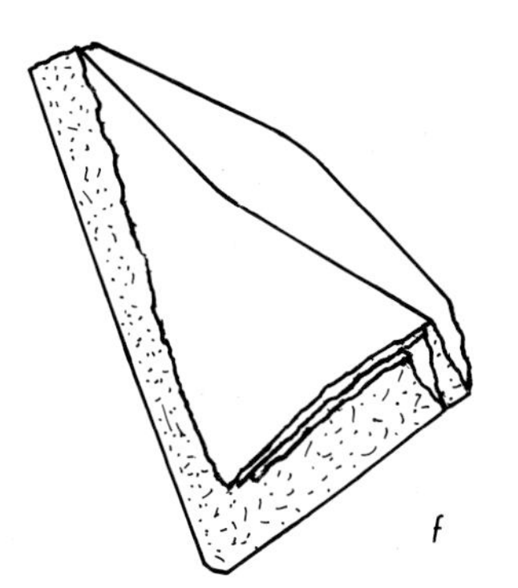

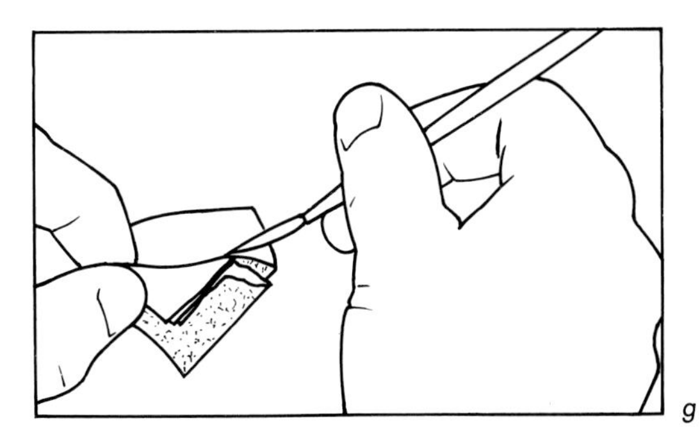

picture develops, start to warm the colour in the cornet (secondary basic colours on the chart) to match the other colours you see in the wood (Fig. 149).

Don't apply pigments continuously to the same spot. Between each group of strokes and at each change of colour, rinse the brush thoroughly in meths and set it in its rack for a few minutes while that last lot dries. When you can rub your fingers over the surface without feeling them drag, you can continue. But first, remove any grittiness you feel with a *very* gentle rub with 4/0 steel wool, working with the grain, remove all traces of dust and minute fragments of steel wool with a lint-free cloth and then fix the area with a wipe of the shellac rubber. You will then be able to see the true effect of your efforts and select the pigments required to further the operation. It is also important not to try to disguise a blemish while standing on the same spot all the time. Remember that the reflectivity of the wood can change as you view it from different directions, so you must move round the piece as you work, adjusting the colours you apply as you see the surface from different angles. Also, if practicable, turn the piece of furniture from time to time so that the surface you are working on catches the light from different angles. It is often necessary to have two, or even three, cornets on the go at the same time, each with a mixture which matches the various aspects.

There will be no set number of stages to go through in developing the basic pale, cool colour by the addition of the warmer tones. Obviously, the least pigment you can get away with the better, for a build up can become an eyesore if you are not careful. Your first attempt may end up as a visible ridge, in which case there will be nothing for it but to flatten it. Wait until the shellac is absolutely dry, next day preferably, then rub the area very gently with worn 320 grit silicon carbide paper, taking care to abrade the pigmented area only. It may not be necessary to remove all the pigment; clean off the dust before you go right through, wipe the shellac rubber over a couple of times and see what it looks like (quite often the effect of the pigment dramatically improves, as this cutting back exposes intermingled flecks of colour which were not apparent while you were working). When you decide to let well enough alone, give the surface you are working on (the entire surface, not just the pigmented area) a few wipes with the shellac rubber and you are ready for the next stage, which may be either bodying up or staining.

149. Stages in disguising a blemish. The progression from cool, pale colours of pigment through to the warm, darker colours is demonstrated in this sequence of disguising five burns on a piece of mahogany.

Staining

Three sorts of stain are useful for adjusting the colour of surfaces which are already finished with shellac or are compatible with it: vandyke, water stain and spirit stain. The techniques described do not actually involve staining in the accepted sense of the word, for no stain is allowed to penetrate the wood. Staining bare wood it not a process which can be controlled accurately enough for restoration purposes and mistakes are nearly always irreversible. In the techniques described here, the stain is contained between layers of shellac, producing the desired effect while being entirely reversible should the need arise.

Vandyke

This is, to all intents and purposes, a water stain, but such are its characteristics and versatility that it merits separate description. The original and proper form of vandyke, sometimes called walnut crystals, is produced from the coloured pigment extracted from the husks of walnuts. It is obtainable as granules, which vary in size from minute up to ½", or as a powder. Sometimes the powdered form is labelled 'vandyke substitute', which is fine if it is powdered walnut extract but do check the stuff before you use it (or better still, before you buy it). Some suppliers have been known to sell aniline dye as vandyke substitute, which is useless for the methods of preparation and use described here. The way to check is simple enough: drop a few grains of the powder into cold water and observe it as it starts to dissolve. Proper vandyke will dissolve into swirls of an even, dark brown, whilst aniline will give you all the colours of the rainbow. Very beautiful but useless.

To prepare enough vandyke to last a few weeks, heat about quarter of a pint of water in a saucepan until it is good and hot but not boiling. If you are using crystals, crush a few ounces fairly small (the smaller the better) whilst the water heats up. When the water is hot enough add vandyke a little at a time, stirring each lot until it dissolves. As you add more and more it will become difficult to stir but persevere, for the mixture must be of uniform consistency. When you have got to the point where no more crystals will dissolve and you have a hot, stiff paste in the pan, turn the stuff out into a jar (an old stoneware pot looks the part in a restorer's workshop) and allow it to cool until solid.

Vandyke is a most effective medium for a number of finishing processes, not only as a stain but for reproducing the shading and the darkened areas which are features of much old furniture and for replacing graining and other surface marks obliterated by the pigmenting of blemishes.

Staining with vandyke

To stain large areas, pour a few drops of water into the vandyke pot and mix it in thoroughly with a 1" paint brush, working the mixture until it has the consistency of thin cream. Make sure that the surface to be treated is fixed with a few wipes of the shellac rubber and is completely dry. Dampen and squeeze almost dry a clean linen rag and form this into a rubber – not a precision job like the polishing rubber but so that there are no lumps or loose threads about – and have another piece of rag to hand. Apply the vandyke mixture with the brush and then distribute it evenly with the rag rubber. Work quickly, as the object is to get an even coat over the whole surface before the water evaporates, which it can do with alarming rapidity. Work with smooth strokes with the pattern of grain and figure, wiping the face of the rag rubber with the spare piece of rag if you feel a gritty accumulation forming, and change the face of the rubber to a clean area if too much wet vandyke prevents the surface drying or creates streaks. Don't rub hard. The vandyke, being slightly abrasive, can cut through the shellac to smear any previous applications or leave streaks in the finish below. Work with quick light strokes and if, when the vandyke is dry, you don't like the look of things, simply wipe it off with a damp rag, allow the surface to dry and try again. The result of a successful treatment with vandyke is an even mellowing and slight darkening of the colour, with no telltale streaks cutting across figure patterns. When you are satisfied that you have achieved this and the vandyke is absolutely dry, give the surface a wipe over with a dry hand to make sure that no gritty particles have been left behind, then fix with a couple of wipes of the shellac rubber. If you decide that another application of vandyke will improve the appearance, give the surface a few more

a

b

c

150. Preparing vandyke.
a. Vandyke crystals.
b. Crystals are crushed into a powder, slowly added to hot water and stirred until dissolved.
c. The near-solid mass of prepared vandyke is turned out into a pot to cool.

a

b

c

d

151. The effectiveness of vandyke demonstrated on a piece of carving.
a. The carving as it looked when it arrived in a box of oddments.
b. Applying a sealing coat of shellac polish with a mop.
c. Brushing on a thick mix of vandyke.
d. Wiping with a damp cloth to produce variations and highlights.
e. The carving with a few coats of shellac, dulled and waxed.

e

coats of shellac to make sure that the first is well sealed in, then allow it to dry thoroughly before proceeding. Or you may decide to body up straight away.

Shading and darkening

Following the principle of not overcleaning a piece of antique furniture, the effect of the dark traces which are allowed to remain on surfaces and in nooks and crannies must be reproduced on repaired areas. In nearly every case vandyke will be ideal for this purpose. As before, all new wood must have had its grain filled and be well sealed with shellac polish beforehand.

On flat surfaces a heavy consistency of vandyke mixture will be required, so if it has been used for staining as described above, the contents of the pot might be too wet for the purpose. Leave the lid off until the stuff looks dry on the surface and let the brush dry out a bit as well, then dab the brush onto the vandyke and transfer it straight to the area to be treated. Immediately stipple the patch of vandyke with the edge of your palm using a quick, light chopping action and moving the hand outwards from the centre, spreading the stain until it begins to dry out. It probably will not look dark enough at this stage but you must not put more on to the same place until it is fixed with shellac. Wait until the vandyke is perfectly dry, rub *very* gently over with 4/0 steel wool, working with the grain, to remove any grittiness, dust off and wipe with the shellac rubber. You may then find that the desired effect has, in fact, been achieved.

If you have to shade and darken the recesses in carving, turnings and mouldings, yet another consistency of vandyke is called for. This time, sprinkle a few drops of water onto the dry surface of the vandyke in the pot and mix with a barely damp brush. The resulting thick mixture can then be stippled into the required parts with the brush and the highlights immediately produced by wiping gently with a slightly damp rag. When the vandyke is dry, a further gentle buffing with a dry rag should complete the effect. Fix with a 50/50 mixture of shellac polish and meths, applied with a polisher's mop or large sable brush.

Graining and other surface marks

A thin mixture of vandyke will nearly always be right for the reproduction or enhancement of grain and other surface marks which have been covered in any process of pigmenting. If the colour is not quite matched, put a little vandyke into a small pot or saucer and alter it with made up water stain (described below). Apply the stain with a fine sable brush, and don't try to do too much, particularly when graining, before allowing it to dry and fixing with a wipe of the shellac rubber to assess your progress.

Distressing

It is appropriate to discuss distressing here, since vandyke is such an essential part of the process. Many of the blemishes which are so much a part of the overall effect of a piece of antique furniture are more than just surface effects which can be reproduced by the means described above. Hundreds of minor knocks over a period of centuries, polished over, rubbed and knocked again, produce an effect of colour and reflected light which is beyond the understanding of the average botcher. Some damage is too prominent, distracts and has to be corrected by patching or filling. All repairs, major or minor, *must* be made to blend in with their surroundings for, left unattended, they

152. A botched job of distressing. Not only is the work an eyesore but no attempt has been made to match the grain or reflectivity of the wood.

153. A more convincing example of distressing. Varying the implement used and the pressure and direction of the blows takes time but produces an effect which is not eye-catching.

154. Handy-sized stones (3″ diameter and 4″ and $1\frac{1}{2}$″) which are ideally suited for the purpose of distressing.

can present an appearance which is almost as unsightly as the original damage. Distressing is a fairly descriptive word for what the restorer has to do to give new wood the right look and, often, the right feel.

The object, as with so many restoration processes, is to change appearances without being obvious. Because it is virtually irreversible, distressing has to be done properly first time. The use of flailing chains and repeated bashing with a hammer are easily recognized methods, but nonetheless frequently used. Even some supposedly random distressing can be all too obvious, as can be seen in Fig. 152, and Fig. 9 on page 18. Anything which will leave a convincing mark may be used, but the important thing to remember is to use each implement only a few times in different places, tapping, scratching or rolling it on the surface with varying amounts of pressure and angles of attack. A stone which has lots of irregularities but no sharp bits (such as those illustrated in Fig. 154) makes an ideal tool.

The best stage at which to do the distressing on shellac-finished surfaces is after all staining (including the use of any water stain) has been completed. When you have pounded and tapped to your satisfaction, fix the surface and weigh up the effect. Usually some colour will be required to give the indentations their proper effect. This is achieved with a thick mix of vandyke well rubbed into all the marks, followed immediately by a light wipe, with the grain, with a slightly-dampened rag. You will then have to wait patiently for the vandyke to dry completely, before fixing it with a mop charged with 50/50 shellac and meths. You may then decide to add a few very shallow indentations which will not be coloured and/or rub those areas which are prone to more wear than the rest with well-worn silicon carbide paper, cutting through previously-applied layers of stain or not, depending on the effect you need. When all is done you can fix and body up as you think fit.

When distressing is required on an area which is to be finished with the burnished wax process, the surface should be fixed if necessary with a wipe or two of the shellac rubber, distressed, then have vandyke applied before the layers of beeswax are built up.

Water stain

Water stains come in a variety of colours, in powder form (see Appendices, p. 150). They should be stored in jars with well-fitting lids, particularly those which are hygroscopic, or you will soon have a solid mass instead of powder. Water stain is best mixed fresh for each job as the consistency you require is bound to vary. Experience will show you how much to use but start with a little water in a small pot and add minute quantities of the powder until the colour looks right. Of course, you won't be able to tell if it is quite right until you have tried it on the surface you are treating, but you can easily adjust it with more powder or water.

As when staining with the thin mix of vandyke, the surface must be fixed with shellac polish beforehand, so that if things go wrong or the colour is not right a wipe with a damp rag will allow you to start again. When the colour proves to be satisfactory, allow it to dry completely before fixing it with shellac. As with vandyke, don't expect or try to achieve a perfect match with one application. A few thin coats, fixed thoroughly between applications, will build up the desired colour gradually and controllably.

Spirit stain

Spirit stains really only come into their own when it is necessary to add a trace of transparent colour to the polish itself, perhaps with a trace of pig-

155. The repaired bracket foot illustrated in Fig. 106 is finished with a few dabs of vandyke followed by coloured size.

ment, in repairing a tinted finish. They are best applied thinly in a 50/50 mixture of shellac and meths, using a mop or sable brush, as appropriate. If you are applying more shellac with the rubber after this, start with light strokes so that the stain is not lifted and spread to other areas.

Care of brushes

Do look after the brushes used in these pigmenting and staining processes. Obviously, separate sets are required for water- and spirit-based processes. Whenever they are not in use, they must be rinsed in the appropriate solvent then brought to a point before being stood in the rack – never leave a brush standing in a pot of solvent, for irreparable damage is likely. Before you first use brushes or mops for a shellac process you will be well advised to suspend them in a jar of shellac for a couple of days to make sure you don't lose hairs from them as you work.

Coloured size

Whilst much of the unpolished wood of antique furniture can be matched by the chemical colouring process which was described at the beginning of this chapter, you are likely to come across many pieces of case furniture which have their backs and underneaths coated with a matt finish. Whether this was the original finish for these parts or not, it is best to treat any repairs to them with a matching finish. This is made by dissolving a spoonful of soaked pearl glue in a little hot water (a couple of fluid ounces should be enough for quite a large job), then keep this size hot while adding a teaspoonful of whiting and enough of the appropriate dry pigments to give the brew the right colour. Don't make the wash too thick. A couple of thin coats, applied with a paint brush, will give the best effect; and if you want to give a bit of variation, a few random dabs with the vandyke brush before the wash is applied will do the trick. Leave the job until next day to dry completely, then a rub over with your dry hand will remove any grittiness and soften the appearance.

The Finishing Touches

Do not underestimate the time you will need to spend on the bits and pieces which come after the main restoration work is done. An amazing amount of time goes on sorting out problems with metal fittings. Woodworm treatment can only be done when all woodwork and finishing have been completed. Leather and baize liners which didn't look too bad on those wrecks you bought now look decidedly scruffy, and that cracked pane of glass is getting on your nerves.

CHAPTER 11
Metal fittings

There cannot be many pieces of antique furniture outside collections which are complete with their original metal fittings, especially those which are susceptible to changes in fashion, such as handles and escutcheons. It is easy to understand why you come across replacement hinges and castors, which are subject to considerable strain, but even locks, for some mysterious reason, are often odd replacements or are missing altogether. To establish whether a fitting is original or not is usually quite straightforward. Take one off and look behind it: if there are no other marks to indicate other fastenings, such as screw holes in positions which do not match the holes in the existing fitting, and if there is a 'shadow' of unfaded wood which matches the fitting, then it's highly likely that it is original. (On the other hand, you might be looking at the work of an extremely skilled exponent of the techniques described in the previous chapter.) Check also on the type and method of manufacture of screws and nails which secure the fittings, as discussed in Chapter 3.

Handles and escutcheons

By now you will have gathered that the handles and escutcheons on your piece of furniture are possibly the latest in a long line of replacements. Original Georgian handle plates may have been replaced with a series of others, then Victorian knobs used to modernize the piece, followed by today's 'Hepplewhite' oval plates put on to conceal the mess of holes and

156. The evidence of several changes of handles on the drawers of an oak dresser.

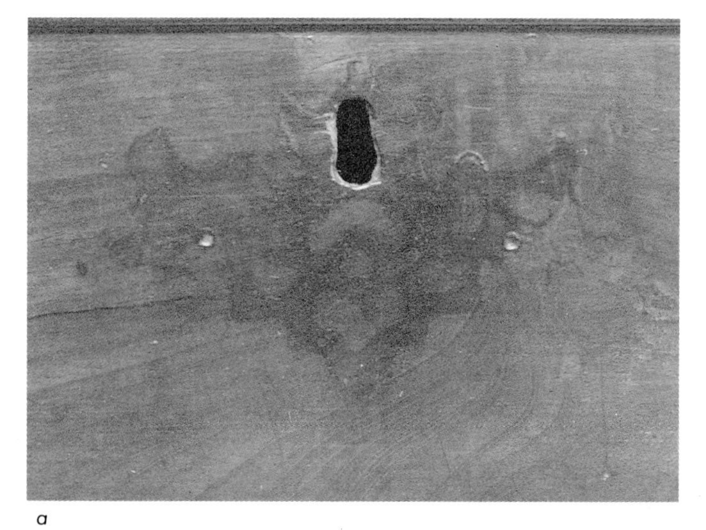

a

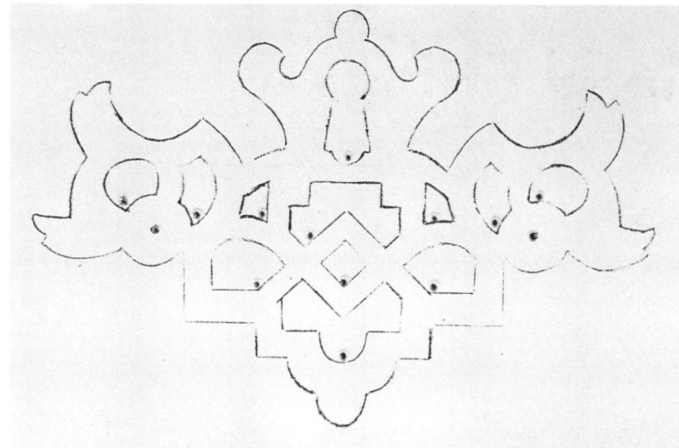

b

c

d

157. Re-creating a pierced brass handle/escutcheon plate from a 'shadow' of the original.

a. These faint marks of the original plate are better than most for the purpose of designing a replacement. A tracing is taken from the marks and checked against those on other drawers. Also checked is the distance between the post holes of all the handles so that the tracing bears the average distance.

b. A piece of $\frac{1}{16}$ thick aluminium sheet is cut, of sufficient size to allow a bit of waste all round, bearing in mind that it will need to be within the capacity of the piecing saw so that the point is not reached where the work cannot be turned to follow the direction of the cutting line. If all points of the outline cannot be reached with room to turn the blank to any angle, then a fret saw will have to be used, cumbersome as it is for this sort of work. A photocopy of the traced pattern is attached to the aluminium with double-sided tape and fine holes drilled on the scrap side of each sawing line as a starting point for each cut. The burrs formed by the drill are removed from the back of the blank to avoid damaging the sawing table.

c. When the sawing is complete the paper is removed and edges and bevel worked with files. The outer piece of scrap is not discarded as it makes a useful frame in which to send the model to the foundry.

d. Some cost is saved by asking the foundry to supply the castings unpolished.

e. A casting trimmed and burnished.

e

a

b

158. Antique and modern. An eighteenth-century cast plate (a) still shows crispness of detail and fine bevelling whilst its modern descendant (b) reveals all the signs of mass-production.

159. Patinating brass fittings.
a. The plate prepared in Fig. 157, together with handle bail and posts, has been patinated with the chemical concoction described in the text (Method 1).
b. These fittings show the variation in patination which can be achieved using the ammonia vapour process (Method 2).

scars which disfigure the wood. You could find that the patching, filling and refinishing necessary to correct faults beneath existing plates turns out to be your biggest single restoration problem. However, since handles and escutcheons are often the most eye-catching features of a piece of furniture, all efforts must be made to rectify the damage.

Having determined that the handles and escutcheons are later replacements and decided that they must be replaced, the first job will be to find out what is behind them all, not just the sample which you took off. Once they are removed, you will need to clean off the accumulated dust and metal polish (use the cleaner described on p. 90) before you are able to make out all the traces left by other fittings – other holes are obvious but the faint signs of original handles will usually be impossible to detect unless the surface is carefully cleaned (Fig. 157a is an exception). Differences in colour of the wood, a slight ridge of dark, solidified dirt or a shallow depression where an edge has pressed into the wood all help to recreate the outline of an earlier fitting. Even the most complex of Georgian pierced handle plates can be re-created by tracing all the marks from all the handles and using them to build up a composite picture. Once the evidence has given you all the detail you need, the next stage is selecting the handles and escutcheons.

You can look through the catalogues of suppliers of cabinet fittings (or send them a copy of your drawing) to see if they have a perfect match. The Appendix on p. 152 gives two suppliers. One provides only copies of old fittings individually cast in brass, including handle posts and nuts; the other supplies mass-produced reproductions, the plates for handles and escutcheons being stamped out of brass sheet with post threads and nuts made from steel. The patterns of many of the reproductions are fairly close to the old ones (Fig. 158) but, although the cast copies are two or three times the cost of the reproductions, there is no doubt that they are more in keeping with fine old furniture. Much can be done to improve the appearance of reproduction fittings. Some patient work with files to sharpen details, particularly the bevels on handle plates and escutcheons, and emery cloth to reduce the thickness of plates and handle bails, followed by a good burnish with metal polish and patinating to taste and the only thing which will let you down is the steel nuts and bolts showing on the inside.

The chances of finding exactly the right sort, size and shape of handle and matching escutcheon are slim at best, so if you are determined to have your

a

b

fittings looking as original as possible, you will incur some expense. If there is just one handle and one escutcheon left on the piece, the specialist metal-workers mentioned on p. 152 will be able to produce perfect copies for you. Do ask them for a price first though, then the bill will not be so much of a shock. If, however, there is nothing to copy but the drawings you made from the marks, you will need to make patterns for the foundry to work from. These can be made in brass, which will give you the best idea of what the finished job will look like, but there is lots of sawing and filing involved, so you may prefer to use aluminium. The ease of working aluminium is only slightly offset by its tendency to clog finer saw blades and files, but this is overcome by using fairly coarse blades (1 and 0 gauge will be about right) and keeping fine files for finishing off. Fig. 157 shows the stages in preparing patterns.

It may be that there is no useful evidence of previous fittings on your piece of furniture, so you will obviously then have to settle for reproductions in keeping with the original style. In deciding whether to go for the cast copies or pressed reproductions, three points are critical. First, of course, the style must be correct for the piece. Second, where handles are secured by two posts, the distance between the centres of the (original) holes is most important. Third, the overall size and proportion of the handle above and below the posts affects the whole appearance of the piece. If the size is wrong, the brasswork can overwhelm the wood or be lost on it, and the proportions of the handles are frequently overlooked, leading to an unbalanced appearance. The distance between top of drawer and handle plate was nearly always intended to be the same as between bottom of drawer and handle plate or, in the case of swan-neck handles, top of drawer to post plate and bottom of drawer to bottom of handle bail.

Your new fittings, whether reproduction or castings, may be supplied polished to a bright finish, or patinated. Unfortunately, the patination on reproduction fittings is usually less than convincing, and that on castings tends to be uniform, which is seldom the case with fittings which have been in place for a couple of centuries. So you may wish to improve the effect by polishing high spots and deepening the patina of other areas to re-create the effects of natural oxidization and the sheen produced by regular handling and dusting. There are several methods of patinating brass, the effectiveness of each depending largely on the composition of the metal. Two very successful processes are described here. One gives a mellow, greenish patina but involves messy and time-consuming preparation of the brew; the other is simple (if pungent) and produce a patina which can be varied from pale green to black and pitted.

Method 1. For this process you will require:

	IMPERIAL	METRIC
Copper carbonate	1½ oz	45 g
Copper acetate	½ oz	15 g
Ammonium chloride (sal ammoniac)	½ oz	15 g
Sodium chloride	½ oz	15 g
Purified cream of tartar	½ oz	15 g
Dilute acetic acid (10%)	4 fl oz	120 ml

Mix these together in a glass jar of at least one litre capacity, for as the chemical reaction progresses the concoction will rise and thicken, requiring several good stirs to reduce the volume and consistency – not just once but several times over a period of time. You will need to start the mixing operation in the morning and keep an eye on it all day. Eventually, it will settle down and then it will need to be stored in a glass jar with a secure and corrosion-resistant lid.

Before applying this mixture, make sure that the brass to be treated is well polished and degreased. Stir the mixture to an even, creamy consistency, then paint it onto the metal (with an old paint brush), covering it completely and keeping the brush moving. After a few seconds you should see the colour of the surface changing, the copper content of the brass determining how quickly it changes and therefore how long you will need to leave the stuff on. When the colour appears to be right, wash the fitting in cold water, dry it thoroughly, burnish the high spots if you wish, then polish it with wax. The success of this process does depend on the metal having a formula which is reasonably close to that of old brass. Some of the modern brass fittings, particularly those pressed from sheet brass, may not respond with a convincing colour – in which case, try the second method.

Method 2. Half to three-quarters fill a tough container of clear (or nearly so) plastic with fine wood shavings (the sort produced by planing machines are ideal, but any will do). The quantity of shavings and the size of container will depend on the size and number of fittings you are likely to need to treat. The container must have an airtight lid if the contents are to remain effective for any length of time. Pour 5–10 ml of .880 ammonia over the shavings and seal the lid immediately. Rubber gloves and goggles are essential, and hold everything well away from the face, for ammonia fumes spread quickly and will do more than clear your tubes! An extractor fan above the workbench comes in handy for such operations. Shake the container for a few minutes to disperse the ammonia throughout the shavings, then leave it overnight to ensure complete absorption – the shavings should sound dry when the container is shaken.

Again, make sure that the brass is polished and completely free from grease, then slip it into the container, leaving the lid open for the briefest time possible and keeping your face well away. Shake the container for a few minutes and observe the change in colour, which can be quite rapid. Depending on the composition of the brass and the length of time it is left in the shavings, the colour can be varied to suit. When it looks right, manoeuvre the fittings to the top of the shavings so that you are not searching for them in that fumy atmosphere, using tweezers through the half-opened lid if necessary. Wipe the metal with a damp rag, dry it and, depending on the effect you want, either leave it as it is, burnish high spots and/or wax it and buff it. If the patination you have produced is not even but speckled or patchy, the reason is probably either that the shavings are too wet or that the container has been allowed to stand for too long without being shaken. If you have put in too much ammonia, add another handful of shavings to the container, shake and leave overnight before trying again.

The results possible with these two processes are illustrated in Fig. 159.

Hinges

Avoid replacing old hinges which are damaged if you can possibly save them, especially stopped hinges (the sort that have the knuckle modified to allow a lid to open to about 100°), which are almost unobtainable now. Even if half a hinge is missing it is preferable to get a replacement piece cast from the matching part of another hinge rather than to fit a modern replacement, which will seldom be exactly the same and therefore necessitate alterations to the cabinetwork. Bent hinges should be removed and straightened and loose pins replaced with pieces from a suitable size of round nail.

Castors

The most frequent problems with brass castors are collapsed horns (which support the wheel) and a flat spot on the wheel caused by it seizing up on accumulated grit. Cabinet-makers' suppliers (see p. 152) can get both these faults rectified, at no great expense. If replacement castors are essential, the range available today is large enough for you to be fairly sure of getting a good match, and one which does not entail modifications to the woodwork. Repairs to castors which have wheels of wood or leather are another matter, since these types of castors are likely to be fitted to a rare piece of furniture, so you are recommended to leave their repair to the specialist restorer.

Locks and keys

Most locks you will come across in English antique furniture will not present too many difficulties when fitting keys to conform to their mechanisms (with two notable exceptions). Once the lock is removed and the cap taken off (see p. 32) you will discover if it is a back-spring, tumbler or lever mechanism you have to deal with.

Back-spring locks

The back-spring lock is the easiest to fit with a key (Fig. 160). Make sure that the pipe of the key blank you buy (or old key you are adapting) is a snug fit on the pin of the lock and that the outside of the pipe clears the keyholes in both wood and the cap. The range of key blanks available from cabinet-makers' suppliers is not large, so if you are using one you might have to adapt the pipe to fit the pin and keyholes. When you have the key fitted to the pin, adjust the bit to the keyhole in the cap, then place it on the pin and mark the positions of any wards. *Don't be tempted to knock the wards off to make a key fit*. Saw or file the appropriate wards in the key bit and then test the operation of the lock. You will probably find that a small amount has to be filed from the bottom of the bit before the bolt operates smoothly. Now you can cut the back of the bit in order for it to fit with the cap in place, then cut any wards necessary to match those on the cap. Next replace the cap and hold it firmly in place to test the action. If no adjustments are necessary, fit the cap permanently on its lugs and replace the lock in position. Finally, check that the lock is working properly *before* closing the door or drawer – you may find that it will lock all right and then refuse to unlock because of pressure on the cap due to overtightened screws.

Lever locks

One of the locks difficult to fit with a key is one of the earliest types of lever lock: the Chubb 'detector' lock (illustrated on page 35), which was designed to jam if the wrong key was used or any attempt was made to pick it. If you are faced with a Chubb's patent lock you are strongly recommended to send it to Chubb & Son for their expert attention. Their address is given on p. 152.

a

b

160. Cutting a key to fit a warded back-spring lock. With the cap removed and the parts visible, cutting a new key for this type of lock is straightforward. However, the lugs securing the cap of this lock have been so well peened over that access to the inside would not be accomplished without causing damage. In such a case the method of determining the positions of the wards is as described on p. 135 for dealing with a locked drawer or door.
a. The pipe of the key blank is adjusted to fit the pin of the lock and the key bit cut to pass through the keyhole.
b. The bit is held above a candle flame until it acquires a good coating of soot.
c. When the bit is rubbed against the wards their positions are clearly marked (the lock illustrated has only one ward).
d. A few minutes' work with hacksaw and file has the lock operating.

c

d

Fortunately, run-of-the-mill lever locks are only a bit more complicated to fit with a key than back-spring locks (Fig. 161). Again, the first step is to make sure that you get a key which fits the pin and keyholes. Take off the cover and remove all the levers, lining them up in the order in which they come off. Place the key blank on the pin and see if it will operate the bolt – you will probably have to file a little off the bottom of the bit before it operates cleanly. Now fit the first lever next to the bolt and see how it moves when the key is turned. It will almost certainly be lifted so far that the gate passes beyond the position where the stump on the bolt can pass through without catching. The bit will require filing at the point of contact with the lever until the stump can pass through the centre of the gate. *Do not file the gate wider to allow passage for the stump*. Place the next lever in position and repeat the process, remembering to hold the levers firmly in position (a function normally performed by the cap) when testing the action, in order not to end up with misaligned steps on the bit. With all the levers back, test the action with the cap secured before refitting the lock.

161. Cutting a key to fit a lever lock.
a. The key is fitted to the lock pin.
b. With the levers removed the bit of the key is adjusted to operate the bolt, seen here half thrown.
c. The first lever is replaced and the bit filed at the point where it makes contact with it. Progress is tested frequently and the filing stopped when the lever can be lifted far enough for the lug on the bolt to pass cleanly through the gating.
d. The bit is filed to operate the second lever. The operation of the lock must be tested once the cap has been screwed on and again as soon as the lock is refitted.

162. Making a modern key blank look the part. Some work with files and emery cloth can transform a modern key to look quite in keeping with antique furniture.

Tumbler locks

The fitting of keys for this sort of lock is basically the same as for lever locks, except that it is usually simpler, most only having one tumbler to deal with instead of several levers.

Broken locks

If a lock will not operate it is usually for one of four reasons:

i You are using the wrong key!

ii The lock is dirty. Clean out loose fluff and dust and wash out congealed oil with a stiff brush and paraffin. Rinse a couple of times with meths, let it dry completely and then lubricate with a little powdered graphite.

iii The pin is misaligned, loose or missing. A missing pin is easily replaced with a piece of round nail which is a good fit in the pipe of the key. If you are not equipped for silver-soldering, your local clock repairer or silversmith may be persuaded to do the job.

iv A spring is broken. In the case of a back-spring lock, the spring was usually formed as an integral part of the bolt as it was being forged; later ones have a strip of tempered steel fitted into a slot in the top. These are seen in Fig. 47 and 55, respectively. The latter is obviously easiest to repair: a piece of lock spring from the hardware shop is simply cut to length and fitted into the existing slot, which may have to be closed a little to hold the spring, using hammer and punch. When an integral spring has broken, cut off the remaining piece at the join with the bolt, then saw a fine slot to take a piece as described above (note the angle of the slot in the bolt in Fig. 164).

In tumbler locks and early lever locks, the spring or spring comb is fitted into the case (Figs. 49 and 53), which makes it more difficult to repair. A piece of spring will need to be shaped to match the old one and silver-soldered into the case – a most laborious process when you are dealing with a multi-lever lock and one which you might well delegate to the professional metalworker.

The replacement of a lever spring in later locks (Fig. 54) is perfectly straightforward. The hardware shop will supply you with a strip of spring of the appropriate dimensions for a few pence, from which a piece is soon cut and fitted into the lever.

Bramah locks

When you have once had the opportunity of inspecting the innards of a Bramah lock, such as the one illustrated in Fig. 163, you will realize that this is the other type which is difficult to fit with a key, and understand why you are recommended to leave all repairs and cutting of keys to the experts. Bramah's address is given on p. 152.

Locked drawers and doors

Should you be confronted by a drawer, cupboard door, etc., which is locked and the key lost, never try to prise it open – all you will do is cause unnecessary damage to the woodwork. Try one of the following approaches, depending on the circumstances.

a

b

163. A Bramah patent drawer lock. *a* (front) shows the boss, containing the keyhole which projects through the drawer front. *b* shows the bolt face. This lock has not been taken apart to show its mechanism because of the small size of the components and the complexity of assembly. *c* (opposite) Fig. 133 from George Price's 1856 *Treatise on Fire and Thiefproof Depositories and Locks and Keys*, proves the wisdom of the decision! This lock is believed to be the first in which the key does not operate directly onto the bolt but via the mechanism, as do today's Yale locks.

If you have some old furniture keys, these will obviously be your first recourse. If there are other locks in the piece, check to see what type they are, select all the appropriate keys and try them. If it is a warded lock, which a peep through the keyhole will establish, try to see the spacing and height of the wards to save trying a lot of useless keys. Don't use force when you test the keys, as you can do without a broken key bit in the lock to add to the problem. It is unlikely that your odd keys will work, so next check to see if you can get access to the back of the lock to remove the screws or nails holding it in place. This is often a lot easier than it sounds: take a few screws or nails from a back panel and you may be able to reach through and unfasten the lock. Sometimes this operation is complicated by a securely-nailed back (which should not be disturbed), by dustboards between drawers and interior fittings in the way.

The next ploy is to see if other locks in the piece are of the same construction as the offending lock, and cut a key for one of them. If the resulting key doesn't do the trick, the chances are that this is the one odd lock in the piece!

If you can establish that the problem lock is a back-spring type, there is one more way to get it undone without causing any damage – pick it. (The picking of lever locks and some tumbler locks requires tools which would take longer to make than is worthwhile.) For this operation you will need the usual key cutting equipment, plus a lighted candle. First, inspect the lock through the keyhole to see if there are any wards which, for the purpose of this exercise, there are assumed to be. (An unwarded back-spring lock will often respond to a piece of steel rod with its end bent to fit into the talon of the bolt.) Hold the bit of a suitable key blank in the tip of the candle flame until it is well blackened with soot (Fig. 160). Carefully insert the key until the front of the bit makes contact with the wards (or the deepest ward), turn it from side to side to rub the soot at the position of the ward(s), remove the key and see if you have a clear mark. Saw and file at the marked areas until the bit fits right down on the pin and over all the wards, re-blackening and marking again as necessary. With the front (case) wards taken care of, remove any waste from the back of the bit until it fits comfortably inside the cap, blacken the bit again and insert it through the keyhole without removing any soot from the sides of the bit, for it is on the sides that you will get the marks of the back wards by gently turning the key until contact is felt. After cutting these wards, a small adjustment to the bottom of the bit will usually have the key working.

When all else has failed, there is one last chance, but this does depend on the lock not being held in too firmly. If there are other locks in the piece, check to see how these are held in place (large or corroded screws may indicate that the lock is held firmly) and test to see how secure the fastenings are. If there's a chance that things are not too secure, take a short length of rod of the largest diameter which will fit through the keyhole, place an end of the rod against the lock just below the pin (making sure that you haven't covered a ward) and tap the other end once with a hammer. If there is any give at all, a few more light taps should release the lock. The slight damage you will need to rectify should be confined to the screw holes, which are likely to need drilling out and plugging. If that first tap does not loosen the lock, don't persist unless you are sure that its case, and the woodwork, will stand it. And *don't* strike the pin of the lock with a punch, as is often recommended, for you are likely to loosen it or even push it through the case.

If you still haven't got in, call the locksmith!

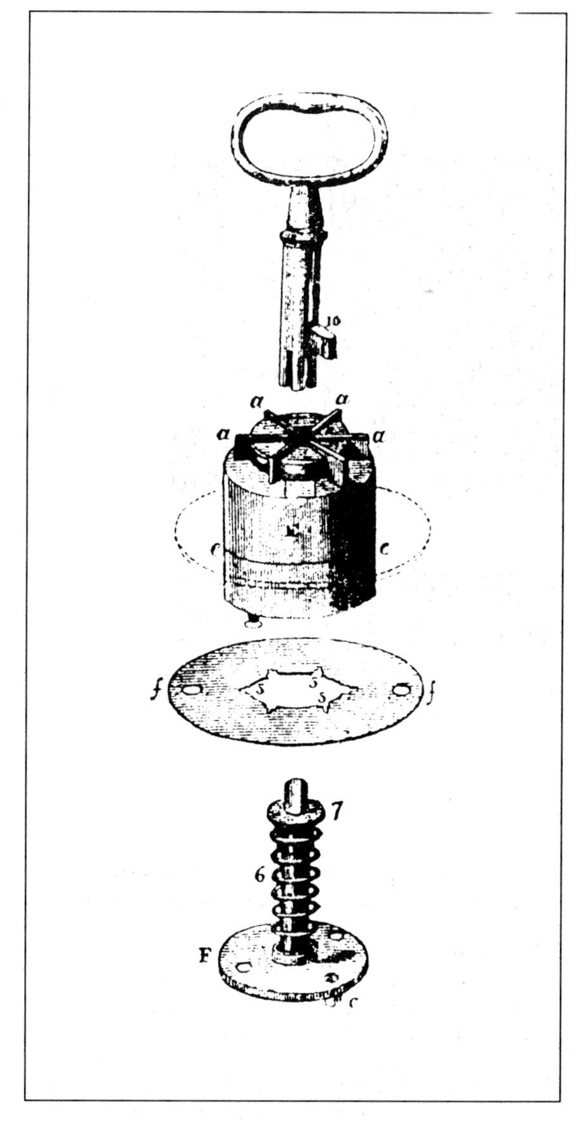

C

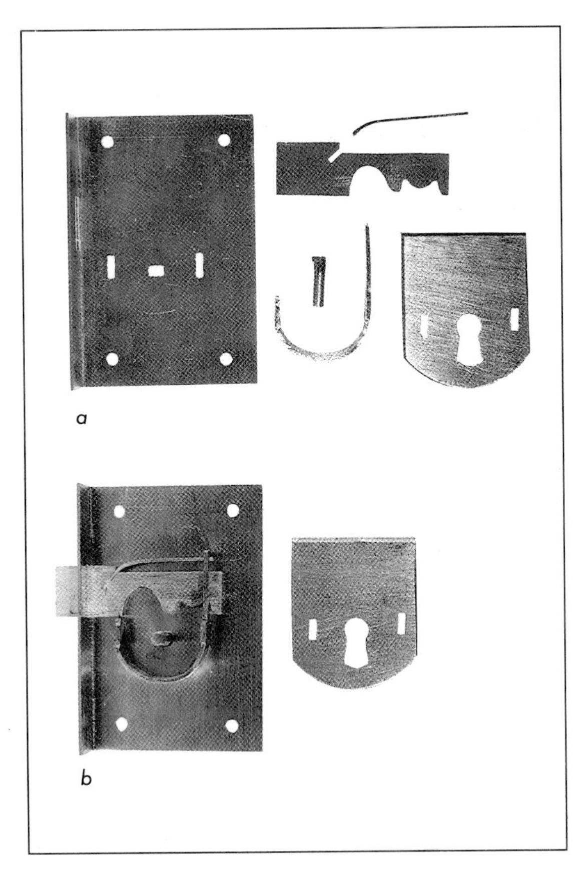

164. A hand-made lock. The simple components of the back-spring lock are not too difficult to produce providing that accurate measurements have been taken.
a. The components.
b. Assembled.

Missing locks

If a lock is missing and it is essential to replace it (that is, if it is the only means of keeping a door closed, as with most cabinets and longcase clocks) then it is acceptable to fit a modern lock but *only if it does not require the cutting away of wood to make it fit*. Locks of clock case doors, interior cupboards of bureaux, etc., were usually so small that no modern equivalent size is available. In such a case it it well worth the time and effort to make a replacement lock. Stick to the pattern of the old back-spring lock, the components of which are reasonably simple to make and assemble, and make sure you spend adequate time on the crucial measuring and sketching necessary before you start (see Figs. 164 and 165). Then it's up to your skill at cutting, bending and filing. The fitting of the bolt spring is described under **Broken locks** above. The pin and cap spacer are best silver-soldered into the case, leaving cap lugs to be peened over when you assemble the lock.

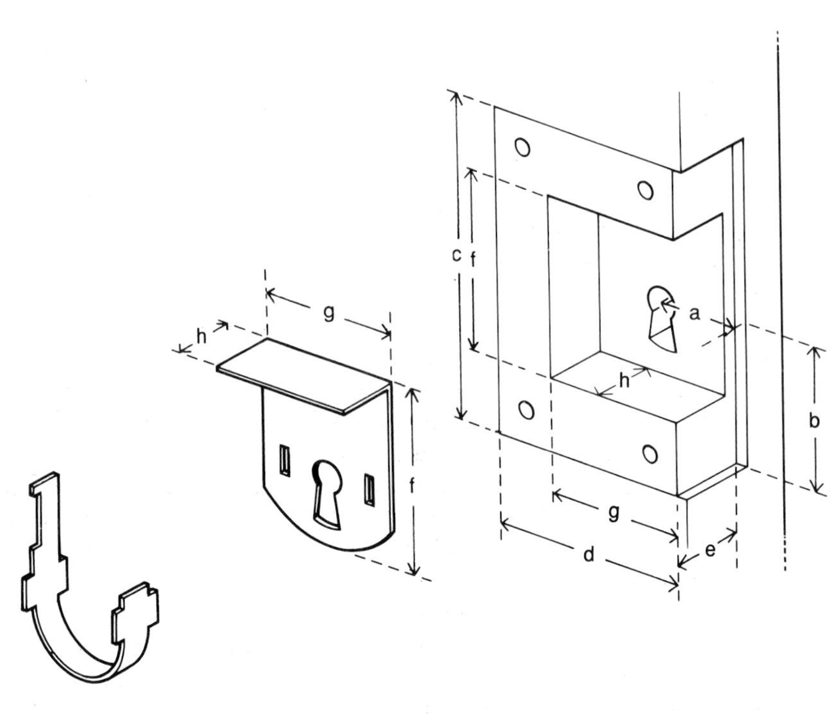

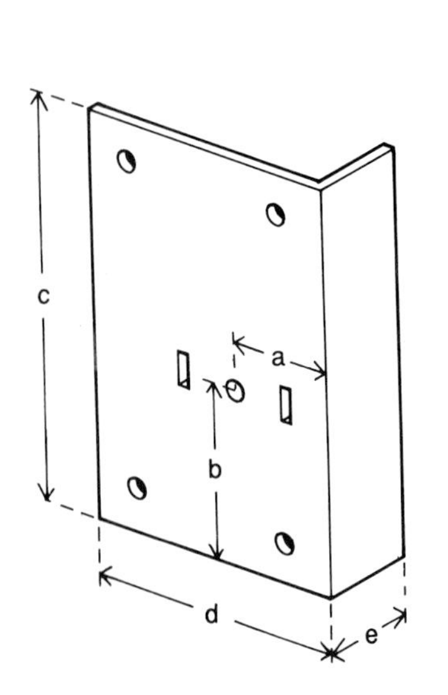

165. Dimensions to note before making a back-spring lock:

a. Outer edge of bolt face to centre of keyhole and pin.
b. Bottom of lock case to centre of keyhole and pin.
c. Height of case.
d. Width of case (inside).
e. Depth of case (inside).
f. Height of cut out.
g. Width of cut out.
h. Depth of cut out

CHAPTER 12
Leather and baize liners

In Chapter 2 it was suggested that relining a leather-topped article should be considered as a last resort, only to be undertaken after all attempts to revive the old one had failed. There's not much that can be done for badly torn and crumbling leather, but many liners which look as though they are beyond recovery actually only need feeding to restore their natural suppleness and texture. For this purpose a concoction known as 'British Museum Leather Dressing' remains unequalled. You will require:

	IMPERIAL	METRIC
Beeswax	$\frac{1}{4}$ oz	7 g
Hexane	$\frac{1}{2}$ fl oz	15 ml
Anhydrous lanolin	$3\frac{1}{2}$ fl oz	100 ml
Cedarwood oil	$\frac{1}{2}$ fl oz	15 ml

Shave the beeswax finely into a glass jar, pour in the hexane and leave it until all the beeswax is dissolved, stirring occasionally. Add the lanolin and cedarwood oil and shake well. Apply this mixture with a soft cloth, being careful not to tear off loose fragments of coloured surface leather. When the surface has dried thoroughly (give it a few hours) you will be able to judge whether or not the treatment has been successful. If the leather is still crumbly and unyielding, a further application can be tried, but should this be ineffective you may decide, not least for functional reasons, to replace it.

The first step is to decide what to replace the old leather with: hide or skiver. Skivers, being sheepskin, are quite small and, therefore, large areas have to be made up with three pieces – usually a large centre panel flanked by small side panels, the joins of which are embossed with the same pattern which decorates the border. Against this disadvantage must be set the cost of hide which, although capable of covering a large top in one piece, is many times the price. So, whilst in theory you should replace hide with hide, this rule need only be obeyed with high-value pieces of furniture on which economies would not be justified, and skiver may be used for most replacements.

Removal of an old leather is usually no problem, for it will part company from the ground wood easily and the glue beneath can then be washed off. When measuring up for the new leather, don't forget to check that the diagonal measurements are equal: only if the edges are absolutely square to each other should you rely on sending measurements to the supplier. Generally, it is best to prepare a template, and essential when odd shapes are to be relined.

Colours of leather and styles of tooling vary from supplier to supplier, so it is advisable to check your local directory and get samples of both from listed leather merchants and also ask for prices, which vary considerably around the country. Your new leather will arrive with a good surplus around to allow

a

b

c

166. Laying a leather liner. It is important to have a guide to help locate the leather accurately on its ground. Strips of masking tape (a) with which the guide lines on the leather can be aligned (*b*) will make for a perfect result when the surplus is trimmed off and the edges pressed down (*c*).

for small variations in the edges of the top, and there will usually be faint lines marked on it to indicate the dimensions you have specified.

Although the original leather was almost certainly held down with animal glue, you will be best advised to use a good wallpaper paste made up to the consistency of thick cream. This will give you plenty of time to lay the liner and allow you to make small adjustments as you do so; and it will hold leather perfectly securely after a short time. Prepare the paste, and while it is soaking get everything ready for the laying operation. You will find that a guide to the positioning of the corners of the liner is essential, and is achieved by lightly applying pieces of masking tape at the corners of the top to indicate the positions of the edges (Fig. 166).

When the paste is ready, brush it onto the ground wood and spread it evenly over the whole surface, making sure that the edges get their fair share. Wipe off any paste which has strayed onto the polished surround, then immediately apply the leather, lining up the intersecting edge marks on it with your tape markers. When you judge that the leather is exactly in position, smooth it down with a wad of soft cloth, starting in the middle and working outwards to disperse any air bubbles. Press down at the edges to feel the position of the lip up to which the leather must butt, and check the alignment with the edge markings. Only if things are completely misaligned are you likely to need to lift the whole leather, in which case you will probably need to apply an additional very thin film of paste.

Now that the leather is accurately positioned, you have to trim off the waste. For this operation you will need a scalpel with a new no. 15 blade (see p. 47) and a guide which conforms to the required cutting line. If all the edges are straight, a steel straight-edge will serve as the guide, but if there are lots of curves to cut you will find that a hardboard template will be helpful (Fig. 167e) and certainly more accurate than trying to follow a curve free-hand. When cutting, the scalpel must not be pressed hard up to the guide for this can lead to accidents: hold the blade lightly against the guide, angle it to 10–15° to undercut the leather, and you will get a neat edge with no pale bits showing. When all the waste is off, press the edges of the leather down against the edges of the surround with your hardwood scraper, wipe any remaining paste off polished surfaces and leave the job overnight to dry. The next day, give the liner a polish with a pale leather wax and the job is complete.

Where the liner is baize you will not usually have to do too much soul-searching to decide whether to replace it or not, since many existing ones are themselves replacements. However, if the baize is original and has an embossed pattern around the edge, you may decide that you can live with a moth hole or two. Many colours of baize are available but you might have to shop around to find the perfect match. The Appendix on p. 152 gives suppliers who provide a postal service.

The procedure for removing an old baize liner and preparing the ground is the same as that for leather. New baize may also be secured with wallpaper paste, but a more satisfactory result is achieved by using animal glue (Fig. 167). Prepare a thin mix of Scotch glue as you would for securing veneer, brush it evenly over the ground wood and leave it for a few minutes to gel. Wash off any glue that has got onto the polished surround and into the join of folding tops. Heat up a large flat-iron until it is just bearable to touch. Lay the baize in position, smooth it out and put a square of clean, white linen on top (a piece of a couple of square feet is ample, as there is no need to cover the entire surface). Apply the hot iron to the linen and work it steadily, without undue pressure, being careful not to let it ride up over the wood

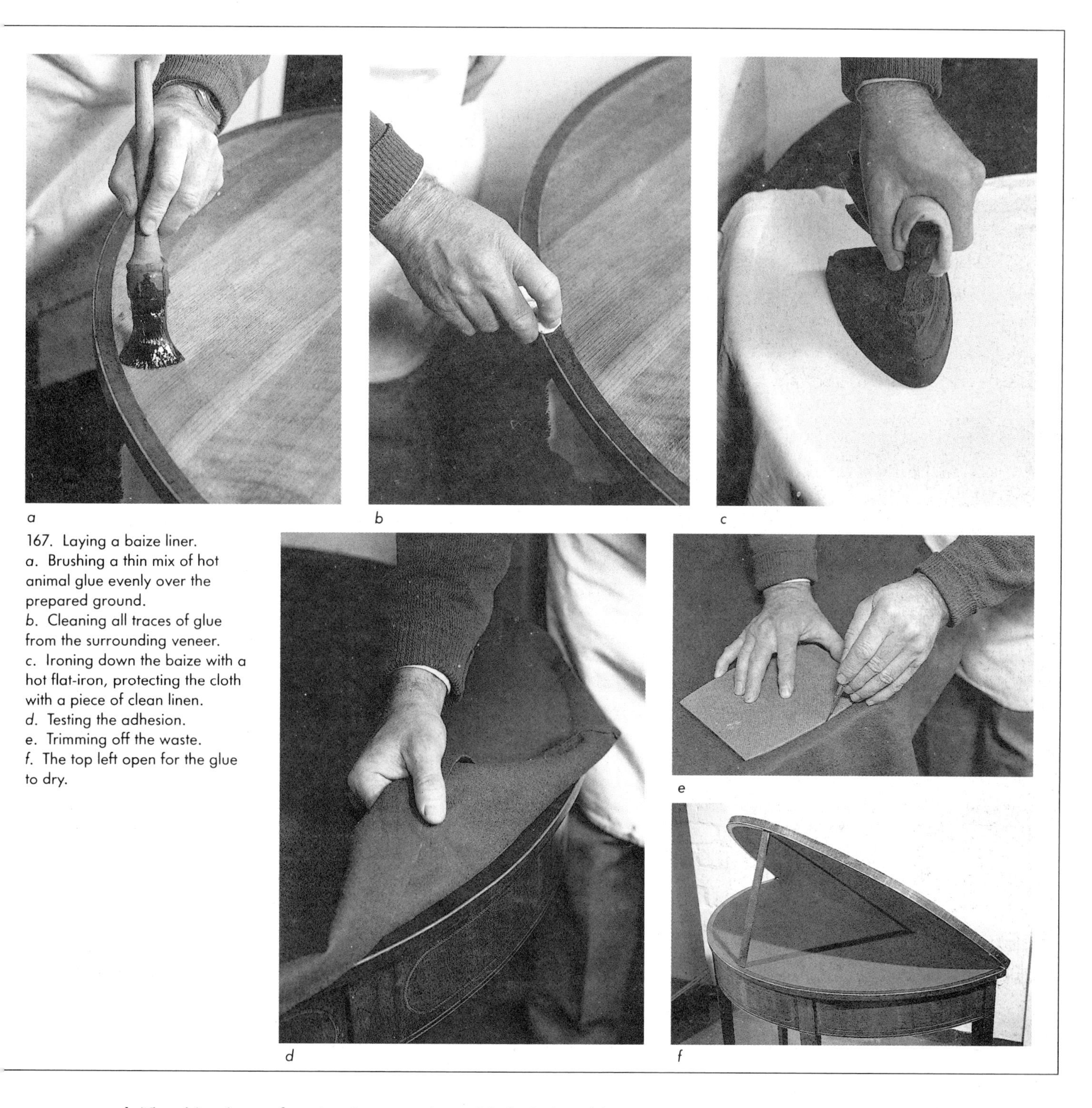

167. Laying a baize liner.
a. Brushing a thin mix of hot animal glue evenly over the prepared ground.
b. Cleaning all traces of glue from the surrounding veneer.
c. Ironing down the baize with a hot flat-iron, protecting the cloth with a piece of clean linen.
d. Testing the adhesion.
e. Trimming off the waste.
f. The top left open for the glue to dry.

surround. The object is to soften the glue enough to stick the baize without penetrating it, so check by gently lifting the edge of the baize to get an idea of the tackiness of the glue. When it is just holding the material, move the linen on to another area and repeat the operation. When the whole top has been treated in this way, trim off the waste as described for leather liners (except that it is not necessary to angle the scalpel to undercut the baize). Finally, check that the edges of the material are secure and iron over any that tend to lift, then leave overnight to dry. In the case of folding tops, common to most baize-lined tables, make sure that the cloth is well secured at the fold edges and leave the top propped open a few inches to allow the glue to dry (and the smell to dissipate!).

CHAPTER 13

Glazing

Old glass, with its imperfections and concentric ripples, is a highly-prized feature of antique furniture, so unless a cracked pane really offends the eye it should be left alone. When you have to replace broken glass, you may be able to find some old stuff with the right characteristics by searching through old picture frames in junk shops or auction rooms. If this proves difficult, then there is some fairly decent thin modern glass, with a good aqua colour, to be had from specialist glaziers.

Having decided to replace a pane, the first job is to remove the door from the piece of furniture and put it flat, putty side up, on a couple of newspapers on the workbench, where it is easier to work on (and take down any tools that are hanging in the vicinity!). The secret of removing that old putty which, after so many years, will have acquired the consistency of rock, is to warm it first. An extraordinary amount of damage can be done to delicate glazing bars and to other glass by attempting to chip out hard putty, whereas a few seconds of heat and the old oil remaining in it will soften and allow the putty to be peeled out. The ideal tool for this job is an electric soldering iron, adapted with the special putty softening bit described in on p. 48. (You can use the soldering iron without this bit, but the small amount which it can soften at one time makes the job somewhat tedious.) Fit the softener bit and let the iron get to full heat. Then hold one face of the bit as flat as you can on the putty and think about something else for a minute, after which time (more or less) you should be able to get the tip of a chisel under the putty and peel it out in one piece, cleanly, right down to the wood. There's no need for a sharp chisel – in fact, a blunt one is to be preferred, for no force is necessary if the putty is properly softened. When you have got the hang of this technique you will be able to remove putty with one hand and control the soldering iron softening the next area with the other. Look out for loose glazing bars. It is often only the glass and putty which are holding them together, so when you are dealing with two or more damaged panes adjacent to each other, remove the inside putty from all of them before taking any of the glass out. When you come to take the old glass out and clean out the remaining putty, make sure that the bars, and the rest of the door, are well supported.

Once the bars and frame are cleaned up, the next step is to make a cardboard template for each piece of glass. No matter how square a frame appears to be, a template made to fit inside, with $\frac{1}{16}''$ to $\frac{1}{8}''$ clearance, depending on how much room you have to play with, will save time when it comes to cutting the glass. And if you prefer, as most do, to leave glass cutting to the local glazier, a template will be appreciated.

When you have sorted out the glass, it is time to think about the putty. Modern putty is fine for the job but seldom the correct colour, although the brown variety may often be close to that required. No matter, for you can soon adjust the colour to an exact match by kneading in a little of the ap-

168. Removing putty from a door frame. This putty was rock hard before the application of heat; now it peels out easily.

propriate colour(s) of earth pigment, working it well for a few minutes to make sure you have an even colour. Roll some of the putty into a ball big enough to fit comfortably into the palm of your hand. Squeeze a little into the rebate of the frame, and any glazing bars, with your thumb to form the bed for the glass, and immediately put the pane in position, pressing evenly and firmly round the edges. Be wary of distortions in the frame and insecure glazing bars. Trying to press the glass to equalize the thickness of the bedding putty can put undue stress on the door, with predictable results, so make sure that only just enough putty comes off your thumb to fill the angle of the rebate. With the glass bedded in, apply the facing putty and smooth it to conform to the bevel of the putty in any other panes or, in any case, so that the putty does not extend beyond the edge of the rebate to become visible from the outside. Scrape off excess putty from the inside, trim and remove any small amounts of bedding putty which show outside, then leave the door in a safe place for two or three days for the putty to form a skin before you set about cleaning the glass. Then mix an equal amount of meths and water, dampen a piece of clean linen with it, and wash off the smears. Woodwork may then be cleaned with a little of the preparation described on p. 90 and polished with wax if necessary. When you are re-hanging the door, do try to remember that the putty will still be soft!

CHAPTER 14

Woodworm treatment

The larvae of the furniture beetle (*Anobium punctatum*) are the cause of more unnecessary damage to antique furniture than they, as a species, actually do. How many times have you heard the cry: 'Burn it, it's infested!'? So on to the bonfire it goes, in ignorance of the fact that not only have the little beasts been eating away at the wood for at least two years, and up to five, before those first holes appeared (and could have been stopped without trace during that period), but also that irreparable structural damage will take a long time to accomplish. Any piece now in such a state has been totally neglected in the face of evidence of many years of woodworm activity (Fig. 169).

It is good housekeeping to treat all your furniture, not just antiques, with woodworm fluid every year, as a preventative measure. The best time to do it is in spring, before the larvae which have burrowed up to just below the surface to pupate can hatch into beetles and bore through to the outside world to start the life cycle again. The first treatment will have to be the most thorough. Check all over each piece of furniture for 'worm holes', the flight holes of the mature beetle. Active woodworm is indicated by fresh holes, which are easily recognized by their sharp edges with pale, clean wood

169. A chair leg with severe woodworm damage. Treatment at an early stage would have saved a costly repair.

showing inside and an amount of fine powder (frass) about, which is gritty to the touch (not to be confused with the talc-smooth dust so often found on and around drawer runners, which frequently causes panic). Look out, too, for the beetles themselves. They are most often seen in mid-summer, but any warm spell can entice them out of the wood to breed. If you find small ($\frac{1}{8}''$ to $\frac{3}{16}''$ long) beetles with distinctly narrow, dark reddish-brown bodies, reach for the 6× magnifying glass. If this reveals rough, longitudinal ridges on their backs, start searching for the centre of activity. Treatment is simple and effective. Get yourself a gallon (5 litres) of woodworm fluid (with a decent quantity on hand you won't be mean with the stuff) and one of the purpose-made injectors which has a fine, pointed nozzle surrounded by a sealing ring, with a squeezy container to hold the fluid. This sort gets the insecticide right into the galleries and penetrates all the infected wood, not only stopping existing larval activity but making the wood unpalatable for future generations.

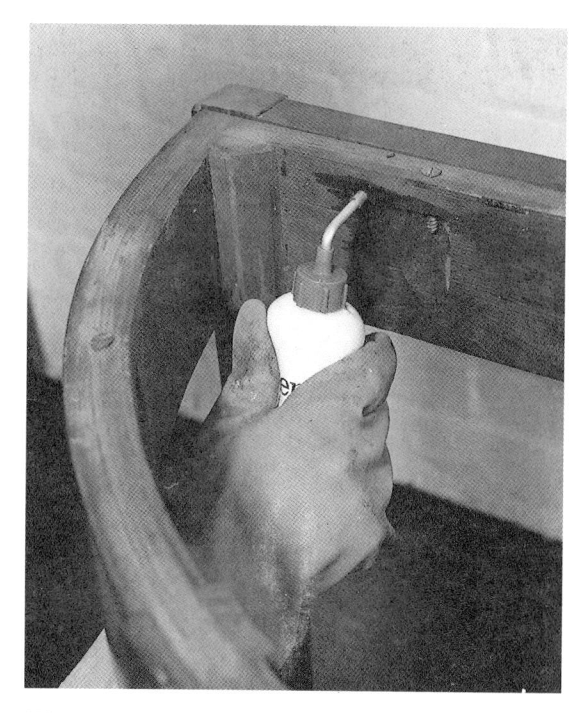

170. Injecting insecticide. Note how this simple device forces fluid into the larvae's galleries – an essential operation if infestation is to be completely eradicated.

Wearing rubber gloves and goggles, give all worm holes and dusty corners a good penetrating squirt of fluid. Goggles are essential, because when you have got the sealing ring firmly pressed around a worm hole and given the bottle a too-vigorous squeeze, a stream of fluid may shoot out of another hole several inches away. Don't squeeze the bottle hard as soon as you have located the nozzle in a hole – start gradually until you are sure that fluid isn't gushing out somewhere else, then build up the pressure until you can see fluid seeping to the surface along the woodworm galleries (Fig. 170). When you have treated all holes and crevices, wipe any runs of excess fluid over surrounding bare wood, thoroughly clean polished surfaces of all oily traces with clean rag, then set the piece in a well-ventilated place for a couple of days to air off. This takes care of the first and major treatment. When you are satisfied that the insecticide oil has dried sufficiently (the time will vary according to where the piece of furniture is normally kept – the warmer and better-ventilated, the sooner it will dry), you can fill all the holes with small pieces of matching beeswax stopping (p. 102). This is a time-consuming and unutterably boring business but you will greatly improve the appearance of the piece and make the detection of any further activity much easier.

Treatment in future years should, if you have been thorough with that first one, involve little more than a check for fresh holes and a precautionary injection of any crevices which look a bit dry and dusty in case any eggs are laid in them.

Treatment for woodworm in a piece of furniture which also requires other repairs (often replacement tenons, as the dried-out crevices at the interfaces of joints are one of the egg-laying places which tend to focus attention on woodworm activity – when the thing collapses) must wait until repairs are glued and all refinishing is completed, for the oil in the insecticide will inhibit these processes. So when all other work is completed, go through the routine described above, and keep up the annual checks. If the damage is such that you have to get the infestation treated before you start work, get the piece fumigated. Remember, though, that the fumigation process only kills the active larvae and for long-term protection the fluid treatment will be required. Really extensive worm damage is best left to the professional restorer to rectify, because the consolidants needed for such work are not generally available in the small quantities required for individual jobs.

APPENDICES

Checklist of machinery, tools and equipment

Bandsaw, 2-wheel, 7 ft (approx) web size, with 2 webs each size $\frac{3}{4}$" (or $\frac{1}{2}$") & $\frac{1}{4}$"
Bench hook**
Bradawl
Cabinet scrapers, 20 gauge (for scratch stock blades): 2
Callipers, internal and external, 6"
Chisels, firmer and bevel-edged: full range $\frac{1}{4}$" to 1" each type
Compasses, 6" minimum
Cramps: G-cramps, 3", 4", 6" & 8": 2 each size*
  Klemmsia cramps, 2 ft and 3 ft: 2 each size*
  Sash cramps, T-bar, 3 ft and 5 ft: 3 each size*
  Webbing cramp
Cutting gauge
Drills: Archimedean drill stock and bits
  Electric drill, 2-speed (variable), $\frac{3}{8}$" chuck capacity, with set of high speed steel bits $\frac{1}{16}$" to $\frac{1}{2}$" in $\frac{1}{16}$" steps, plus counter-sink bit and plug cutters $\frac{5}{16}$", $\frac{3}{8}$" and $\frac{1}{2}$"
  Hand drill (enclosed)
  Ratchet brace with Jennings pattern bits $\frac{1}{4}$" to 1"
Files: assorted half-round, round, flat and rat-rail
File card
Glue pot, cast iron (or similar), 1 pint size
Gouges, firmer and scribing: full range $\frac{1}{4}$" to 1" each type
Hammers, Warrington pattern: 10–12 oz. and 4 oz
Heat gun (Black & Decker)
Hotplate, electric, with two rings
Mallet, rubber head
Mallet, wooden, cylindrical head
Marking knife
Metal detector (DIY wire-finding type)
Mitre box**
Mortice gauge
Oilstones: coarse, medium and fine
Pallet knives, large: 2 (or old, flexible steel table knives)
Pans: 2
Pincers: 6" and 8"
Planes, metal: jack, smoothing, jointer, block, low-angle (end grain), bullnose, rebate
Planes, wooden moulding: rounds and hollows size 2 to 18
Pliers: 6", 8" and snipe-nosed
Profile copier
Punches: centre punch, $\frac{1}{16}$" and $\frac{1}{8}$" nail punches
Putty softener**

Router, to take $\frac{1}{4}$"-shank bits, with single- and double-flute cutters $\frac{1}{8}$" to $\frac{1}{2}$"
Rules, stainless: 6" and 12"
Saws: 18–24" panel saw with 8–12 tpi
24–30" rip saw with 4–6 tpi
12" heavy back saw (tenon) with 14 tpi
6" light back saw (gents) with 24–32 tpi
Coping saw, with blades
Fret saw (for blades, see piercing saw)
Hacksaws, full size and junior, with blades
Piercing saw with blades sized 6 down to 2/0
Sawing table, marquetry**
Scalpel, Swann-Morton no. 3, with blades nos. 10A and 15
Scrapers, hardwood**
Scratch stock**
Screwdrivers: 10 ranging from $\frac{1}{8}$" wide tip of $\frac{1}{64}$" thickness and 4–6" blade length, to $\frac{5}{8}$" wide tip of $\frac{1}{16}$" thickness and 10" blade length
Shooting board**
Sliding (adjustable) bevel
Slipstones: course, medium and fine
Soldering iron, low-wattage electric, with $\frac{1}{8}$" diameter bit
Spanner, adjustable, 8–10"
Spokeshave, metal, with 2" cutter
Straight edge, 3 ft minimum
Tape measure, steel, 10 ft
Torch, butane gas
Torch, electric
Trestle, 4'×4', 12–15 high**
Try squares: 6" arm and 12" arm
Tweezers, various
Veneer hammer**
Vice, engineer's, 3". mounted on 6"×4"×4" wood block
Whetstone, horizontal stone, electric, with course stone
Workbench, with large capacity quick-release vice, end vice and dogs

* Minimum requirement
** Made to your own requirements

Checklist of miscellaneous materials and equipment

Abrasives:	
Carborundum powder, 100 grit	500 gms
Papers:	
Garnet paper, A OP, 150 grit (4/0)	25 sheets
Garnet paper, A OP, 320 grit (9/0)	25 sheets
Silicon carbide paper (Lubrisil), A OP, 320 (9/0)	25 sheets
Pumice powder, fine	500 gms
Steel wool (Liberon), 2/0	2 rolls
Steel wool (Liberon), 4/0	2 rolls
Aprons, white woodworkers	2
Brushes:	
Dulling	1
Glue, bridled, no. 12	2
Polisher's mop, no. 10	1
Watercolour, sable, nos. 0, 2, 6, & 8	2 each size
Fire extinguisher, inert gas (halon) type	1
Gloves, household rubber	2 pairs
Glue, scotch (animal), pearl	1 kilo
Goggles	1
Graphite, powdered	1 tube
Magnifying glass, 6×	1
Masks, aluminium face (Martindale), with refills	1
Metal polish (Brasso)	200 ml
Mutton-cloth	500 gms
Oil, thin mineral	250 ml
Rags, cotton	1 kilo
Syringe, hypodermic	1
Tapes:	
Double sided, 2″	1 roll
Gummed paper, 2″	1 roll
Masking, ¾″	2 rolls
Wadding, grey skin	1 yard

Woods used for the construction and decoration of English furniture

Common name (Alternatives in brackets)	Botanical name	Chief characteristics of unfinished wood	Principal uses
Amboyna	*Pterospermum indicum*	Made up of curls with many small 'bird's eye' knots, in pale brown and honey colours.	Veneer and banding.
Apple	*Malus spp.*	Hard, pinkish-white, very fine grain.	Inlay and marquetry
Ash	*Fraxinus excelsior*	White, with long, usually straight, lines of grain.	Country furniture, particularly chairs.
Beech	*Fagus sylvatica*	White to pinkish-brown; distinctive fine fleck which shows as satin-brown markings on transverse cuts.	Chairs and carcase-work; gilded and painted furniture.
Birch	*Betula spp.*	Hard, white to pinkish-brown with fine, regular grain.	Framework for tables and chairs.
Box	*Buxus sempervirens*	Pale yellow, with no distinguishable grain. Works crisply, leaving a glossy surface.	Inlay, stringing and banding; fine turning.
Brazil-wood	*Caesalpinia brasilensis*	Rich red, with a grain similar to a close-grained mahogany.	17th century inlay, and again in the 19th century.
Calamander	*Diospryos quaesita*	Light brown, mottled and striped with black.	Crossbanding and veneer.
Cedar: West Indies North America	*Cedrela odorata* *Juniperus virginiana*	Soft and smooth-textured with reddish to greenish-brown colour; characteristic fragrance.	Linings of drawers, presses and in solid for boxes and chests.
Cherry	*Prunus avium* & *spp.*	Hard and attractively figured with close grain; creamy to red-brown	Small furniture.
Chestnut, Sweet (Spanish)	*Castanea sativa*	Colour and grain very similar to oak but without medullary rays.	Chairs. Also replacement for oak in drawer linings.
Coromandel	*Diospyros melanoxylon*	Resembles rosewood, but light stripes are pale brown.	Veneer and banding.
Cypress	*Cupressus sempervirens* (Mediterranean)	Hard, close-grained; reddish.	Linings of chests.
Ebony	*Diospyros spp.*	Heavy and black, some with grey-green to brown stripes.	Inlay, marquetry; banding and stringing.
Elm	*Ulmus procera* (English) *Ulmus glabra* (Wych)	Light reddish-brown with distinctive figure and grain, often including conspicuous golden-brown fibres.	Country furniture.
Holly	*Ilex aquifolium*	White, hard with close grain and fine flecked markings.	Inlay and marquetry, sometimes stained.
Kingwood (Prince's wood)	*Dalbergia spp.*	Similar to rosewood, except that the light and dark bands are more regularly spaced.	Veneer and crossbanding.
Laburnum	*Laburnum vulgare* & *spp.*	Distinctive rich olive-green to brown heartwood with bright yellow sapwood – usually used together.	Oyster veneers on cabinets and desks of the late 17th century.

Lignum vitae	*Guaiacum officinale*	Dark brown to green in contrasting streaks, with yellow sapwood. Extremely hard and difficult to work.	Veneers in 17th century.
Lime	*Tilia vulgaris*	Close-grained, light and soft; white to pale yellow.	Carving.
Mahogany:			
West Indies (Cuban or Spanish)	*Swietenia mahogani*	Rich dark brown to plum-coloured; hard and brittle; often with white (silica) in the grain.	Second and third quarters of 18th century, in solid and veneer.
Honduras (Baywood)	*Swietenia macrophylla*	Paler than Cuban and lighter in weight. More open grain, again containing silica.	Mid-18th century to early 19th century, in solid and veneer.
Maple	*Acer campestris* (same genus as Sycamore (q.v.) and easily mistaken for it)	White, close-grained with shaded veining.	Veneer.
	Acer saacharum (Sugar Maple)	Produces the 'bird's eye' veneers.	Regency period veneer.
Oak	*Quercus spp.*	Uniform colour, varying with species from white to dark brown. Distinguished by its grain; medullary rays prominent on end grain and quarter-sawn cuts.	In solid to late 17th century, thereafter for some carcase-work. Continued use in solid for country furniture.
Olive	*Olea europaea*	Hard and close-grained; yellowish-green with dark blotches.	Parquetry and veneer.
Pear	*Pyrus communis*	Hard and fine-grained; cream tinged with red.	Marquetry, inlay and banding. Often stained to imitate ebony.
Pine	*Pinus spp.*	Soft with straight figure; white to pale yellow.	Carved and gilded furniture; carcase-work.
Plane	*Platanus acerifolia*	Pale yellow to pale red; quarter-sawn shows lacey effect.	Gilded furniture.
Plum	*Prunus domestica*	Hard and heavy; yellow, streaked brown to red.	Inlay and turning.
Purpleheart	*Peltogyne spp.*	Grey-brown when first cut, changing to bright purple on exposure to light.	Crossbanding.
Rosewood	*Dalbergia spp.*	Purple-brown with often highly-figured black bands and markings. Unmistakable fragrance when cut.	Veneer. Some solid work, usually turned pieces or carved detail.
Satinwood:			
West Indian	*Fagara flava*	Rich yellow, displaying fine, highly-reflective and variegated figure.	Fine-quality late 18th century furniture, veneered and solid.
East Indian	*Chloroxylon swietenia*	Paler then the West Indian, and without the same depth of reflectivity.	Introduced afer the West Indian; same uses.
Sycamore	*Acer pseudoplatanus*	Milky-white with fine, close grain.	Inlay and veneer. Stained to a grey-green colour it was known as Harewood.
Thuya	*Tetraclinis articulata*	Wavey figure in rich browns, interspersed with 'bird's eye' markings.	Veneer and inlay.
Tulipwood	*Dalbergia spp.*	Straw-coloured with pink stripes.	Crossbanding.
Walnut	*Juglans regia* (European) *Juglans nigra* (American or Black)	Pale purple-brown to red-brown, with dark brown to black veining; *nigra* usually more variegated.	Predominantly from mid-17th to early 18th century, first in solid then as veneer.
Yew	*Taxus baccata*	Heaviest and hardest of the softwoods, yet extremely supple. Heartwood varies from purple-brown to orange, with thin white sapwood. Turns particularly well.	High quality chairs and small tables in the solid. Veneer.
Zebrawood	*Pithecolobium racemiflorum*	Light brown with regular wide bands of deep brown.	Veneer and crossbanding.

Checklist for basic stock of woods

	Proportional quantity			Form in which usually available				
				Solid wood		Veneer		Stringing Banding (new)
	S	M	L	New	Breaker	New	Breaker	
Apple	●			●				
Ash		●		●				
Beech			●	●				
Birch		●			●			
Box		●		●				●
Cedar	●			●	●			
Cherry	●			●				
Chestnut	●			●	●			
Ebony	●			●				(Stained)
Elm		●		●				
Holly	●			●				
Lignum vitae	●			●				
Mahogany, West Indian		●			●		●	
Mahogany, Honduras			●		●		●	
Oak			●	●	●			
Pear	●			●		●		
Pine			●	●	●			
Rosewood		●			●		●	
Satinwood		●		●		●		●
Sycamore		●		●				
Tulipwood	●					●		●
Walnut, European			●	●	●	●	●	
Walnut, Black		●		●	●	●	●	
Yew	●			●				

Other, exotic timbers may be ordered as required.

Checklist for stock of finishing materials

Please note that some of the items listed below could be hazardous if not properly used. Section 6 of the Health and Safety at Work Act 1974 (as amended by the Consumer Protection Act 1987), places a duty upon suppliers of substances for use at work to ensure, so far as is reasonably practicable, that the substances are safe and without risk to health when properly used. The duties specifically include requirements for testing and the provision of information about hazards and precautions which should be taken. The Classification, Packaging and Labelling of Dangerous Substances Regulations 1984 also contains specific requirements about the type of warning labels which should be fixed to containers of dangerous substances. If any product you are buying does not come with proper information about its correct method of use and any precautions which should be taken, either on the container or in a separate data sheet, you should ask the supplier about possible hazards.

Note also that if you buy acids in concentrated form to dilute for yourself, always **add acid to water**, never water to acid.

The suggested stock quantities should be sufficient for the home workshop where constant use is made of these items, bearing in mind economical order quantities and shelf lives. Most are now sold in metric measures.

Acids:	
Acetic acid B.P. (33%)	1 litre
Nitric acid B.P. (33%)	250 ml
Oxalic acid crystals	500 gms
Ammonia .880	100 ml
Bleach, 2-part pack (A & B) or (1 & 2)	500 ml each
Dewaxing solution	1 litre
Methylated spirit	5 litres
Paint stripper, solvent wash type	1 litre
Pigments: Burnt Turkey, Umber, Raw Umber, Yellow Ochre, Raw Sienna, Brown Umber, Burnt Sienna, Orange Chrome, Yellow Chrome, Flake White, Vegetable Black	100 gms each
Potassium bichromate	100 gms
Shellac flakes	500 gms
Shellac polish, Special Pale Button	1 litre
Shellac sanding sealer	1 litre
Soap, liquid (Teepol)	1 litre

Sodium Chloride B.P.	100 gms
Stains, spirit powders: bismark (brown), black, green, yellow	50 gms each
Stains, water powder: mahogany, oak, brown, black, green	50 gms each
Turpentine, pure	1 litre
Vandyke (walnut) crystals	500 gms
Waxes:	
Beeswax, yellow and white	500 gms each
Carnauba wax, grey and yellow	500 gms each
Paraffin wax	500 gms
White spirit	1 litre
Whiting	500 gms
Woodworm insecticide	1 litre

Suppliers of materials and services

There are many suppliers of the materials and services mentioned in this book, most of whom offer first-class products and workmanship: their names are listed in directories and specialist magazines. However, should you have difficulty in finding what you need locally, the following firms offer a postal service:

Baize (and leather) for table liners:
Woolnough Ltd.
23 Phipp Street
London EC2A 4NP
0171-739 6603/8975

Cabinet fittings (reproduction):
Martin & Co.
97 Camden Street
Birmingham B1 3DG
0121-233 2111

Cabinet-makers and finishing materials (specialize in small quantities):
Restoration Materials
Proctor Street
Bury
Lancs BL8 2NY
0161-764 2741

Castings in brass (copies of old fittings, from stock):
Optimum Brasses
7 Castle Street
Bampton
Tiverton
Devon EX16 9NS
01398 31515

Castings in brass (from your pattern):
Devon Metalcraft Ltd.
2 Victoria Way
Exmouth
Devon EX8 1EW
01395 272846

Humidifiers:
Air Improvement Centre Ltd.
23 Denbigh Street
London SW1V 2HF
0171-834 2834
0171-821 8485

Leather liners (hand-coloured hides and skivers):
The Antique Leathercraft Co. Ltd.
108 New Bond Street
London W1Y 9AA
0171-361 8191
0171-499 9192

Lock repairs and key cutting:
Bramah Security Ltd.
30/31 Oldbury Place
London W1M 3AP
0171-935 7147
0171-486 1739/1757

Chubb Lock Company Ltd.
(Customer Services Department)
PO Box 197
Wednesfield Road
Wolverhampton WV10 0ET
01902 55111

Veneers, stringing and banding:
J. Crispen & Sons
92–96 Curtain Road
London EC2A 3AA
0171-739 4857

Summary of recipes

1 oz = 28.125 g
1 fl oz = 28.5 ml

Cleaner (page 90)

	IMPERIAL	METRIC
Pure turpentine	8 fl oz	200 ml
Methylated spirit	4 fl oz	100 ml
Acetic acid B.P. (33%)	2 fl oz	50 ml
Teepol (liquid soap)	1 fl oz	25 ml
Brasso (metal polish)	1 fl oz	25 ml
Ammonia .880	½ 5 ml medicine spoon	

Wax polish (page 91)

	IMPERIAL	METRIC
Carnauba wax	1 fl oz	30 ml
Paraffin wax	1 fl oz	30 ml
Beeswax	½ fl oz	15 ml
Mansion Wax (or similar) polish	½ fl oz	15 ml
Pure turpentine	4 fl oz	120 ml

Patination of brass (page 129)

	IMPERIAL	METRIC
Copper carbonate	1½ oz	45 g
Copper acetate	½ oz	15 g
Ammonium chloride (sal ammoniac)	½ oz	15 g
Sodium chloride	½ oz	15 g
Purified cream of tartar (potassium bitartrate)	½ oz	15 g
Dilute acetic acid (10%)	4 fl oz	120 ml

British Museum Leather Dressing (page 137)

	IMPERIAL	METRIC
Beeswax	¼ oz	7 g
Hexane	½ fl oz	15 ml
Anhydrous lanolin	3½ fl oz	100 ml
Cedarwood oil	½ fl oz	15 ml

Recommended reading

Antique furniture

Edwards, Ralph, *Shorter Dictionary of English Furniture* (Hamlyn, London, 1959).

Fastnedge, Ralph, *English Furniture Styles from 1500-1850* (Penguin Books [Pelican], London, 1970).

Metalwork

Butter, F.J., *Encyclopaedia of Locks and Builders' Hardware* (Josiah Parkes & Sons Ltd, Willenhall, 1958).

Commissioners of Patents, *Patent Abridgments*, 1873: Locks, Latches, Bolts and Similar Fastenings, 1774–1866, Vol. 60. Nails, Rivets, Bolts, Screws, Nuts and Washers, 1618–1866, Vol. 58.

Dickinson, H. W., 'Origin and Manufacture of Wood Screws', *Newcomen Transactions XXII*, 1941.

Dodd, George, *British Manufacturers; Metals* (Charles Knight & Co., London, 1845).

Price, George, *Treatise on Fire and Thiefproof Depositories and Locks and Keys* (Simpkin, Marshall & Co., London, 1856).

Index

Page numbers in *italics* refer to relevant illustrations and captions.

Abrasive, carborundum powder 45
garnet paper 47, 80, 93, 116, *117*
pumice powder 109, 110
silicon carbide paper 47, 103, *103*, 107, 116, *117*, 118, 122
steel wool 47, 94, 95, 97, 98, 109, 114, 118
stocks of 146
Acid, acetic, in bleaching process 99, 100, *100*
acetic, in cleaner 90
acetic/iron solution *113*, 114
nitric 112–14, *112*, *113*
oxalic, in bleaching process 99, 100, *100*
oxalic, in colouring *113*, 114
stocks of 150
Adhesives *see* glue
Air drying, finishes etc 100, *113*, 114, 139, 143
timber 67
Aluminium, sheet *127*, 129
Amboyna 147
Ammonia, in cleaner 90
patinating brass *128*, 130
stock of 150
Antique, definition of 6, 22
Antique dealers/shops 10, 11–12
Antique furniture, buying 9–39
Antique or Fake? (Hayward) 14–15
Antiques fairs 10, 12
Apple 147, 149
Ash 147, 149
Auctions 10–12

Back-spring locks *see* locks
BADA *see* British Antique Dealers' Association
Baize *see* liners
Banding *86*, 87
Bandsaw 23, 25, *25*
Barron, Robert *34*
Beading 16, 46, 79–81, *81*
Beech 147, 149
Beeswax *see* wax
Birch 147, 149
Bleaching 98, 99–101, *99–101*, 111, 114, 150
Blistered veneer *see* veneers
Bodying up 107, *107*
Botching 13, 15, *16*, *17*, 19, 22, 62, 63, *63*, *72*, 121, *122*
Boulle 46, 85–7, *87*
Box 147, 149
Bracket feet 70–73, *72–73*, *123*
Bramah lock *see* locks
Brass, colour and patina 31
handles and escutcheons 31–2, *31*, *32*, 126–9, *126*, *127*, *128*
patinating *128*, 129–130
see also boulle
Brazil-wood 147
Breakers 50–52, *52*
British Antique Dealers' Association (BADA) 6, 12
British Museum Leather Dressing 137, 153
Brushes, pigmenting and staining 116, *117*, 121, 123, 146
Bun feet 70
Burnished beeswax finish *see* wax
'Butterflies', masking tape 80, *80*

Calamander 147
Carborundum powder *see* abrasive
Carnauba wax *see* wax
Castings *127*, 129, 152
Castors 131
Catalogues, auctioneer's 10–11
Caustic solutions 95, *95*
Cedar 147, 149
Cherry *50*, *113*, 147, 149
Chestnut 147, 149
Chipped surfaces 74–5, *74*, *75*
Chisels *see* edge tools
Chubb lock *see* locks
Circular saw 23, 25, *25*
Clamping strips 18, *18*, 30, *67*
Clamps *see* cramps
Classification, Packaging and Labelling of Dangerous Substances Regulations (1984) 150
Cleaner for finishes 90–91, *91*, 128, 141, 153
Cockbeading *see* beading
Colour and patina (of wood) 15, 16, *17*, 19, 36, 50, *50*, 52, 75, 89, 93
see also brass
Coloured size 123, *123*
Colouring, chemical 111–4, *113*
Condition (of furniture) 15–22, *16–21*
see also botching
Construction, firmness of 15–16, *16*, *17*
Consumer Protection Act (1987) 150
Copying and faking 7, 14–15, 19, 20, 22, 23–39, *24–39*
see also reproductions
Coromandel 147
Cramps and formers 47, 54–5, *54*, *61*, *62*, 65, *65*
Crossbanding *18*, 75
Cut clasp nails 27, *27*
Cypress 147

Dating furniture 14
Dateline for antique furniture 6
Deburring *see* sharpening edge tools
Dents, filling 101–3, *102*
steaming 77–8, *78*
Dewaxing solution 94, 150
Distressing *18–19*, 19, 121–2, *122*
Dovetails *see* joints
Dowelled joints *see* joints
Drawer rails 69–70, *69*, *70*
Drawer runners 69, *69*
Drawer stops 68–9, *68*, *69*
Dulling 107, 109, *120*

Ebony 147, 149
Edge tools 42–6, *43*
Elm *50*, 147, 149
Embossing (tooling) on leather 19–20, *20*, 137
Escutcheons *see* brass
Ethics (of restoration) 7, 22, 115

Faking *see* copying and faking
Figure (of wood) 16, 50, *50*, *51*, 52, 75
Finishing materials 150–151
Five-clout nail 27–9, *27*
Flat iron *see* ironing
Formers *see* cramps and formers
Fox wedging 59, *59*, 63
Frame saw 23, *23*, *24*, 25
Frass 143
French polishing 104

Garnet paper *see* abrasive
G-cramps *see* cramps and formers
Glass, glazing 20, 140–141, *141*
Gloves *see* protective clothing and equipment
Glue, animal (Scotch), pearl 53–5, *53*
baize liners, securing 138–9, *139*
preparation and use 53–5, *53*, *55*
rubbed joints 65, *65*, 72, 73
washing off 52, 53, *57*
Glue, wallpaper paste 138
Gluepot 48, 53, 144
Goggles *see* protective clothing
Gouges *see* edge tools

Grain 50, *50*, 52, 75
filling 101, 103, *103*, 107
imitating *51*, 121
raising 80, 93, 99
Graphite, powdered 134, 146

Hand-worked wood 23–5, *24*
Handles and escutcheons *see* brass
Health and Safety at Work Act (1974) 150
Heat gun 57, 144
chemical colouring *112*, *113*, 114
removing veneer 51–2, *52*
Heelball *see* wax
Hide 137
Hinge joints *see* joints
Hinges 66, *66*, 130–131
Holly 83, 147, 149
Holzer drill 48, *49*, 57–9, *58*
Honing *see* sharpening edge tools
Humidifiers 68, 152
Humidity, relative 67–8, 106
Hypodermic syringe *see* syringe

Inlay 16, 81–5
Ironing, baize 138–9, *139*
blistered veneer *see* veneer
see also dents

Joints, dovetail 63
dowelled 64
hinge 65–7
knuckle 65–6, *65*
loose and broken 15–16, *16*, *17*, 56–67, *59–63*, *65*, *66*, 69–70, *70*
mortice and tenon 59–63
pegged 25, *26*, 37–9, *38*, *39*, 64
replacement tenon 59–60, *60*, *61*, *62*, 63, *63*
rubbed 65, *65*, 72, 73, *73*
rule 66–7, *66*, *74*
taking apart 53, 56–7, *56–7*, *58*
wedged through-tenon 63, *63*
see also fox-wedged tenon

Keys 131–5, *132*, *133*
Kingwood 147

Labels, makers 13, *13*
Laburnum147
LAPADA *see* London and Provincial Antique Dealers' Association
Leather *see* liners
Lever locks *see* locks
Lignum vitae 148, 149
Lime 148
Liners, baize 137, 138–9, *139*, 152
leather 19–20, *20*, 137–8, *138*, 152
Liquid soap 90, 151
Locks, back-spring, 32,*33*,*33*, *35*, 131,*132*, 134,135, 136, *136*
Bramah 134, *134–5*, 152
broken, repairing 134, 152
Chubb *35*, 131, 152
lever 33, *34*, *35*, 131–2, *133*, 134, 135
locked 134–5
missing 136, *136*
picking 135
tumbler 32–3, *33*, *34*, *35*, 134, 135
London and Provincial Antique Dealers' Association (LAPADA) 12

Machine-worked wood 23, 24, *24*, *25*
Mahogany 16, 20, 21, *30*, *50*, *51*, 52, 68, 71, 118, 148, 149
Maple 148
Marquetry 18, 46, 67, 81–5, *82–4*
Masking tape 80, *80*, 146
Metal detector 42, *42*, 57, 144
Metal polish 90, 146
Metalwork 46, 126–136, *127*, *128*, *132*, *133*, *136*
Methylated spirit 44, 52, 101, 134
beeswax polishing 110
cleaner for finishes 90
pigmenting 118
shellac polishing 105,106, 107, 108, 109
staining 121, 122, 123
stock of 150
stripping 95, 97, 98, 99
surface preparation 94
with water, to clean glass 141
Moisture content (of wood) 67–8
Mortice and tenon joint *see* joints
Mosaic banding *see* banding
Mouldings 46, 48
cross-grained *79*, 80, *80*
gluing 80
straight grained 79–80, *79*, *80*
Mutton-cloth 90, 92, 110, 146

Nails, dating 25–9, *27*
embedded 57–9, *58*
hidden 42, *42*, 60
Nettlefold, John Sutton 29
Newton, William Edward *28*
Nitric acid *see* acid

Oak 20, 23, *24*, *50*, *67*, 68, 71, 148, 149
Oilstones 42–5, *43*, 144
Olive 148
Oxalic acid *see* acid

Paint stripper *see* stripping
Paraffin wax *see* wax
Patches, repair *51*, 74–5, *74*, *75*
Patina *see* colour and patina
Pear 83, 148, 149
Pearl glue *see* glue
Pegged joints *see* joints
Picking locks *see* locks
Piercing saw 46, 82, *83*, *127*, 129, 145
Pigment, cornet 116, *117*, 118
in glazing putty 141
in stopping 101, 102
Pigmenting 111, 115–8, *115*, *117*, *118*, 121
Pin blocks 77, *77*, 79, 114
Pine 148, 149
Pit saw 23, *24*
Plane 148
Planes *see* edge tools
Plum 148
Polisher's mop 109, *120*, 121, 122
Polishes, polishing 91–2, 104–110
see also french polishing; shellac polishing; wax; wax finishes
Polishing rubber *see* shellac polishing rubber
Potassium bichromate (dichromate) 112, *113*, 114, 150
Price, George 134, 154
Protective clothing and equipment 47, *95*, *96*, *97*, 98, 99, 103, 112, 130, 143, 146
Provenance 13, *13*, *14*
Pulling over 107–9, *108*
Pumice powder *see* abrasive
Purpleheart 148
Putty softener *see* soldering iron

Raising grain *see* grain
Receipts for purchases 10–11, 12, 13–14
Recipes, summary of 153
Reflectivity *51*, 52, 74, 82, 118, *122*
Reproductions 14
see also copying and faking
Restoration *passim, et*
cabinetwork 41–87
cost and time 15, 16–17
finishes 89–143, 150–51
previous 20–22
v conservation 22
Reused wood 30
Reviving, finishes 90–92
leather 137
Rosewood 16, *50*, 52, 77, *91*, 148, 149
Rubbed joints *see* joints
Rubber *see* shellac polishing rubber
Rule joints *see* joints

Salt (sodium chloride) 112,*113*, 114, 150
Sanding sealer *see* shellac
Sand scorching *84*, 85
Satinwood *50*, 52, 148, 149
Sawing table 48, *49*, 83, *83*, 145
Scalpel 47, 74, 81, 138, *139*, 145
Scotch glue *see* glue
Scrapers, cabinet 79, 94, 144
paint 98
wax 48, *48*, 103
Scratch stocks, 48, *48*, 79–80, *79*, *80*
blades 79, 79, 145
Screws, dating 25–8, *28*, *29*
development of *28*, 29, *29*
embedded 57–9, *58*
removal of rusted 26–7
Seasoning of timber 67
Sharpening edge tools 42–4, *43*
Sheepskin *see* skiver
Shellac, pigmenting 111, 116, 118
polishing 79, 94, 104–9, 111, 113
polishing rubber 52, 104–9, *105*, 116, 118, 119, 121, 122, 123
sanding sealer 103, *103*
staining 119, 121, 122, 123
and see stopping
Shrinkage (of wood) 18, *18*, 26, 30, *30*, 37, *68*
Silicon carbide paper *see* abrasive

Size *see* coloured size
Skiver 137
Slipstones 42–4, *42*, 145
Sloane, Thomas J. 28
Softening blocks 54
Soldering iron 47, 145
  removing rusted screws 27
  removing dents 77–8, *78*
  repairing blistered veneer 76–7, *78*
  softening glazing putty 48, *48*, 140
Spirit stain *see* staining
Staining 111, 118–23
  spirit stain 118, 122–3, 151
  water stain 118, 121, 122, 151
  vandyke (walnut crystals) 85, 118–21, *119*, *120*, 123, *123*, 151
  see also colouring
Steaming dents *see* dents
Steel wool *see* abrasive
Stopping 101–3, 111
  hard (shellac) 101–2, *102–3*
  soft (beeswax) 101, 102–3, *103*, 143
Stringing *18*, *86*, 87, *87*
Stripping finishes 93, 94–8, *95*, *96–7*, 99
Style and rarity 14–15
Sycamore 148, 149
Syringe 48, *56*, 57, 76, 146

Tacks 27, *27*, 29
Tempering edge tools 45, *45*
Tenon *see* joints
Thuya 148
Titter & Co. *13*, *65*
Tooling, leather *see* embossing
Tools and equipment 42–8, 144–6
  to buy 45–8, *42*, *44*
  to make 48–9, *48*, *49*
Tortoiseshell 85, 87, *87*
Trades Description Act 12
Treatise on Fire and Thiefproof Depositories and Locks and Keys (Price) 134, 154
Treenails (pegs) 25, 26, *26*, 37, *38*
  see also joints, pegged
Tumbler locks *see* locks
Tulipwood 148, 149
Turpentine 90, 91, 92, 109, 151

Value of antiques 13
Vandyke *see* staining
Varnish 36, 94, 95, 104
Veneer hammer 47, *76*, 77, 78, *78*, 145
Veneers 16, 18, *18*, 20, *21*, 37, *39*, 53, 67, 71, 74, 86, *91*, 95, 112, 152
  blistered and split 75–7, *76*, *77*
  bracket feet 71
  dents in *see* dents, steaming
  eighteenth-century 30–31, *30*
  marquetry 81–5, *82–4*
  removing from breakers 51–2, 52
  reveneering 54–5, 78–9, *78*

Wadding 104, 105, *105*
Wallpaper paste *see* glue
Walnut 16, 26, *50*, 71, *80*, 148, 149
Walnut crystals *see* staining
Warpage 18, 67, *67*, 68, *68*
Washing finished surfaces 90
Water stain *see* staining
Wax, beeswax, burnished 104, 109–110, 111, 122
  beeswax, in heelball 81
  beeswax, in polish 91–2
  beeswax, in stopping 101, 102–3, *103*
  carnauba, fake patination 36, *36*, 38
  carnauba, in polish 91–2
  finishes 90, 91–2, 104, 109–110, 120, 122
  paraffin, in polish 91
Wear and tear 19–20, 22, 36, *37*
Wedged through-tenon *see* joints
Wood screws *see* screws
Woods, characteristics of 50, 51, *50*, *51*, 52, 147–8
  see also individually named
Woodworking methods 23–5
Woodworm, damage 20, *21*, 22, *62*, 63, 70, *82*, *142*
  treatment 142–3, *143*, 151

Yew *50*, 148, 149

Zebrawood 148